CIPS STUDY MATTERS

ADVANCED DIPLOMA
IN PROCUREMENT AND SUPPLY

COURSE BOOK

Operations management in supply chains

© Profex Publishing Limited, 2016

Printed and distributed by:

The Chartered Institute of Procurement & Supply, Easton House, Easton on the Hill, Stamford,
Lincolnshire PE9 3NZ
Tel: +44 (0) 1780 756 777
Fax: +44 (0) 1780 751 610

Email: info@cips.org
Website: www.cips.org

First edition October 2012
Reprinted with minor amendments June 2016

Contents

Preface

Welcome to your new Study Pack, consisting of two elements.

- A **Course Book** (the current volume). This provides detailed coverage of all topics specified in the unit content.
- A small-format volume of **Revision Notes.** Use your Revision Notes in the weeks leading up to your exam.

For a full explanation of how to use your new Study Pack, turn now to page xi. And good luck in your exams!

A note on style

Throughout your Study Packs you will find that we use the masculine form of personal pronouns. This convention is adopted purely for the sake of stylistic convenience – we just don't like saying 'he/she' all the time. Please don't think this reflects any kind of bias or prejudice.

A note on structure

This Course Book contains full coverage of the Unit Content for *Operations Management in Supply Chains*, as indicated in the cross-referencing to chapters in the Unit Content section on page vii. You will note, however, that the structure of the Course Book does not follow the structure of the Unit Content sequentially. We have done this to ensure that the sequence of learning flows logically, so what you learn in later chapters builds on what you learned in earlier ones.

The Office of Government Commerce

The Course Book refers several times to the UK's Office of Government Commerce (OGC). The OGC no longer functions in its original form and its responsibilities have been allocated to different areas within the UK Government, principally the Crown Commercial Service (CCS). However, the OGC's publications remain an authoritative source of guidance on best practice in procurement and definitions of terminology. It is perfectly valid to cite the work of the OGC in these areas when answering exam questions.

June 2016

The Unit Content

The unit content is reproduced below, together with reference to the chapter in this Course Book where each topic is covered.

Unit purpose and aims

On completion of this unit candidates will be able to explain plans, designs, processes or systems for the improved control or improvement of operations.

This unit is designed to enable those involved in procurement and supply to appraise the main techniques that improve organisations' operations. Operations management refers to the process of converting input resources into the outputs of products or services that occur across a wide range of sectors such as in manufacturing, construction, retail, services and public sectors.

Learning outcomes, assessment criteria and indicative content

Chapter

1.0 Understand the concept and scope of operations management in supply chain organisations

1.1 Analyse the role and activities of operations management in organisations

- Definitions of operations and operations management   1
- The extent of operations management in organisations   1
- Operations management in different types of organisations   1

1.2 Critically assess the objectives and strategies of operations management

- From implementing to supporting to driving strategy   2
- The stages of development of operations strategy   2
- The performance objectives of operations management (quality, speed, dependability, flexibility and cost)   2
- Top down and bottom up perspectives of operations strategy   2
- Order-qualifying and order-winning objectives of operations management   2

1.3 Evaluate main operations processes

- The 'input-transformation-output' model of operations management   3
- The dimensions of operations processes (volume, variety, variation and visibility)   3
- The activities of operations processes   3

1.4 Analyse the application of operations management across different supply chains in the main sectors

- Operations management in manufacturing, services, retail, construction, and public sector supply chains   1
- The impact of operations management on global sourcing   1
- Examples of operations management in different supply chains   1

4.0 Understand the main improvement methodologies that can be applied in operations management

How to Use Your Study Pack

Organising your study

'Organising' is the key word: unless you are a very exceptional student, you will find a haphazard approach is insufficient, particularly if you are having to combine study with the demands of a full-time job.

A good starting point is to timetable your studies, in broad terms, between now and the date of the examination. How many subjects are you attempting? How many chapters are there in the Course Book for each subject? Now do the sums: how many days/weeks do you have for each chapter to be studied?

Remember:

- Not every week can be regarded as a study week – you may be going on holiday, for example, or there may be weeks when the demands of your job are particularly heavy. If these can be foreseen, you should allow for them in your timetabling.
- You also need a period leading up to the exam in which you will revise and practise what you have learned.

Once you have done the calculations, make a week-by-week timetable for yourself for each paper, allowing for study and revision of the entire unit content between now and the date of the exams.

Getting started

Aim to find a quiet and undisturbed location for your study, and plan as far as possible to use the same period each day. Getting into a routine helps avoid wasting time. Make sure you have all the materials you need before you begin – keep interruptions to a minimum.

Using the Course Book

You should refer to the Course Book to the extent that you need it.

- If you are a newcomer to the subject, you will probably need to read through the Course Book quite thoroughly. This will be the case for most students.
- If some areas are already familiar to you – either through earlier studies or through your practical work experience – you may choose to skip sections of the Course Book.

The content of the Course Book

This Course Book has been designed to give detailed coverage of every topic in the unit content. As you will see from pages vii–ix, each topic mentioned in the unit content is dealt with in a chapter of the Course Book. For the most part the order of the Course Book follows the order of the unit content closely, though departures from this principle have occasionally been made in the interest of a logical learning order.

Each chapter begins with a reference to the assessment criteria and indicative content to be covered in the chapter. Each chapter is divided into sections, listed in the introduction to the chapter, and for the most part being actual captions from the unit content.

All of this enables you to monitor your progress through the unit content very easily and provides reassurance that you are tackling every subject that is examinable.

Each chapter contains the following features.

- Introduction, setting out the main topics to be covered
- Clear coverage of each topic in a concise and approachable format
- A chapter summary
- Self-test questions

The study phase

For each chapter you should begin by glancing at the main headings (listed at the start of the chapter). Then read fairly rapidly through the body of the text to absorb the main points. If it's there in the text, you can be sure it's there for a reason, so try not to skip unless the topic is one you are familiar with already.

Then return to the beginning of the chapter to start a more careful reading. You may want to take brief notes as you go along, but bear in mind that you already have your Revision Notes – there is no point in duplicating what you can find there.

Test your recall and understanding of the material by attempting the self-test questions. These are accompanied by cross-references to paragraphs where you can check your answers and refresh your memory.

The revision phase

Your approach to revision should be methodical and you should aim to tackle each main area of the unit content in turn. Read carefully through your Revision Notes. Check back to your Course Book if there are areas where you cannot recall the subject matter clearly. Then do some question practice. The CIPS website contains many past exam questions. You should aim to identify those that are suitable for the unit you are studying.

Additional reading

Your Course Book provides you with the key information needed for each module but CIPS strongly advocates reading as widely as possible to augment and reinforce your understanding. CIPS produces an official reading list of books, which can be downloaded from the bookshop area of the CIPS website.

To help you, we have identified one essential textbook for each subject. We recommend that you read this for additional information.

The essential textbook for this unit is *Operations Management* by Slack, Chambers and Johnston.

Examination

This subject is assessed by means of four exam questions each worth 25 marks, each testing a different learning outcome.

CHAPTER 1

The Role and Activities of Operations Management

Assessment criteria and indicative content

1.1 Analyse the role and activities of operations management in organisations

- Definitions of operations and operations management
- The extent of operations management in organisations
- Operations management in different types of organisations

1.4 Analyse the application of operations management across different supply chains in the main sectors

- Operations management in manufacturing, services, retail, construction, and public sector supply chains
- The impact of operations management on global sourcing
- Examples of operations management in different supply chains

Section headings

1 Defining operations management
2 The extent of operations management in organisations
3 Operations management in different types of organisations
4 Product vs service operations
5 The impact of global sourcing
6 An example of operations management

1 Defining operations management

Overview

1.1 An operation is defined by the Collins English Dictionary as 'a process, method or series of acts especially of a practical nature'. The definition covers all human activity of a productive and organisational nature and is directly applicable to business operations. An operational activity may appear insignificant when viewed in isolation but it is the result of an integrated set of operations that together deliver effective operations or processes.

1.2 A process may be viewed as a particular course of action intended to achieve a desired result or more specifically a set of logically related tasks performed to achieve a defined business outcome.

1.3 A process exists to achieve a purpose. It is also useful to think of roles and responsibilities in this way. A person's job is not to carry out a process but to achieve a result. Michael Hammer, regarded as the father of business process re-engineering, defined process as 'a related group of tasks that together create a result of value to a customer'.

1.4 Processes consist of a series of integrated single operations that take inputs, add value to them and deliver outputs. The process must be designed, formalised and linked to other processes in order to effectively deliver the desired operational activity.

- As an example one complaint to an organisation may be ineffective but if it is delivered via a call centre where calls are monitored and records kept, a pattern of problems can emerge and remedial actions put in place leading to an overall improvement.
- A delivery of components to form part of a production run requires other operations to enable it to reach the production line. The delivery must be recorded, notification of delivery must be available, storage must be available, location must be recorded, machinery is needed to move the components to the right point.

1.5 With the above examples (one a service, the other from manufacturing) the operations and operational activities are different but the effective integration of the operational links serves to form part of the value-adding activities that underpin organisational operations. It is the integration and effective co-ordination and management of the operational activities involved that together help form operations management.

Definitions of operations management

1.6 Operations management has its development roots during the manufacturing era. In consequence many definitions still allude to this period. This is not necessarily incorrect but the definitions must often be extended to modern day work practice, in particular the supply chain concept and the growing importance of services.

- 'Operations management consists of those activities which are concerned with the acquisition of raw materials, their conversion into finished product, and the supply of that product to the customer'. (R L Galloway).
- 'Operations management is concerned with creating, operating and controlling a transformation system that takes inputs and a variety of resources, and produces outputs of goods and services needed by customers'. (J Naylor)
- 'Operations management is the term used for the activities, decisions and responsibilities of operations managers who manage the production and delivery of products and services'. (Slack, Chambers and Johnston)
- Operations management is 'the direction and control of the processes that transform inputs into finished goods and services.' (Krajewski and Ritzman)
- Operations management is 'the management of any aspect of the production system that transforms inputs into finished goods and services.' (Jones, George and Hill)

1.7 Operations management concerns itself with the effective and efficient management of any operation. Although originally manufacturing based, the degree to which a physical component or product is involved is largely irrelevant. Operations management can be equally applied to a TV news programme, a hospital ward or a local authority where the objective is more toward service delivery than product delivery.

1.8 The role of operations management is crucial to the success of any organisation as it seeks to improve effectiveness, ie to ensure that operations are carried out so as to meet customer requirements and to improve efficiency.

1.9 Increasing effectiveness will increase profitability or contribution by making the organisation leaner, more responsive and more competitive. Improvements in efficiency will reduce costs but these cost savings must not be made at the expense of effectiveness. Measures must be put in place to evidence improvement gains achieved through increasing effectiveness. Measuring performance allows judgement by setting targets and evaluating feedback leading to discussions on future improvements, efficiency savings or new approaches.

1.10   Efficiency can be defined as the relationship between inputs and outputs achieved. The fewer the inputs (both goods and services) used by an organisation to achieve a given output, the more efficient is the organisation.

1.11   Effectiveness is the degree to which an objective or target is met.

The 'restricted sense' and the 'broader sense'

1.12   Two interpretations of the term 'operations management' must be clearly understood.

- Operations management in the **restricted** sense concentrates on organisational aspects such as planning, organising and controlling the production process together with the management of interface functions in order to achieve organisational objectives. This is not necessarily restricted to production management but can equally apply for service or not-for-profit organisations, but these operational aspects are the core functions of operations management.
- Operations management in the **broader** sense sees a **wider** remit in every activity of the organisation. We might ask: 'Do you sense that many managers within your organisation could be said to have some operational management role?' The answer will usually be yes. Most management roles focus on the efficient use of resources to meet company goals. In the broader sense we need to consider the interfaces between the functions of the operation so as to achieve the best overall delivery of customer service irrespective of functional boundaries.

2   The extent of operations management in organisations

Introduction

2.1   The role of operations is concerned with any productive activity. Operations management is concerned with ensuring that these activities are carried out effectively and efficiently. In its broader sense operations management is about ensuring the efficient use of resources to meet customer expectations. These expectations are an amalgam of company history and tradition, company resources, company image, brand perception, customer services levels and a host of other related factors that come together and need to be met or exceeded.

2.2   The role of operations management is crucial to the success of any organisation as it seeks to improve effectiveness, ie to ensure that operations are carried out so as to meet customer requirements and to improve efficiency in the design and management of those operations so that they can meet customer service requirement in the most cost-effective and timely manner while maintaining customer service levels.

2.3   Irrespective of the changing nature of operations management the need to use resources effectively and efficiently is central to any organisation. The challenge for those involved is to ensure that this is possible and that resources are used to meet the needs of the organisation and customers, not only now but to meet planned future developments.

2.4   The increasing effectiveness will increase profitability or contribution by making the organisation leaner, more responsive and more competitive. Improvements in efficiency will reduce costs but these cost savings must not be made at the expense of effectiveness. Measures should be put in place to evidence improvement gains achieved through increasing effectiveness. Measuring performance allows judgement by setting targets and evaluating feedback leading to discussions on future improvements, efficiency savings or approaches.

2.5   Operations managers 'make things happen'. They take in goods, ideas and concepts and refine them to deliver the finished article. Many roles have an operations management perspective. Even if the role does not carry the operations management title the areas of operations management form part of many managers' roles.

Responsibility for cost

2.6   Operations management is concerned with managing the resources of an enterprise that are required to produce the goods and services to be sold or provided to consumers or other organisations. Operations managers have responsibility for the design of the operation and the systems and processes involved in making them.

2.7   The operations function involves managing a large cost centre with an overall responsibility for up to 80 per cent of all the costs incurred by a business. These comprise most, if not all, of the direct costs (employees and materials) and a proportion of overheads that are applicable to specific operations.

2.8   With the high level of costs involved, the operations function has a key role in managing the flow of money through the organisation. Costs are built up as a product or service moves from raw materials or information through processing to result in finished goods or service delivery. The purchase of raw materials, components and items for assembly, and the direct costs involved in the transformation process, must be well managed not only from an operational standpoint but also with regard to the cashflow implications.

Responsibility for activities

2.9   Operations managers have a degree of responsibility for all the activities of the operation that directly or indirectly contribute to the effective production of goods and services. The direct responsibility concerns all the activities involved in the input–transformation–output process. The indirect responsibility concerns the linkages between operations and the other functional areas of the business.

2.10   As organisations have changed to meet the needs and challenges of the modern business environment their management structures have also been altered, often to a flatter and more flexible structure that serves to encourage cross-functional teamworking. The role of operations managers involves an ongoing interface with other business areas such as design, procurement and supply chain management, logistics and finance. This interface role will involve cross-functional teamworking to ensure that all relevant areas linked to a project or issue are discussed and developed as appropriate.

Responsibility for performance

2.11   Operations management places responsibility on managers to continually improve the performance of their operation. The role involves the issue of managing complexity.

2.12   Even where individual tasks are not complex, the drawing together of these tasks in a way that is most appropriate and effective to deliver results may be a challenge. One part of the operation may involve a number of individual tasks that come together to produce the desired outcome but the operations manager also needs to consider how these individual tasks may impact different business areas if they are designed to meet just one operational requirement.

2.13   The need to continually improve, at least as fast as competitors, is a constant pressure across the organisation. As competitors work to improve systems and performance and customers' expectations continue to rise, organisations in a competitive environment must rise to meet the challenge or possibly risk seeing the competition make inroads into their business. The role of operations management is central to ensuring that the organisation is in a fit condition and responsive enough to meet these outside pressures.

2.14   To meet these needs it is essential that operations managers have a strategic plan in place. This operations strategy must align with the corporate strategy of the organisation.

2.15   Operations managers must also try to ensure that problems do not occur in the first place. This responsibility involves operations management in product design, logistics, storage and distribution issues, design of production processes and systems, and quality throughout the organisation through the delivery of the goods or services.

2.16   The design of the operation, the products and the processes is an essential aspect of operations management. Although responsibility for product design may not be a direct operations management role, it is vital for operations managers to become involved in this area. This will ensure that, via cross-functional teamworking, the product can be integrated into the stock management and production processes of the organisation in the most effective manner to deliver the desired outcome.

2.17   Operations managers have a direct responsibility for the planning and control of the operation. This area covers decisions relating to what the operation's resources should be doing and ensuring they are doing it effectively and efficiently. Areas covered include the objectives and activities of operations planning and control, system capacity and system efficiency, and demand management strategies that serve to give a flavour of the complexity and essential nature of this crucial role of operations management.

3   Operations management in different types of organisations

The manufacturing sector

3.1   The role of operations has broadened as the scope of business has expanded. From its original remit of production management the broader term 'operations management' reflects the wider scope of the role and its importance across wider sector environments.

3.2   The conventional aspect of operations management is its production origins. In the manufacturing environment this involves the conversion of raw materials into a final product through a manufacturing (transformation) process. Discussed later in the chapter the input-transformation-output model is fundamental to operations management.

3.3   The input-transformation-output model takes inputs such as components and assembly items to be put into the transformation process where they contribute to the manufactured product then progress through to the output required to meet customer demands. The principal role of operations management is to increase productivity by reducing the amount of inputs, which can include costs, labour and processes, while securing the same level of outputs.

The service sector

3.4   Services are the activities that influence the physical, emotional or intellectual condition of a customer and are an increasing aspect of the operations management role.

3.5   Services include consultancy, retailing, dentistry, solicitors, public service areas etc. They can equally apply the input-transformation-output model (see Chapter 3), taking ideas, people and/or concepts as inputs and transforming then through a series of processes to achieve a defined outcome. As an example, the services provided by a local authority must not only be delivered but the reasoning behind them must be explained and justified to council taxpayers who derive no first-hand benefit from them. Delivery of the service is the first part of the definition and influencing the intellectual condition of the customer is explaining the reasoning.

3.6 Supply activities are those involved in the change of ownership of a physical product. Goods move and change ownership and make-up as they progress along the supply chain (raw material – refined material – component of first production process – delivery to be incorporated into manufacture of the final product) or as ownership is transferred as part of a wholesale or retail process. The supply chain has a direct relevance for operations managers as they are reliant on the timing and quality of delivered goods inputs in order to progress to the transformation stage.

3.7 The service supply chain requires the same consideration from operations managers involved. As an example the production of a text book may require inputs from a number of different writers. These inputs need to be collated and transformed into the finished book before being bound and delivered to customers.

3.8 The role of logistics is a crucial contributor to successful operations. The role is the movement and storage of material in and out of the organisation in the most effective manner. The role of logistics personnel will vary greatly but can involve such areas as storage, stock control and distribution, with the objective of managing these operations in the most effective manner to meet company and customer needs.

3.9 Distribution activities are those involved in the movement and storage of goods including movement by sea, air, road and rail, warehousing, containerisation and all interlinked logistic considerations. These can equally have an operations function. Warehouses can take in bulk deliveries and transform them by breaking the delivery into smaller quantities and adding value by arranging home deliveries.

3.10 The retail operations manager takes deliveries from a number of suppliers and organises the processes that display and support the sales process. Value is added by the transformation process of breaking large quantities and providing smaller quantities to individual customers. The advent of online retailers has demonstrated how effectively technology can be used to bring a fresh approach and reduce costs.

The not-for-profit sector

3.11 When considering not-for-profit organisations such as hospitals, local authorities or charities, increases in effectiveness can be viewed as the contribution these improvements bring to the overall organisation. This is the contribution that comes from better processes, systems and linkages that achieve equal or superior output without an increase in input resources.

3.12 Measuring improvements can be more difficult in a service-orientated environment. Governments have introduced national targets, with mixed success, but they provide a target for bodies to aim for or exceed. The targets can also be used for similar organisations to benchmark their operations against more successful organisations. An example is local authorities where successful improvements and gains are published, along with league tables, on the internet.

3.13 The site allows public sector organisations to learn of successful improvements and how they were implemented, and then apply them to their own organisation in a manner that they find appropriate for their own circumstances.

3.14 It would be a mistake to consider different sectors as operating in isolation. Good operations management requires an interface (in terms of cross-functional teams, information flows and good communications) to be an ongoing feature of the business or service irrespective of the organisational structure used.

The retail sector

3.15 Recent years have seen the retail sector under pressure like never before. The world-wide slow-down in demand has caused many retailers to fail while many others have responded by examining their operations more closely, looking for gains that can be made with minimum or no impact on service.

3.16   Consumers are demanding greater choice, with products being replaced more frequently, resulting in shorter product lifecycles. Consumers want a more exciting shopping experience with innovative stores and shopping centres. All this imposes increased operating costs on the retailer.

3.17   The supply chain in the retail sector is global in scope and requires careful management to reduce lead times, control costs and achieve quick response, highlighting the need for agility in their approach. The Operations Management Retail Sector Special Interest Group recommends that retailers need to ensure that they find the right balance between price, inventory, agility, adaptiveness, innovation and cost cutting in order to maximise success in a competitive marketplace.

3.18   Within the fashion sector, as an example, it is common practice for retailers to deal with manufacturers, with centralised buying and considerable negotiation on prices, quality and delivery schedules. Many supply chains involve intermediaries acting as significant figures in the supply chain. Globalisation has had a profound impact on the fashion industry with many companies either sourcing from overseas, or moving manufacturing to countries with lower labour costs.

3.19   A number of strategies in the textile and clothing supply chain are evident. Just in time (JIT) supply is a common approach, as is the delivery of finished goods to be sold through the supply chain. UK retailers understand the vulnerability of these globalised supply chains and will look to flexible delivery through domestic sourcing as a possible option.

3.20   A key operational approach is improved demand management coupled with a reduction in wasteful activities. The challenge enterprises face is to either focus on speed and efficiency throughout the supply chain to replenish stock to a predetermined level, or to produce exact quantities in response to fulfilling customers' orders.

3.21   Long lead times mean that companies have to rely heavily on long-term forecasts, which may prove to be unreliable. Companies in the fashion industry are increasingly using time as a factor for enhancing competitiveness. Reductions in lead-times assist companies in addressing an increasing demand for variety. Development cycles are shortening, transport and delivery is more efficient and merchandising is presented 'floor-ready'.

3.22   Errors in forecasting can result in lost sales and excess inventory. Products where demand can be accurately predicted should be differentiated from those where determination of demand is difficult. It follows that forecasting and sourcing strategies should reflect that differentiation. In consequence, the role of the buying team is essential to a retailer's success.

3.23   The future will require a combination of optimising the business model, optimising the total value chain, and building trust and understanding throughout the supply chain. Increased sharing of risk, improved communication and increased benefits for all supply chain members will help to develop an improved supply chain.

3.24   From an operations management perspective the challenge is to better understand the underlying factors that influence retail and to put in place management practices that deliver high levels of customer service while effectively forecasting, managing the supply chain and ensuring delivery into the store.

The construction sector

3.25   The construction sector is one of the most diverse areas of business. It can be divided into three broad areas.

- Building construction (including refurbishment)
- Heavy and civil engineering construction
- Speciality trade construction

3.26   This industry is a leader in terms of outsourcing as it relies heavily on subcontractors and suppliers of building materials and equipment. It can also be seen as different from other industries in that it is inherently a site-specific project-based activity.

3.27   These characteristics lead to the industry taking a different approach to channel members. At the project level the relationship can be viewed as temporary or short-term while at the firm level relationships can permit long-term relationship building that reflects good supply chain management practices.

3.28   Planning is a key area in construction projects. Construction is founded on projects that have a defined start and end. It is based wherever the construction project is located. Sound planning is essential and will pass through four stages.

- The development stage
- The tender stage
- The pre-construction stage
- The construction stage

3.29   The role of operations will reflect the different stages. During the development stage the developer is calculating the financial viability of the potential project. The operations role will be to assist in the cost build-up. During the tender stage Procurement could be considered as holding the operations role. During the pre-construction phase operations involves planning and discussing the project with the objective of ensuring smooth delivery. Operations will take on its more traditional role prior to and during the delivery of the project (the construction stage).

3.30   Construction operations managers make sure that projects meet building and safety standards and they regularly check on the progress and quality of construction. They apply for permits and licences when necessary, and read and review blueprints. In addition, a construction manager prepares contracts and bids; estimates costs and makes schedules; and ensures projects stay within budget.

3.31   Health and safety considerations are paramount in constructions operations. There are strict regulations. In the UK, for example, all accidents must be reported to the Health & Safety Executive who have the power to close a site if there are serious on-site issues. There are numerous pieces of legislation concerned with health and safety. Other considerations will include the disposal of waste in accordance with environmental regulations and the secure storage of hazardous material.

3.32   The construction operations administrator must monitor the progress of each individual aspect of the construction project. To do this, they will meet with the management to discuss any delays or additional costs that may occur. Operations will then update the timeline of the project and inform the client of any significant changes.

3.33   Construction covers a wide business area. Operations management in this sector is usually very 'hands-on' with those making the week-to-week, day-to-day decisions having a depth of experience in the business area whether it be building, drilling, demolition etc. Every project has its own characteristics – no two building projects are the same.

4 Product vs service operations

The mix of goods and services

4.1 The outputs of a business may be either goods or services or a mix of the two. The proportions of goods and services in the mix will vary from industry to industry. Here are some examples (with percentages included for illustration only).

Table 1.1 *The mix of goods and services in different industries*

OPERATION	GOODS	SERVICES
Mining	95%	5%
Vending machines	95%	5%
Low-cost consumable goods	80%	20%
Home computers	75%	25%
Fast-food operation	60%	40%
High-quality restaurant meal	30%	70%
Car breakdown service	25%	75%
Local authority	25%	75%
Teaching	5%	95%

4.2 With mining the purpose is to extract raw materials. Little emphasis is placed on the delivery of support services with the exception of transportation to a port or for refinement.

4.3 A fast-food restaurant offers a mix of a limited product range with a standardised approach to service; a more upmarket restaurant provides better facilities and specialised advice; a local authority provides goods in terms of refuse collection, street cleaning etc, but concentrates more on offering a range of support services that meet the needs of the community.

4.4 This analysis demonstrates that most operations produce a mix of goods and services.

4.5 We are seeing major changes in two key areas that affect the goods-service mix.

- **Customer service requirements**. Customers are becoming more demanding and require better and consistently high levels of customer service. One approach is to use this to the supplier's benefit and 'add value' to the customer experience. Delivery in 24 hours, late product customisation, 'delighting' the customer with unexpected upgrades and improvements at no extra cost, are all examples. The reward can be better customer relationships and retention, leading to an improvement in the operation overall.
- **The impact of information technology**. Information and communication technologies can allow for the provision and standardisation of services in a way that can be easily understood by customers. A well designed website can provide company information, product information and purchase information together with a secure method of purchase and detail on subsequent delivery.

Aspects of tangibility

4.6 Products are tangible, which means that they have a physical presence (unlike services which have no physical presence). The essence of services is that they do not result in the ownership of anything.

Table 1.2 *Characteristics of goods and services*

GOODS	SERVICES
Tangible	Intangible
Can be inventoried	Cannot be inventoried
Little customer contact	Extensive customer contact
Standard customer contact	Flexible customer contact
Long lead times	Short lead times
Capital intensive	Labour intensive
Quality easy to assess	Quality very difficult to assess

4.7   Services have been defined by Kotler as: 'any activity of benefit that one party can offer to another that is essentially intangible and does not result in the ownership of anything. Its production may or may not be tied to a physical product'.

4.8   Service delivery differs from the operational aspects of goods delivery in a number of crucial ways. The operations and marketing roles, in particular, face a number of distinct problems that require different approaches to address the issues raised. The characteristics of services that make them distinctive are as follows.

- Intangibility
- Inseparability
- Variability (also referred to as heterogeneity)
- Perishability
- Ownership

4.9   **Intangibility** refers to the lack of substance that is involved in service delivery. Unlike goods there are no physical aspects, no taste, no feel etc. This can inhibit the choice of a customer to use a service, as they are not sure what they will receive.

4.10   **Inseparability**. A service often cannot be separated from the provider of the service. The creation or the performance often occurs at the same instant that a full or partial consumption of it occurs. Goods must be produced, then sold, then consumed (in that order). Services are only a promise at the time they are sold; most services are sold and then are produced and consumed simultaneously.

4.11   **Variability**. Many services face a problem of maintaining consistency in the standard of output. Variability of quality in delivery is inevitable because of the number of factors that can influence it. It may prove difficult or impossible either to attain precise standardisation of the service offered or to influence or control perceptions of what is good or bad customer service.

4.12   To minimise the impact there is a need to monitor customer reactions. A common way of addressing this problem involves applying a system or business format to deliver a service that can then be franchised to operators. The franchisor can set precise guidelines throughout its business in areas such as customer service, dress code and design and layout that can serve to standardise the offering.

4.13   **Perishability**. Services cannot be stored. Seats at a concert, provision of a lecture, services of a dentist consist of their availability for periods of time. Perishability presents specific marketing problems. Meeting customer needs in these operations depends on staff being available as and when they are needed. This must be balanced against the need for a firm to minimise unnecessary expenditure on staff wages. Anticipating and responding to levels of demand is a key planning priority.

4.14 **Ownership**. Services differ fundamentally from goods in that purchase does not result in a transfer of property. The purchase of a service only confers on the customer access to or rights to use a facility – not ownership. This may lower the customer's perception of the service's value.

4.15 Services involve a higher degree of customer contact and presentation than with the selling of a product. The physical delivery of a service is less of a problem as the service element is intangible. However, other areas take on a more important role.

- **People**: have a crucial role in providing service. Customer satisfaction can often depend on the person providing the service, because the service is inseparable from the person delivering it. As a result, there is an increased emphasis on staff training and development.
- **Physical evidence**: the ambience surrounding the service being provided. As an example the ambience surrounding a top hotel may serve to convey the nature of the product, reinforce the image of the hotel, engender rapport, imply qualities and transmit messages.
- **Process**: this refers to the methods used to provide the service and is directly related to the role of operations management. Procedures for dealing with customers and for supplying the service must be carefully planned and managed so as to reduce variability.

Quality issues

4.16 Quality is key to service delivery. Only the customer can judge quality.

4.17 Quality of service is an increasingly important performance measurement tool in both the public and private sectors. With the move to a more service-orientated economy and greater transparency and accountability being expected in the public sector, the area of service is increasingly being placed under scrutiny.

4.18 Quality of service to customers is, by its nature, subjective and qualitative. Gathering the information provides greater challenges than would be the case with a product, where measures such as rejection rates or percentage for scrap could be used. Questionnaires are commonly used (either by mail, email or over the telephone), although the response rate can be low.

4.19 Two categories of data are relevant.

- **Quantitative** (also known as hard data) based on figures (eg variances, profit, sales, costs, ratios, indices)
- **Qualitative** (also known as soft data) based on opinions and feedback

4.20 Judgement on quality of service provision can be formalised by linking feedback from questionnaires with some quantitative measures that can be used in connection with it. Ratios such as returns to sales or complaints per units sold are one tool. Delivery targets (eg 95 per cent delivery in two days) can be measured against actual achievement. Speed of service at supermarkets and calls waiting at call centres are all performance measures that together can give a realistic and rounded assessment of the quality of service being delivered.

4.21 The role of operations management must be measured to be fully evaluated in its effectiveness. Measurement highlights areas for improvement, permits benchmarking where appropriate and allows for the setting of realistic targets and objectives. The role needs to be fully appreciated at the strategic level of an organisation in order to reach full potential and should be fully supported as a strategic objective. The role is becoming more complex as business pressures continue to grow.

5   The impact of global sourcing

Globalisation

5.1   The period since the second world war has seen a considerable growth in the numbers, size and spread of multinational companies who have benefited from factors such as the reduction in tariff barriers, the growth in technology, the impact of worldwide communications, the increasing standardisation of trade-related documentation and the harmonisation of customs tariff numbers among many others.

5.2   Organisations confront a challenging set of problems in the form of global competition, emergence of developing economies, formation of trade blocs, environmental neglect, economic stagnation and recessions, and low labour skills. Alongside this, new opportunities are being offered in the form of larger global markets, environmental clean-up operations, infrastructure regeneration and reconstruction, and the ongoing development of the worldwide financial and telecommunications markets.

5.3   The impact of technology and the development of new service markets, programmes for upgrading human skills and the survival of lean producers and lean marketers are all part of the modern trading environment. The ability to succeed in today's economic community will require much more awareness of global issues and the global market place than has previously been the case.

5.4   The globalisation of business has, in many ways, been permitted by the impact of enhanced communications. Systems can be integrated within organisations, regardless of international boundaries, and can add value to a firm's performance by reducing stockholding, ensuring efficient materials usage and cost effective manufacture, and saving on labour costs amongst other areas.

5.5   With developments in IT and communications, particularly the internet, smaller organisations can now cost-effectively start to view the world in a similar way, as a global market for their products or services. International communications and other developments enable marketing, in particular, to be viewed in the global context.

Marketing in a global economy

5.6   The convergence of global consumer markets has been emphasised by the widening of marketing from a national or pan-national approach to a highly developed global perspective being taken by organisations.

5.7   Factors that have enhanced this global approach include the following.

- **Branding:** customers want products or services they are familiar with and that they trust. The use of international media to establish a 'brand identity' and the status factor in using internationally established brands has led to branding becoming an important consideration for any company wanting to establish its identity in overseas markets.
- **Market positioning:** it is now easier to identify and target user and consumer segments in many international markets. For the international marketer this means that market planning can be more effective and that promotion can be better targeted.
- **Promotion:** developments in international media coupled with the speed and effectiveness with which messages can be relayed have led to a more global outlook on promotional campaigns. A global approach to advertising will influence whatever type of medium is being used (trade fairs, television, magazines etc), and will often stress the brand in using the brand logo, brand colours and brand identity to reinforce the image in the mind of users and consumers.
- **Distribution:** the increase in global trade has been aided by a growth in the number and efficiency of services for transporting goods internationally. In today's international trading environment there may be a need to site manufacturing in the most cost effective locations or to purchase components from different countries. An effective global physical distribution and logistics network is essential to underpin the globalisation of world trade.

- **Pricing:** the implications of pricing strategy are significant to the international company. Differential pricing (adopting different prices in different markets) can often lead to difficulties as importing from lower priced countries for re-selling in more expensive markets can be damaging to a company's brand integrity, may introduce legal problems and can result in loss of profit.

5.8 Global marketing requires a different approach from traditional exporting in that it aims towards economies of scale in production and distribution and towards a gradual convergence of customer needs and wants on a global basis.

5.9 The global corporation seeks competitive advantage by identifying worldwide markets and then developing a manufacturing strategy that supports the marketing strategy. Global marketing needs (according to Chris Noonan in *Export Marketing)*:

- an organised strategy
- active market management and policies
- a flexibility recognising local market differences.

5.10 To the operations manager within this global concept there is the need to gain competitive advantage in manufacturing. This advantage can then be used to underpin the global marketing strategy by delivering goods of the appropriate quality, on time and in a manner that meets customer needs.

5.11 The Japanese writer Kenichi Ohmae coined the phrase 'Think Global – Act Local' as a way in which global corporations should view their markets. Organisations should always remain aware of local tastes and preferences, local culture and law, and should adapt the marketing mix to suit different needs while also being consistent in the approach to marketing strategy on a global scale.

Socio-cultural variety

5.12 The convergence of consumer preferences has occurred widely, particularly in regard to globally branded and technologically based products. However, wide socio-cultural differences and varying perspectives exist.

5.13 The socio-cultural environment consists of those physical, demographic and behavioural differences that influence business activities in different markets. Success will come from an understanding and knowledge of the country and the people you are dealing with. In today's competitive global economy you will need to fight hard for customers; appreciating their wants and needs is arguably more crucial in international trade than in any other area of marketing.

5.14 Culture has been defined as learned responses to recurring situations. Much of human behaviour is learned and cultural factors have a considerable influence on a customer's or business partner's values and attitudes. As individuals mature, their family, friends, school, religion, country and many other factors influence them. As they socialise they adopt sets of values, perceptions and preferences that influence the way they react to others or respond to events and which will strongly pattern their behaviour as adults.

5.15 Each country has its own values and customs – the dos and don'ts that make up the cultural pattern of the people. The international trader has to be able to recognise the similarities that bring customers together but must be sensitive to understand and value cultural differences. To work effectively in a variety of markets it is necessary to appreciate the need and be aware of and show respect to other cultures, in both attitude and behaviour.

5.16 Awareness of culture is an important element for any individual or organisation carrying out business overseas. Cultural appreciation helps in assessing the needs and wants of customers. Differences in attitude and belief may affect:

- Attitude toward ownership of an item

- Strength and direction of attitude
- Reason for desire or antipathy
- Perception of appropriate style and design
- Meaning of colours, symbols or words

5.17   It is clear there has been a convergence of consumer preferences in many areas. Using branding and telecommunications as examples there is the opportunity to either add value or reduce costs and an organisation must decide on the strategy appropriate to it.

5.18   For many organisations production and sourcing will be on a global basis looking not only at price but also at location of manufacturing sites and quality of product as key areas. This approach widens the remit of operations to give an international perspective.

5.19   The operations management role, initially production based, has been extended to incorporate service delivery and can now be viewed within an international perspective with international manufacturing and sourcing contracts and decisions often forming an integral part of the operations role. This broadens the remit of the operations manager who needs to take existing skills into overseas operations and develop and refine them to ensure delivery often in multi-site and multi-country operations.

The impact of globalisation on operations management

5.20   Globalisation has been defined by Ruud Lubbers as 'a process in which geographic distance becomes a factor of diminishing importance in the establishment and maintenance of cross border economic, political and socio-cultural relations'. The definition highlights the way in which communications are reducing geographic issues and enabling an approach that can view the world as one market.

5.21   This view of the world extends to production as well as marketing. The industrialised world has over recent years seen much of its manufacturing base move to overseas markets. The reasons are often discussed but the reality is that many overseas countries offer lower production costs because of lower rates of pay and overheads and can often match or improve on quality.

5.22   Globalisation has affected operations management as the operations manager, whether in goods or services, needs to deliver the efficiencies and effectiveness called for in a diverse mix of markets.

5.23   The management of overseas operations, whether outsourced or company-owned, calls for a wider appreciation of cultural, ethical and communication issues than is the case when operating only in the domestic market.

5.24   Many organisations throughout the world are now taking a global perspective on their strategies to take advantage of the current situation. The globalisation of production has opened new opportunities for countries such as China and Indonesia. The globalisation of services has opened new opportunities for India, in particular as high computer literacy coupled with English language skills have led to a growing IT support and call centre industry.

5.25   World best practice demonstrates that organisations should take commercial advantage of these opportunities in order to meet the increasing demands of customers in terms of quality and cost.

5.26   The best overseas manufacturers and service providers are constantly in demand. The role of the operations manager may involve training and updating certain providers to ensure expected standards are met but in many cases the provider may be more advanced because of their ability to specialise and their knowledge of the requirements of global companies.

Increased competition

5.27   The globalisation of business coupled with the economic growth in global economies has combined to lead to a highly competitive global environment. Organisations must be sure of their strategies and be responsive to customer needs in order to survive.

5.28   Professor Michael Porter identifies five competitive forces in the environment of an organisation. The impact of globalisation is serving to widen the impact of these factors.

- The threat of new entrants to an industry. A new entrant will bring extra capacity and poses a threat as established organisations may lose market share and economies of scale. With the increased globalisation of business new entrants may often mean established international firms looking for new markets.
- The threat of substitute products or services. Substitutes pose a threat as they limit the ability of an organisation to charge high prices for its products so that demand for products becomes relatively sensitive to price
- The bargaining power of customers. Customers will look for better quality products and services at lower prices. Factors such as differentiation by adding value in areas such as delivery or customer service, the ability to switch between products and the importance of the spend, can reduce this strength
- The bargaining power of suppliers. This depends on a number of factors including the business relationship, the number of suppliers, the importance of the supplier's product and the cost of switching from one supplier to another.
- The rivalry amongst current competitors in the industry. The intensity of competitive rivalry will influence the profitability of the industry as a whole.

5.29   The influence of Porter's Five Forces leads companies to consider their competitive position. Competitive position describes the market share, costs, price, quality and accumulated experience of an entity or product relative to its competitors.

5.30   Competition forces most organisations to look for cost savings or value-added activities that enhance marketability. One of the key roles of operations management is to make improvements in efficiency and effectiveness in order to increase productivity. Operations managers will seek to increase productivity but also to enable value-added production through areas such as design, flexibility in manufacture and late customisation of product.

Shorter product lifecycles

5.31   The product lifecycle (PLC) concept is based on the premise that products pass through various stages in their sales life. The basic principle of the PLC is that products have a finite life (although exceptions can be found to this rule). The length of the PLC will be different for all products. For example the length of the PLC for Mars bars will be different from specific models of mobile phones.

Figure 1.1 *The product lifecycle*

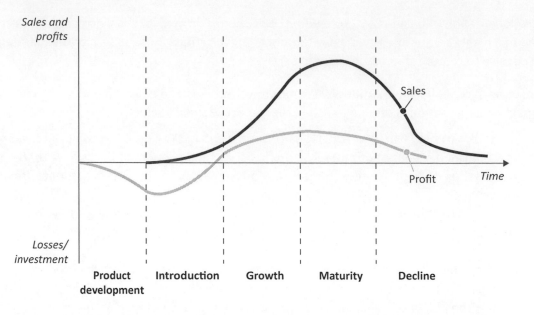

5.32 Increased competition, when linked to increasing customer demands, forces companies to review their product offerings more frequently. Product lifecycles are shortening in response to increased competition, advances in technology and customer demand.

5.33 The use of computer aided design and manufacture enables faster product development and manufacture. Organisations that can bring new and innovative quality products to market can gain a substantial competitive edge over the competition. CAD/CAM systems permit faster times (from concept through to manufacture) while permitting simulation of use where appropriate. Simulation means that, often, models and mock-ups are not required as computer-generated information can carry out testing on a virtual model. This not only saves money but also speeds up the product development to launch process.

5.34 Globalisation widens the remit of the operations role. Greater emphasis is placed on adopting world best practice. This can be achieved through monitoring technical developments and applying benchmarking where appropriate. The operations role is to understand the manufacturing and service developments needs of globalisation and apply the benefits to work practices.

6 An example of operations management

6.1 The indicative content suggests that you may be required to describe examples of operations management in practice. You should build up a file of examples you come across in your work or in the press. In the meantime, we illustrate the kind of issues you should be focusing on by referring to the example of McDonald's, the fast food restaurant chain.

Product planning

6.2 The planning of products and services is one of the most important operations of any type of organisation. Product planning involves designing products with both economy and quality in mind, which a customer will find attractive, be able to understand and quickly able to use with minimum risk and which delights by its performance or flavour or durability etc.

6.3 In McDonald's, product planning is a key operation. The restaurant has to keep adding new products to its menu in order to meet the needs of the customers, whose preferences are constantly changing. As an example, the increasing preference of consumers towards healthy food made the restaurant add healthier options to its menu. This change has also been driven by competitive pressure, notably from Subway, whose more healthy product range has impacted on McDonald's business.

Capacity planning

6.4   The second operational decision important for organisations is capacity planning. Capacity planning and control is the task of setting the effective capacity of the operation so that it can respond to the demands placed upon it. This normally means determining how the operation should respond to fluctuations in demand.

6.5   Operations managers usually distinguish between short-term, medium-term and long-term capacity decisions. For short-term and medium-term capacity planning, the capacity level of the operation is adjusted within the fixed physical limits that are set by long-term capacity decisions. This is also referred to as aggregate planning and control because it is necessary to aggregate the various types of output from an operation into one figure.

6.6   In McDonald's, the operations managers have to set the capacity of making food items in such a way that it responds quickly to the demand for those items in peak hours. It also has to make sure that it has enough stock of ingredients to prepare food items. This is important because if one ingredient falls short then the whole process of making food may halt.

Location planning

6.7   Location planning is one of the important operations that every organisation carries out. It is one of the critical success factors for many organisations. Therefore it is very important for businesses to choose an ideal location. They may do so on the basis of various factors such as proximity to the source of raw material, cost-effectiveness, proximity to customers or suppliers, competition in the area, transportation availability and cost, availability of resources, and availability of the right labour.

6.8   McDonald's have to plan their location in such a way that maximum customers visit their restaurants. They will look for locations that will have a large customer base, transport access and availability of parking space. They also prefer locations that are suitable for raw materials delivery.

Process planning

6.9   After developing the product a business has to develop processes for making and supporting the product. Organisations have to identify appropriate processes which will be needed to achieve a required level of output of the planned goods and services at the right quality standards. In McDonald's, the operations manager develops and establishes the process of cooking the food items in such a way as to maintain the speed of production and the quality of the food. Processes are designed to ensure that health, safety and hygiene issues are taken into consideration. The equipment market is constantly monitored to ensure that the best technology is being applied.

Layout

6.10   Layout is the arrangement of a facility to provide working, service and reception, storage and administrative areas. The layout is designed by traditional techniques using templates, scale plans, string diagrams, and travel charting, which have been proved as low-cost methods of achieving either optimal or near optimal layout plans. Poor layouts can greatly reduce the overall capacity and overall productivity.

6.11   In McDonald's, layout design is a very important operation. A proper layout of the equipment in the kitchen is essential to ensure preparation of quality food in less time and in compliance with health and safety standards. It will also help to minimise any need for supervision, therefore reducing cost.

6.12   The customer-facing internal layout is standardised as much as possible, with necessary adaptations across global markets. Generally colours, seats, table layout, and merchandising will be as consistent across the chain as possible, providing customers with a comfortable, well-understood experience.

Job design

6.13   Job design consists of formal specifications and informal expectations of an employee's work related activities. The job design should try to meet the needs of both the job holder and the organisation. Each job must be a reasonable compromise of technical, economic, and behavioural feasibility.

- Technical feasibility: the person holding the job must be capable of performing the required tasks with the resources available to him.
- Economic feasibility: the cost of providing a salary to the employees, providing equipment and maintaining the organisational environment must remain within the organisation's capabilities.
- Behavioural feasibility: the feeling that people derive from a job affects their motivation to perform it.

6.14   Job design is also an important operation in McDonald's. A particular set of tasks is allocated to each staff member. For example, some crew members cook food items in the kitchen, others work on the counter, while others look after the customers in the lobby. Also there are employees who manage the crew members and look after overall wellbeing of the restaurant. While designing these jobs the technical, economic and behavioural feasibility is taken into consideration.

Supply chain management

6.15   Supply chain management allows McDonald's to get the right goods and services to the place they are needed at the right time, in the proper quantity and at an acceptable cost. Efficiently managing this process involves overseeing relationships with suppliers and customers, controlling inventory, forecasting demand and getting constant feedback on what is happening at every link in the chain. In McDonald's, supply chain management is a global operation and management of suppliers is clearly crucial. Individual stores will complete regular supplier reports.

Inventory management

6.16   Inventory management is another important operation. It involves choosing the best method of inventory control. While doing so, managers must keep in mind the expected demands for the products. The bases on which managers choose their methods of inventory control may differ but the common idea is to ensure that the mix of inventory types is able to satisfy customer needs and deliver the required profitability and cashflows.

6.17   In McDonald's, the inventory is managed on a first-in-first-out (FIFO) basis. This is because most of the inventory consists of perishable items. Deliveries of inventory will occur three or more times a week, perhaps daily depending on the business of the restaurant. Inventory is stored in freezers with proper packaging so as to ensure the freshness of the food items.

Quality management

6.18   Quality management is important to McDonald's. One of the key factors in successful franchising is the consistency of the product. It is important so as to keep up the reputation of the organisation. To manage and maintain the quality of the products and services the organisation may adopt a number of practices such as quality checks.

6.19   Quality of food can be very difficult to maintain and therefore McDonald's carry on a number of practices to make sure that quality food is served. Examples include visits by the food inspector from the head office, supervisor checks etc, with feedback promptly acted upon.

t timescale (technology, operations); or it may be able to apply new technologies effectively and in
a way as to give it an advantage over competitors (operations, technology, marketing).

rations must work toward developing the management, technological and manufacturing processes
systems that allow it to meet its stated objectives as defined in the strategic plan. It must look beyond
strategic plan into the vision of the organisation in order to focus on critical areas that will help drive
organisation forward.

of business strategy

third and arguably the most difficult role of operations is its role in driving strategy. The objective of
rations driving business strategy is to differentiate the company from others by giving it an advantage
its competitors. By excelling in key areas such as on-time deliveries, responsive manufacturing times
or new product development and delivery – or whatever areas are required by the organisation –
rations can go beyond its remit and develop a role that drives business success in the company.

Stage Model of Hayes and Wheelwright (HW)

Hayes and Wheelwright model, which has been well known and accepted for many years, is used to
ribe the contribution of operations to a company's competitiveness. It can be related to the three
s of the operation as discussed above. Moving from Stage 1 to Stage 2 of the HW model requires the
ty to implement strategy; moving from Stage 2 to Stage 3 requires the ability to support strategy;
ing from Stage 3 to Stage 4 requires operations to drive strategy with its unique capabilities.

e 2.1 *Hayes and Wheelwright's Four Stage Model*

e 1	**Internal neutrality**: here operations react to strategies that have been designed. The role of operations makes little contribution to the competitive advantage of the enterprise. It aims for 'internal neutrality', not by doing anything positive but by avoiding mistakes. It is essentially reactive to situations.
e 2	**External neutrality**: the operation looks outside the confines of its own organisation and compares itself with similar external enterprises. Benchmarking against other enterprises enables the operations role to adopt the best ideas, practice and norms of their competitors and bring them into the business. Although still being predominately reactive, new ideas and the integration of improvement areas into the business start to introduce a proactive approach.
e 3	**Internally supportive**: the operations role strives to be the best in the market. While the current levels of operations are already adequate, managers seek improvement. They try to gain superiority by analysing appropriate business strategy and then developing the best operations to support it. The operation is 'internally supportive' by providing a credible operations strategy. The operations role is proactive in looking for development areas that would benefit the enterprise.
e 4	**Externally supportive**: the final stage is one where the operations function is seen as providing an important foundation for the organisation's future success. Enterprises seek to be ahead of the competition in the way in which they design and develop products and services and in the way their operations are organised. Outward looking and proactive in nature, the operations role is integral in delivering competitive advantage.

conceptual model which allows organisations to consider how good their operations are. It is not a
ise tool for measuring operations excellence.

rent parts of operations can be at different stages to others. An airport could have check-in facilities at
e 4 but baggage handling at Stage 2. The overall customer experience would be mixed, particularly if
bags are lost. Identifying the stages gives operations the opportunity to improve.

Chapter summary

- In a restricted sense, the role of operations management is to obtain inputs, convert them using a transformation process, and produce outputs that can be sold to customers. In a broader sense, most managers can be said to have an operations role.
- Operations managers have responsibilities for costs, activities and performance. Ultimately they are concerned to ensure that outputs satisfy customer expectations.
- The role of operations management has its roots in the manufacturing sector. However, it is now recognised that principles of operations management are applicable in other sectors too: services; not-for-profit organisations; the retail sector; and the construction sector.
- Many organisations produce outputs that are a mix of products and services. The nature of services gives rise to additional challenges for operations managers.
- In recent decades we have witnessed increased globalisation of both sales and procurement. Operations managers are increasingly required to address issues of socio-cultural diversity, increased competition and shorter product lifecycles.
- In a typical operations management project, there may be issues of product planning, capacity planning, location planning, process planning, layout planning, job design, supply chain management, inventory management and quality management.

? Self-test questions

Numbers in brackets refer to the paragraphs above where your answers can be checked.

1 Define operations management. (1.6)

2 What is the difference between the 'restricted sense' and the 'broader sense' of operations management? (1.12)

3 Explain how an operations manager has a responsibility for cost control. (2.8)

4 Responsibility for product design is a direct operations management role. True or false? (2.16)

5 Can we apply the input – transformation – output model to services? (3.5)

6 List three broad areas of the construction sector. (3.25)

7 Describe two recent influences in the mix of goods and services in the economy. (4.5)

8 How does Kotler define services? (4.7)

9 Describe factors that have led to an increase in global marketing by selling organisations. (5.7)

10 How does Lubbers define globalisation? (5.20)

11 What are Porter's Five Forces? (5.28)

Strategic choice involves understanding the nature of stakeholder expectations, identifying strateg options, and then evaluating and selecting strategic options.

Strategic implementation is often considered the hardest part. When a strategy has been analyse and selected, the task is then to translate it into organisational action.

Strategy at different levels of a business

1.4 Strategies exist at several levels in any organisation, ranging from the overall business (or group of businesses) through to individuals working within it.

- *Corporate strategy* is concerned with the overall purpose and scope of the business to meet stakeholder expectations. This is a crucial level since it is heavily influenced by investors in the business and acts to guide strategic decision-making throughout the business. Corporate strategy is often stated explicitly in a **mission statement**.
- *Business unit strategy:* is concerned more with how a business competes successfully in a particular market. It concerns strategic decisions about choice of products, meeting needs of customers, gaini advantage over competitors, exploiting or creating new opportunities etc.
- *Operational strategy* is concerned with how each part of the business is organised to deliver the corporate and business-unit level strategic direction. Operational strategy therefore focuses on issues of resources, processes, people etc.

1.5 Operations strategy is 'the pattern of strategic decisions and actions which set the role, objectives and activities of the operation' *(Slack et al)*. Operations strategy is conventionally viewed in two aspects.

- *Content.* The content of operations strategy comprises the decisions that shape the way in which the role of operations will meet the company strategic plan. It consists of the role, objectives and activities which when developed should enable operations to deliver as required by the strategic plan.
- *Process.* The method used to make specific content decisions. The process of operations strategy refers to the procedures which are used to formulate operations strategies. It is the way we go about the activity of devising strategy.

From implementing to supporting to driving strategy

1.6 It would be anticipated in any business that the contribution of operations would improve over time. When a new or revised strategy is introduced much of the practicalities of delivering success over the long term will come from the way in which operations management in the company is successful at implementing the strategy. A second consideration is how the operations strategy supports the business strategy and a third is how operations drives strategy by surpassing its competition or excelling in its role.

1.7 Well-implemented strategic planning provides the vision, direction and goals for the organisation, but operational planning translates that strategy into the everyday tactics of the business that will ultimately produce the outcomes defined by the strategy. Simply stated, operational planning is the conversion of strategic goals into managed execution.

1.8 Corporate strategy can be thought of as a message that must be passed through the organisation, understood by all and acted on together. If the message is garbled, ambiguous or not communicated well, the intent will be lost in translation and operational execution will become misaligned with the corporate strategic goals.

1.9 Superior operational planning requires proactive and innovative thinking to enact strategy within the operational layer of the business. Operational planning must produce the planned outcomes while managing constraints on time, money and other resources.

1.10 *Slack et al* identify three roles for operations management. These are not e operation has to be one of them, but they all contribute to making up the three roles are as follows.

- The implementer of business strategy
- The supporter of business strategy
- The driver of business strategy

1.11 There are two important considerations in understanding these roles.

- Firstly, they are stated in ascending order of difficulty and of importan strategy is a very basic responsibility for operations; supporting busine operations should aspire to; but driving business strategy is only possi have unique capabilities.
- Secondly, they are cumulative in the sense that an operation cannot b strategy unless it has skills as an implementer, and cannot drive busine skills to support the business strategy.

The implementer of business strategy

1.12 The fundamental role of operations is to implement strategy. This will need already functioning environment with schedules to be kept and demand to management this presents a challenge that does not face the strategic plan at resources, location, skills as well as further business considerations. Ope the strategic planning process but the strategic plan needs to be implemen company are continuing.

1.13 Strategy implementation is fundamentally connected with organisational cl strategic implementation (ie making the strategy work in practice), fails to argued that the operational aspect is sometimes perceived to be the less 's essential that operational planning has to be done and organisations need

1.14 Operational planning requires a different skill set and discipline as compare biggest difference is to adjust our thinking to the day-to-day business opera constraints, inhibitors and accelerators that must be evaluated and factore discipline required is in many ways a mix of a practical application of strate project management.

The supporter of business strategy

1.15 Supporting strategy is an approach that goes beyond the implementation s succeed, it means developing and improving on the capabilities that allow improve.

1.16 Organisations will have a set of characteristics that are instrumental in thei resources, competencies and capabilities). Key success factors (KSFs) are wl competent at carrying out or concentrating on in order to succeed.

1.17 An organisation needs to understand its own KSFs. In order to do this succe its customers and understand why they differentiate between competitors need to determine how customers differentiate between similar offerings a organisation will differentiate itself from these competitors and gain and su

1.18 KSFs can be identified in a number of areas such as technology, distribution As an example the organisation may be adept in transferring design into the

1.19 Ope
and
the
the

The drive

1.20 The
ope
ove
and
ope

The Four

1.21 The
des
role
abi
mo

Tab

Sta
Sta
Sta
Sta

1.22 It is
pre

1.23 Dif
Sta
the

1

Chapter summary

- In a restricted sense, the role of operations management is to obtain inputs, convert them using a transformation process, and produce outputs that can be sold to customers. In a broader sense, most managers can be said to have an operations role.
- Operations managers have responsibilities for costs, activities and performance. Ultimately they are concerned to ensure that outputs satisfy customer expectations.
- The role of operations management has its roots in the manufacturing sector. However, it is now recognised that principles of operations management are applicable in other sectors too: services; not-for-profit organisations; the retail sector; and the construction sector.
- Many organisations produce outputs that are a mix of products and services. The nature of services gives rise to additional challenges for operations managers.
- In recent decades we have witnessed increased globalisation of both sales and procurement. Operations managers are increasingly required to address issues of socio-cultural diversity, increased competition and shorter product lifecycles.
- In a typical operations management project, there may be issues of product planning, capacity planning, location planning, process planning, layout planning, job design, supply chain management, inventory management and quality management.

 ## Self-test questions

Numbers in brackets refer to the paragraphs above where your answers can be checked.

1   Define operations management. (1.6)

2   What is the difference between the 'restricted sense' and the 'broader sense' of operations management? (1.12)

3   Explain how an operations manager has a responsibility for cost control. (2.8)

4   Responsibility for product design is a direct operations management role. True or false? (2.16)

5   Can we apply the input – transformation – output model to services? (3.5)

6   List three broad areas of the construction sector. (3.25)

7   Describe two recent influences in the mix of goods and services in the economy. (4.5)

8   How does Kotler define services? (4.7)

9   Describe factors that have led to an increase in global marketing by selling organisations. (5.7)

10   How does Lubbers define globalisation? (5.20)

11   What are Porter's Five Forces? (5.28)

CHAPTER 2

The Objectives and Strategies of Operations Management

Assessment criteria and indicative content

1.2 Critically assess the objectives and strategies of operations management

- From implementing to supporting to driving strategy
- The stages of development of operations strategy
- The performance objectives of operations management (quality, speed, dependability, flexibility and cost)
- Top-down and bottom-up perspectives of operations strategy
- Order-qualifying and order-winning objectives of operations management

Section headings

1. Stages in the development of operations strategy
2. Performance objectives of operations management
3. Top-down and bottom-up perspectives
4. Order-qualifying and order-winning objectives

1 Stages in the development of operations strategy

1.1 'Strategy is the direction and scope of an organisation over the long term, which achieves advantage for the organisation through its configuration of resources within a challenging environment, to meet the needs of markets and to fulfil stakeholder expectations'. *(Johnson, Scholes and Whittington Exploring Corporate Strategy).*

1.2 In other words, strategy is about the following issues.

- Where is the business trying to get to in the long term?
- Which markets should a business compete in and what types of activities are involved in such markets?
- How can the business perform better than the competition in those markets?
- What resources (skills, assets, finance, relationships, technical competence, facilities) are required in order to be able to compete?
- What external, environmental factors affect the business's ability to compete?
- What are the values and expectations of those stakeholders who have power in and around the business?

1.3 In its broadest sense, strategic management is about taking decisions that answer the above questions. In practice, a thorough strategic management process has three main components: strategic analysis, strategic choice, and strategic implementation (Johnson, Scholes and Whittington).

- Strategic analysis means analysing the strength of a business's position and understanding the important external factors that may influence that position.

- Strategic choice involves understanding the nature of stakeholder expectations, identifying strategic options, and then evaluating and selecting strategic options.
- Strategic implementation is often considered the hardest part. When a strategy has been analysed and selected, the task is then to translate it into organisational action.

Strategy at different levels of a business

1.4 Strategies exist at several levels in any organisation, ranging from the overall business (or group of businesses) through to individuals working within it.

- *Corporate strategy* is concerned with the overall purpose and scope of the business to meet stakeholder expectations. This is a crucial level since it is heavily influenced by investors in the business and acts to guide strategic decision-making throughout the business. Corporate strategy is often stated explicitly in a **mission statement**.
- *Business unit strategy:* is concerned more with how a business competes successfully in a particular market. It concerns strategic decisions about choice of products, meeting needs of customers, gaining advantage over competitors, exploiting or creating new opportunities etc.
- *Operational strategy* is concerned with how each part of the business is organised to deliver the corporate and business-unit level strategic direction. Operational strategy therefore focuses on issues of resources, processes, people etc.

1.5 Operations strategy is 'the pattern of strategic decisions and actions which set the role, objectives and activities of the operation' *(Slack et al)*. Operations strategy is conventionally viewed in two aspects.

- *Content.* The content of operations strategy comprises the decisions that shape the way in which the role of operations will meet the company strategic plan. It consists of the role, objectives and activities which when developed should enable operations to deliver as required by the strategic plan.
- *Process.* The method used to make specific content decisions. The process of operations strategy refers to the procedures which are used to formulate operations strategies. It is the way we go about the activity of devising strategy.

From implementing to supporting to driving strategy

1.6 It would be anticipated in any business that the contribution of operations would improve over time. When a new or revised strategy is introduced much of the practicalities of delivering success over the long term will come from the way in which operations management in the company is successful at implementing the strategy. A second consideration is how the operations strategy supports the business strategy and a third is how operations drives strategy by surpassing its competition or excelling in its role.

1.7 Well-implemented strategic planning provides the vision, direction and goals for the organisation, but operational planning translates that strategy into the everyday tactics of the business that will ultimately produce the outcomes defined by the strategy. Simply stated, operational planning is the conversion of strategic goals into managed execution.

1.8 Corporate strategy can be thought of as a message that must be passed through the organisation, understood by all and acted on together. If the message is garbled, ambiguous or not communicated well, the intent will be lost in translation and operational execution will become misaligned with the corporate strategic goals.

1.9 Superior operational planning requires proactive and innovative thinking to enact strategy within the operational layer of the business. Operational planning must produce the planned outcomes while managing constraints on time, money and other resources.

1.10   *Slack et al* identify three roles for operations management. These are not exclusive in the sense that an operation has to be one of them, but they all contribute to making up the way an operation behaves. The three roles are as follows.

- The implementer of business strategy
- The supporter of business strategy
- The driver of business strategy

1.11   There are two important considerations in understanding these roles.

- Firstly, they are stated in ascending order of difficulty and of importance. Implementing business strategy is a very basic responsibility for operations; supporting business strategy is what most operations should aspire to; but driving business strategy is only possible if the operation really does have unique capabilities.
- Secondly, they are cumulative in the sense that an operation cannot be a supporter of business strategy unless it has skills as an implementer, and cannot drive business strategy unless it has the skills to support the business strategy.

The implementer of business strategy

1.12   The fundamental role of operations is to implement strategy. This will need to be accomplished in an already functioning environment with schedules to be kept and demand to be met. For operations management this presents a challenge that does not face the strategic planner. The strategic plan will look at resources, location, skills as well as further business considerations. Operations will be consulted during the strategic planning process but the strategic plan needs to be implemented while the operations of the company are continuing.

1.13   Strategy implementation is fundamentally connected with organisational change. Much of the area of strategic implementation (ie making the strategy work in practice), fails to match expectations. It can be argued that the operational aspect is sometimes perceived to be the less 'sexy' part of planning, but it is essential that operational planning has to be done and organisations need to do it properly.

1.14   Operational planning requires a different skill set and discipline as compared with strategic planning. The biggest difference is to adjust our thinking to the day-to-day business operations and consider all of the constraints, inhibitors and accelerators that must be evaluated and factored into tactical planning. The discipline required is in many ways a mix of a practical application of strategic planning with effective project management.

The supporter of business strategy

1.15   Supporting strategy is an approach that goes beyond the implementation stage. For the organisation to succeed, it means developing and improving on the capabilities that allow the organisation to evolve and improve.

1.16   Organisations will have a set of characteristics that are instrumental in their ability to succeed (attributes, resources, competencies and capabilities). Key success factors (KSFs) are what the organisation must be competent at carrying out or concentrating on in order to succeed.

1.17   An organisation needs to understand its own KSFs. In order to do this successfully it will need to consider its customers and understand why they differentiate between competitors in the same market. Managers need to determine how customers differentiate between similar offerings and then decide how the organisation will differentiate itself from these competitors and gain and sustain a competitive advantage.

1.18   KSFs can be identified in a number of areas such as technology, distribution, marketing and/or operations. As an example the organisation may be adept in transferring design into the finished product within a short timescale (technology, operations); or it may be able to apply new technologies effectively and in such a way as to give it an advantage over competitors (operations, technology, marketing).

1.19 Operations must work toward developing the management, technological and manufacturing processes and systems that allow it to meet its stated objectives as defined in the strategic plan. It must look beyond the strategic plan into the vision of the organisation in order to focus on critical areas that will help drive the organisation forward.

The driver of business strategy

1.20 The third and arguably the most difficult role of operations is its role in driving strategy. The objective of operations driving business strategy is to differentiate the company from others by giving it an advantage over its competitors. By excelling in key areas such as on-time deliveries, responsive manufacturing times and/or new product development and delivery – or whatever areas are required by the organisation – operations can go beyond its remit and develop a role that drives business success in the company.

The Four Stage Model of Hayes and Wheelwright (HW)

1.21 The Hayes and Wheelwright model, which has been well known and accepted for many years, is used to describe the contribution of operations to a company's competitiveness. It can be related to the three roles of the operation as discussed above. Moving from Stage 1 to Stage 2 of the HW model requires the ability to implement strategy; moving from Stage 2 to Stage 3 requires the ability to support strategy; moving from Stage 3 to Stage 4 requires operations to drive strategy with its unique capabilities.

Table 2.1 *Hayes and Wheelwright's Four Stage Model*

Stage 1	**Internal neutrality**: here operations react to strategies that have been designed. The role of operations makes little contribution to the competitive advantage of the enterprise. It aims for 'internal neutrality', not by doing anything positive but by avoiding mistakes. It is essentially reactive to situations.
Stage 2	**External neutrality**: the operation looks outside the confines of its own organisation and compares itself with similar external enterprises. Benchmarking against other enterprises enables the operations role to adopt the best ideas, practice and norms of their competitors and bring them into the business. Although still being predominately reactive, new ideas and the integration of improvement areas into the business start to introduce a proactive approach.
Stage 3	**Internally supportive**: the operations role strives to be the best in the market. While the current levels of operations are already adequate, managers seek improvement. They try to gain superiority by analysing appropriate business strategy and then developing the best operations to support it. The operation is 'internally supportive' by providing a credible operations strategy. The operations role is proactive in looking for development areas that would benefit the enterprise.
Stage 4	**Externally supportive**: the final stage is one where the operations function is seen as providing an important foundation for the organisation's future success. Enterprises seek to be ahead of the competition in the way in which they design and develop products and services and in the way their operations are organised. Outward looking and proactive in nature, the operations role is integral in delivering competitive advantage.

1.22 It is a conceptual model which allows organisations to consider how good their operations are. It is not a precise tool for measuring operations excellence.

1.23 Different parts of operations can be at different stages to others. An airport could have check-in facilities at Stage 4 but baggage handling at Stage 2. The overall customer experience would be mixed, particularly if their bags are lost. Identifying the stages gives operations the opportunity to improve.

Competitive advantage and competitive priorities

1.24   Many factors shape and form the operations strategy of an organisation, for example the ever increasing need for globalising products and operations and therefore reducing the unit cost, creating a technology leadership position, introducing new inventions, taking advantage of mass customisation, using supplier partnering, and looking for strategic sourcing solutions. All of these factors require an external or market-based orientation; these are the changes that take place in the external environment of the company.

1.25   The emphasis given to these priorities and the state of the organisation determine the nature and level of investments necessary to implement the operations strategy. These investments in operational practices are expected to lead to better operational performance, as measured and evaluated internally using indicators such as reject rates in the manufacturing process, production schedule fulfilment, and others. Through investments, firms create and acquire resources that can isolate them from negative market influences and can serve as a source of competitive advantage for them. These investments can be made in tangible assets (eg machinery and capital equipment) and intangible assets (eg brand names and the skills of individual employees).

2   Performance objectives of operations management

Characteristics of performance objectives

2.1   Individual functional areas will draw up their own strategic plans with due consideration of the interdependence of these areas in combining together to meet the aims and objectives specified by the corporate plan. One of the main corporate objectives is survival. In order to survive organisations must be able to respond to change. The ability to respond to change is essential in today's commercial environment. Plans are drawn up using a set of assumptions such as projected growth, cost of raw materials etc. If these projections are not accurate there must be enough flexibility to adapt, reassess and continue to reach the stated objectives.

2.2   Objectives must be clear and measurable and must have a set time frame. The following areas are among those that will be addressed.

- **Customers**: increasing choice, offering greater value, delighting the customer
- **Finance**: increasing profit and sales, reducing costs and losses
- **Internal results**: increasing the number of products brought to market, speeding up delivery time to customers, introducing and measuring a customer returns policy
- **Growth**: learning and innovation (enabling growth, increasing access to knowledge sources, developing organisational skills, introducing training and education plans, improving access to information)

2.3   At both corporate and functional levels the same three steps are applicable.

- Define a set of workable objectives.
- Balance financial and non-financial measures.
- Track and measure progress against objectives.

2.4   Within the role of operations management objectives must be workable. Objectives should be prioritised and weighted to ensure that those implementing the objective at an operational level are clear on their goals and their time frame.

2.5   Muhlemann, Oakland and Lockyer offer five guides applicable to objectives in the operations environment.

- Where multiple objectives exist, it is unwise to try to satisfy them all simultaneously.
- The greater the diversity, the greater the difficulty.
- Problems become easier if broken into parts.

- Organisations should be kept as small as the market and technology permit.
- Organisational structures should serve the needs of customers.

Influences from the market

2.6   A common view of the operations function is that its purpose is to meet market needs. This view extends into all spheres of the operations function and across both the private and public sectors. Market influences are varied and require differing perspectives from the operations role when viewing performance objectives.

2.7   Most private and public organisations involve a mix of goods and services. Too little emphasis on the service element may lead to customer dissatisfaction; too much may lead to production inefficiencies.

2.8   An organisation should clearly identify the market it is in and set up the operations function to deliver the right balance. This can be difficult to achieve in reality and requires ongoing monitoring of both the product and the service. The product, being tangible, is easier to measure while the service element, being intangible, can prove more complex. Customer feedback should be sought or encouraged to build up a genuine picture. Customer service measures such as order fill, on-time delivery, returns and the number of complaints should be recorded and monitored, and lessons learned.

2.9   Another market consideration is the width and variety of the product range. At one end of the market are organisations with a single offering, such as the utilities sector (electricity, gas, water etc). The danger is that complacency creeps in because of a monopoly situation. To a degree this has been addressed in the utility sector as competition has been introduced.

2.10   R L Galloway in *Principles of Operations Management* gives a good example of lack of variety and the problems it may cause.

'The Ford motor company standardised on the Model T, and its production process became so specialised that, while it was superbly efficient, it could not be changed. The assumption was that no one could want more from a car than the Model T provided. The competition, unable to compete on cost, successfully introduced variety into the market, a move that Ford barely survived.'

2.11   Markets change and the operations function may need to change with them. As mentioned earlier, the greater the diversity, the greater the difficulty. Wide variety must be managed. For the operations manager it provides more complexity in design, stock control, outsourcing, production, customer service requirements etc. The wider the variety the more responsive and flexible the operations function will need to be.

Setting performance objectives

2.12   Slack, Chambers and Johnston identify five performance objectives that can be applied to all operations: speed; quality; dependability; flexibility; cost. These objectives can be achieved in isolation but operations works in an integrated manner. The issue facing operations managers is one of 'trade-offs': attempting to find the optimum blend of the key performance factors to deliver the highest level of service from the resources available while also meeting organisational goals.

Speed

2.13   Within an organisation speed is important. Speed can reduce stockholding, particularly when linked to an efficient materials requirements planning (MRP) or just in time (JIT) manufacturing system, reducing risks involved with carrying large quantities of stock that may become obsolete or surplus to requirements.

2.14 Another market requirement is availability. This has two aspects: the speed with which the goods or services are delivered, and the reliability with which this is achieved. The speed objective has benefit to an organisation in that the customers' view of speedy delivery of goods and services is that it enhances the overall offering. The organisation must be aware that if the speed of the customer offering is not matched with the reliability of supply then reputation can be quickly tarnished.

Quality

2.15 The quality ethos is now well established across many goods and service providers. However, quality has different perspectives depending on the business or service provision you are in. Quality must be adequate to meet customer expectations, but quality that is higher than actually required may result in increased costs with no return.

2.16 Modern methods of quality management can serve to reduce costs, provide increased product reliability and engender an ethos that places quality at the thinking centre of an organisation.

Dependability

2.17 Dependability (ie delivering goods and services when they were promised, or the reliability of products and services) is another important market requirement. Customers judge dependability only after the goods and/or service have been delivered. Dependability relates both to products (meeting their claimed performance) or services (such as trains running on time). Waiting (one of Taiichi Ohno's seven wastes) does not add value; it serves only to add cost. Dependability gives predictability that things will occur or happen on time. This increases customer perceptions and, in consequence, their confidence in an organisation.

2.18 Dependability also has implications within an organisation. Manufacturing schedules rely on dependability: that suppliers will deliver on time, that machines will be ready for use, that order systems track the order from receipt through to delivery and payment etc. Dependability is a key performance objective for the operations function.

Flexibility

2.19 Flexibility is an essential requirement of the operations function in today's fast changing business environment. This includes fast introduction of new products, late customisation to meet customer needs, linked with the service offering (faster deliveries, timed deliveries, special packaging). The operations role must appreciate the need to meet customer demands and this in turn means designing processes that are able to change and adapt to suit differing circumstances.

2.20 Internal flexibility helps keep internal operations flowing. No planning will be totally accurate. Suppliers may deliver late, additional demand may come from customers, a coach may crash causing an increase in workload in a hospital's casualty department. Whatever the situation, the operations role must be flexible enough to adapt. Flexibility must be built in to the operational process and supported with considered contingency planning where events outside the anticipated norm may occur.

Cost

2.21 Finally, control of costs is important to any organisation. Staff, facilities, machinery, technology and material costs (among others) need to be well managed and controlled. Cost is affected by all the performance objectives discussed above and the operations role is to strike an acceptable balance while still meeting the required customer service levels.

2.22 The balancing of the five key performance indicators underpins the operational success of an organisation.

Successful management of these key factors contributes substantially to an organisation's success. With confidence in the operational capability to deliver, then sales and marketing programmes can be developed that build on this operational success.

2.23   The operations manager will need to constantly monitor the trade-offs in place. Organisations and customers change constantly and ongoing monitoring and adaptation to meet these needs is essential.

3   Top-down and bottom-up perspectives

3.1   Operations strategy is ..... 'the decisions which shape the long-term capabilities of the company's operations and their contribution to overall strategy through the ongoing reconciliation of market requirements and operations resource '. (Slack *et al*)

3.2   There are differing views and definitions of operations strategy. Slack *et al* summarise these into four 'perspectives' that together provide an insight into the sometimes conflicting context of operations strategy.

- Operations strategy is a top-down reflection of what the whole group or business wants to do.
- Operations strategy is a bottom-up activity where operations improvements cumulatively build strategy
- Operations strategy involves translating market requirements into operational decisions
- Operations strategy involves exploiting the capabilities of operations resources in chosen markets.

3.3   Strategy requires the matching of resources to requirements and it is here where strategy and operations interface. Effective and efficient operations management is reliant on an appropriate operations strategy. The development of an operations strategy should involve consultation and feedback between the operational and strategic levels of the business to ensure that when corporate plans are raised they are taking into account the resource implications that may constrain proposed developments.

3.4   Operations strategy involves maximising the capabilities of resources in specific markets in a way that meets the aims and objectives given in strategic plans.

Top-down strategies

3.5   With a top-down strategy decisions will be made at the corporate level of organisations and will be formulated by considering a range of factors such as future growth plans, the competitive environment facing the organisation, internal constraints such as manpower, money and machinery, amongst many others. Strategic thinking at corporate level involves developing the future direction of the business.

3.6   Strategic decisions are made at the corporate (board) level. These decisions are passed down to organisational departments to implement (eg finance, production, marketing, procurement). These departments, working together, devise tactical plans as to how the desired decision can be best achieved. These tactical plans then become implemented at an operational level.

3.7   The traditional view of operations strategy is as one of several *functional strategies* which are governed by strategic decisions taken at the top of the organisation. With the 'top-down' approach, overall business strategy sets the direction of the organisation. This, in turn, is then interpreted by the different functional areas of the company (marketing, finance, operations, etc.) in their functional strategies with the overall aim of meeting the demands of the corporate strategy.

Bottom-up strategy

3.8   The top-down perspective provides the textbook view of how strategic objectives are formulated and disseminated throughout the business. Indeed, particularly in larger companies with a hierarchical management structure in place, that approach tends to prevail over other approaches.

3.9   By contrast, many medium and smaller enterprises will adopt a 'bottom-up' strategy. This means that day-to-day experience shapes what operations should do.

3.10   The development of strategy should include a mechanism for those lower down the organisation to provide input. Bottom-up planning allows those at operative or supervisory level to have their views heard and considered. Quality gurus from Deming and Juran onwards have stressed that those actually doing the operational work can make suggestions for improvement that managers, who are more remote from the day-to-day activities, might not consider.

3.11   A bottom-up strategic management model seeks to develop ideas using the brainpower of the entire workforce. This can build morale and a sense of ownership among employees of all levels. Employees will be more actively engaged in the work and will strive harder to reach objectives.

3.12   A formalised approach to bottom-up planning can help operations managers in particular as much of the feedback may be directly relevant to individual processes where improvements or gains can be made. Bottom-up planning also gives those lower down the organisation the sense that they are contributing to the development of the organisation as a whole.

3.13   The bottom-up view of operations strategy is to see strategic decision making as an accumulation of practical experiences. Ideas are formed from their previous experience of dealing with customers, suppliers and their own processes. This is the idea behind *emergent strategies*. These are strategic ideas which emerge over time as an organisation begins to understand the realities of their situation.

3.14   An emergent strategy is a pattern of action that develops over time in the absence of a specific mission and goals, or despite a mission and goals. The concept is that strategy emerges over time based on the business environment surrounding the operation rather than a structured approach that is found in the top-down strategic development method.

3.15   When thinking about top-down versus bottom-up (including emergent) perspectives of operations strategy, remember that they are not 'rival' ideas. In reality we can see both top-down and bottom-up influences on strategy making. What is important to remember is that the pure 'top-down' view of operations strategy is simplistic in the sense that it does not recognise the importance of learning through experience.

4   Order-qualifying and order-winning objectives

4.1   One approach to determining the relative importance of competitive factors is to distinguish between 'order-winning' and 'order-qualifying' factors. The terms were coined by Terry Hill, professor at the London Business School, and refer to the process of how internal operational capabilities are converted to a set of criteria that may lead to competitive advantage and market success.

4.2   Hill argues that the criteria required in the marketplace (and identified by marketing) can be divided into two groups: order qualifiers and order winners. An order qualifier is a characteristic of a product or service that is required in order for the product or service to even be considered by a customer. An order winner is a characteristic that will win the customer's preference over competing products.

4.3   It follows that organisations must provide the qualifiers in order to get into or stay in a market. To provide qualifiers, they need only to be as good as their competitors. Failure to do so may result in lost sales. However, to provide order winners, firms must be better than their competitors. It is important to note that order qualifiers are not less important than order winners; they are a pre-requisite to order winners.

4.4   Hill emphasises the need for interaction and co-operation between operations and marketing. Operations are responsible for **providing** the order-winning and order-qualifying criteria **identified by marketing** that enable products to win orders in the marketplace. This process starts with the corporate strategy and ends with the criteria that either keeps the company in the running (ie order qualifiers) or wins the customer's business (ie order winners).

4.5   Companies must also exercise some caution when making decisions based on order winners and qualifiers. For example, a firm may be producing a high quality product (where high quality is the order-winning criterion). If the cost of producing at such a high level of quality forces the selling price of the product to exceed a certain price level (which is an order-qualifying criteria), the end result may be lost sales, thereby making quality an order-losing attribute.

4.6   Order winners and qualifiers are both market-specific and time-specific. They work in different combinations in different ways on different markets and with different customers. While some general trends exist across markets, these may not be stable over time.

4.7   As an example, in the late 1990s delivery speed and product customisation were frequent order winners, while product quality and price, which previously were frequent order winners, tended to be order qualifiers. Companies needed to develop different strategies to support different marketing needs, and these strategies will change over time. Also, since customers' stated needs do not always reflect their buying habits, Hill recommends that firms study how customers behave, not what they say.

4.8   Most organisations will offer a range of products to consumers. In this situation they need to determine the order-qualifying and order-winning factors for each product or group of products. For an example an insurance company would offer different products to the general public and to corporate customers. Both sets of customers would be looking for different levels of cover and features from their policies. Competitive factors will be different in both cases.

4.9   For example, individual buyers of insurance will consider order winners to be price and range of coverage. Organisational customers may look at price, customisation, and quality. For operations it is now possible to develop a suitable system that focuses on those deliverables.

Chapter summary

- Strategy is the direction and scope of an organisation over the long term. It is common to distinguish between corporate strategy, business unit strategy and operational strategy.
- Individual functions, such as operations management, will establish performance objectives. It is important that such objectives are integrated with those of other functions.
- Formulation of strategy may involve a top-down approach (senior management decide the strategy, and this cascades down to all departments) or a bottom-up approach (managers at lower levels have a voice in the process).
- Terry Hill distinguishes between order-qualifying objectives (must be present for customers even to consider buying) and order-winning objectives (capable of winning business by superiority to competitor offerings).

Self-test questions

Numbers in brackets refer to the paragraphs above where your answers can be checked.

1   Johnson *et al* describe a three-stage process of strategic management. Describe the three stages. (1.3)

2   Explain the distinction between corporate strategy, business unit strategy and operational strategy. (1.4)

3   Describe the four stages in Hayes and Wheelwright's model of the increasing contribution of operations management. (Table 2.1)

4   Describe the three steps in a system of performance management. (2.3)

5   What five key performance objectives of operations management are identified by Slack *et al*? (2.12)

6   Describe what is meant by (a) a top-down approach to strategy formulation and (b) a bottom-up approach. (3.5, 3.10)

7   Distinguish between order-qualifying and order-winning factors. (4.2)

CHAPTER 3

Operations Processes

Assessment criteria and indicative content

1.3 Evaluate main operations processes

- The 'input-transformation-output' model of operations management
- The dimensions of operations processes (volume, variety, variation and visibility)
- The activities of operations processes

Section headings

1 The input-transformation-output model
2 The dimensions of operations processes
3 The activities of operations processes

1   The input-transformation-output model

Inputs and outputs

1.1 Operations management is a field of study that tries to understand, explain, predict and change the strategic and organisational effects of the transformation process. The design of a process should reflect what the customer wants and should be flexible enough to change when customers' preferences change.

1.2 Operations management is the systematic direction and control of the processes that transform inputs into finished goods and services. While procurement is concerned with acquiring the right product at the right time, finance with providing the capital, marketing with creating and developing demand, operations produces and (in many cases) delivers the product or service.

1.3 The transformation of inputs to outputs is central to operations management. All operations produce goods and/or services by developing processes that transform the state of something to produce outputs. The transformation process will change the condition of a product and/or service by taking a set of input resources and transforming them (for example, by a manufacturing process) to produce a more refined output.

Figure 3.1 *The input–transformation–output model*

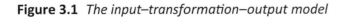

1.4 All operations are input-transformation-output processes. Inputs may be, for example, people, materials, energy, finance, or information. These are converted or aid conversion into a more refined or finished product or service via the transformation process to produce, as an output, the goods or services designed to meet customer needs.

- **People**: the workforce who provide the skills, knowledge and competencies that underpin the operation.

- **Materials**: the raw materials or the assembly items that form part of the finished product.
- **Energy**: the management of costs is central to operations management. Energy management represents just one area for consideration.
- **Finance**: the organisation must have adequate finance for buying and updating capital items (such as plant and equipment) and for working capital (to meet running costs such as wages, purchases and many other related areas of expenditure).
- **Information**: good information is essential to any operational activity in today's workplace. Data processing should be managed to deliver required information as and when required and in a meaningful form to the user.

Operating processes and management support processes

1.5   Processes fall into two distinct categories: 'operating processes' and 'management support processes'.

- **Operating processes** are those that add value to a product or service such as in the transformation process but can also include the addition of value through marketing, customer service and research and development.
- **Management support processes** are those that are needed to keep the operation running as efficiently and effectively as possible. This covers areas such as human resources, information technology and financial management.

1.6   Each is of equal importance in the sense that each requires the other to work effectively to maximise resources. The role of operations is clearly more linked with 'operating processes' but requires input from the 'management support processes' in order to work as effectively and efficiently as possible.

1.7   Central to the transformation processes are facilities: the buildings, machinery, equipment and process technology of the operation and staff; those who operate, manage and maintain the operation. Within this environment a production or operation system is the system that an organisation uses to transform the inputs to outputs.

1.8   The transformation of resources is effected by using the combined effort of all the above factors, in a methodical way, to deliver the desired output. The method or design of the transformation process is central to producing the desired outcome.

1.9   Within an operations environment the production system would involve a number of process considerations that come together as facilitators of the transformation process.

- Capacity
- Type of production or operation
- Level of skills available
- Layout of plant and equipment
- Effectiveness of information technology
- Cost to be achieved

1.10   The transformation of resources is effected by using the combined effort of all the above factors, in a methodical way, to deliver the desired output. The method or design of the transformation process is central to producing the desired outcome.

1.11   The situation is similar in a services environment. Hotels, airlines, hairdressers and a range of other service providers take in inputs (ie people) and transform them by accommodating them, moving them or changing their physical appearance. These can be seen as customer process operations.

1.12   Accountants, market research agencies and news services transform data and information to deliver the required output. These roles can be viewed as predominantly information processors.

1.13   The output stage involves the delivery of the blend of goods and services to meet customer needs.

1.14   All processes will produce by-products or waste. By-products will sometimes have other applications in the production of other goods but in many cases the by-products need careful management and disposal in the appropriate manner.

1.15   'Waste' refers not only to physical waste. The subject has come under considerable scrutiny over the years firstly with Taiichi Ohno, the architect of the Toyota Production System and the 'seven wastes', and more recently with Robert Smith's 'Triangle of Waste' which examines redundant stock, obsolete stock and returned stock as 'waste' areas that organisations are not managing well.

1.16   The 'seven wastes' of Taiichi Ohno are particularly relevant at this stage.

- **Over-production**. From an operations perspective this requires sound stock management procedures and production techniques to ensure that the correct quantities are ordered and made.
- **Waiting time**. This adds no value, only cost and inconvenience. Machines that are not compatible and produce at different rates can cause waiting on the production line. Waiting for the telephone to be answered, the shop to open, the assistant to come back are all examples of service sector incidences of 'waiting'.
- **Unnecessary transporting**. Loads should be maximised, goods should be transported to the correct location and should not require additional transportation.
- **Inappropriate processing**. All processes must be appropriate to the required output, ie they must meet customer requirements.
- **Unnecessary inventory**. Inventory costs money. Except in the most refined just in time systems inventory still needs to be carried. The objective is to carry as little as possible to meet current requirements.
- **Unnecessary motions**. This concerns the design of movement within the working environment in order to ensure that every movement is minimised while still performing the required task.
- **Defects**. Products should be designed so as to build in quality from the outset through good use of design, materials and processes. Defects require an organisation to instigate post-manufacturing inspection processes with consequent costs and may involve re-working of an item or failure to meet customer service requirements.

1.17   The transformation process links a related group of tasks together to create a result of value to a customer (Michael Hammer). The role of the operations manager is to ensure the efficient and effective application of the transformation process. To achieve this will involve the operations manager outside the transformation area to have extensive involvement in both the prior inputs and later outputs.

2   The dimensions of operations processes

Planning and control

2.1   The central role of operations management is the transformation process. To enable the transformation process to operate to its most effective level requires a high degree of planning and control of activities. The role of planning and control in operations is to manage the continuing operational activities in order to satisfy customer demand.

2.2   A plan is a formalisation of what is intended to happen at some time in the future. Control is the process of coping with changes to the plan and the operation to which it relates.

2.3   The plan is the mechanism through which management can visualise the future and objectively evaluate whether it has sufficient critical resources to meet the anticipated demand. All organisations face cost constraints and have only finite resources. Planning and control decisions must be made about the effective deployment of those resources.

2.4 Planning and control is the reconciliation of the potential of the operation to supply products and services, and the demands of its customers on the operation. It is the set of day-to-day activities that run the operation on an ongoing basis. 'Planning and control activities provide the systems, procedures and decisions which bring different aspects of supply and demand together' (Slack *et al*).

2.5 Although planning and control are theoretically separable, they are usually treated together. The balance between planning and control changes over time. Planning dominates in the long term and is usually done on an aggregated basis. At the other extreme, in the short term, control usually operates within the resource constraints of the operation but makes interventions into the operation in order to cope with short-term changes in circumstances.

2.6 In planning and controlling the volume and timing of activity in operations, four distinct activities are necessary.

- Loading, which dictates the amount of work that is allocated to each part of the operation
- Sequencing, which decides the order in which work is tackled within the operation
- Scheduling, which determines the detailed timetable of activities and when activities are started and finished
- Monitoring and control, which involve detecting what is happening in the operation, re-planning if necessary, and intervening in order to impose new plans.

2.7 Two important types of control are 'pull' and 'push' control. Pull control is a system whereby demand is triggered by requests from a work centre's (internal) customer. Push control is a centralised system whereby control (and sometimes planning) decisions are issued to work centres which are then required to perform the task and supply the next workstation. In manufacturing, 'pull' schedules generally have far lower inventory levels than 'push' schedules.

2.8 The ease with which control can be maintained varies between operations. The volume-variety position of an operation (see later in this section) has an effect on the nature of its planning and control. Customer responsiveness, the planning horizon, the major planning decisions, the control decision and the robustness of planning and control are especially affected by volume and variety.

Long, medium and short-term control

2.9 Planning and control of an operation will change over different time horizons. Production is planned using a long-term, medium-term or short-term view. Long-term views focus on the major decisions a company makes that influence capacity, whereas short-term views focus more on using more efficiently what a company already has. Medium-term views focus on adjustments, such as hiring, redundancies, increasing inventory, or expediting back orders.

2.10 Companies will have separate production plans for the different time horizons. While a company can focus its efforts on a particular horizon, even to the exclusion of the others, it is beneficial to maintain a focus on the long term, even if that focus is broad. For example, a company focused on increasing profit margins in the short term might neglect to reinvest some of those profits – a bad idea for any business in the long term.

2.11 Inventory control, while a large part of production planning, is frequently looked at as a minor subset of supply chain management. However, inventory control is a crucial part of the production system. Apart from the determination of the minimum level of stock a company can maintain as safety against a fluctuation in customer demand, inventory control looks at the costs associated with maintaining inventory, both of raw materials and finished product. Inventory control is affected by changes in customer demand, holding costs, ordering costs and back-order costs.

2.12 Capacity planning attempts to match the volume of output the company is producing to customer demand. Maximum output capacity is calculated and an optimal capacity is determined. Too much capacity can result in a low return on asset investment, whereas too little capacity can drive away customers by having too many back orders, or even having to refuse orders. A good capacity plan has a level amount of input (raw materials and other resources) for its output (the actual product) with little to no bottlenecks and little to no downtime.

2.13   Finished inventory is frequently managed through aggregate planning, a method that looks at production, the workforce itself and inventory management. Aggregate plans help match supply and demand while minimising costs by applying upper-level forecasts to lower level, production-floor scheduling. Aggregate plans do this by lumping together resources in a very general way. Plans either 'chase' demand (eg in a flower shop, where the products are made in response to an order) or assume 'level' demand (eg with a clothing manufacturer, where the products are produced at a regular rate and simply stored until demand requires them).

2.14   Regardless of the concept employed in production planning, an extremely useful concept is **rolling horizon**. Production planning depends upon certain assumptions of customer demand and delivery; a rolling horizon means that a company implements a production plan but sets up to review its effectiveness in a short time (such as a yearly production plan being reviewed and adjusted weekly). Using a rolling horizon allows a company to be more flexible and adaptive.

The volume-variety effect on planning and control

2.15   There are contrasting approaches between companies that produce a high variety of products or service in low volume and others that produce more standardised products or services at high volume.

2.16   To understand the different types of operation we differentiate between them by using four dimensions, sometimes called the four Vs of operations. (These are what your syllabus refers to as the **dimensions of operations processes**.)

- Volume – how many products or services are made by the operation?
- Variety – how many different types of products or services are made by the operation?
- Variation – how much does the level of demand change over time?
- Visibility – how much of the operation's internal workings are 'exposed' to its customers?

2.17   In most industries one can find examples at either end of each dimension. So, for example, in transport, a taxi service is low volume while a bus service or mass rapid transport is high volume. In accounting firms, corporate tax advice is high variety because all large corporations have different needs, while financial audits, which have to be carried out to comply with financial reporting legislation, are relatively standardised. In food manufacture, the demand for ice-cream varies considerably depending on the weather, while the demand for bread is far steadier and more predictable. In the dental care industry, dentists operate high visibility operations (it's difficult for the dentist to work on your teeth if you are not there) but rely on dental technicians in factory-type laboratories to make false teeth etc. These dimensions are most useful in predicting how easy it is for an operation to operate at low cost.

2.18   With regard to the **volume dimension**, in the low levels of volume, the company's operations have specific characteristics such as having low repetition in the everyday procedures. Each staff member performs more than one job; in other words they are multifunctional, with less systemisation and high unit costs. In the high levels of volume, the company's operations have specific characteristics such as high repeatability in the everyday procedures. There will be specialisation, systemisation, more capital intensive operations and low unit costs.

2.19   With regard to the **variety dimension**, on the high side of the scale there will be more flexibility in the operations procedure. The company will make sure to match customer needs and of course the unit cost will be high. By contrast, for a company on the low side of the scale the procedures will be well defined, there will be routine, standardisation, and of course low unit cost.

2.20   The **variation in demand** has many implications that can be seen from the company's characteristics. If the company is in the high levels of demand variation then it has changing capacity, anticipation for what the customer might demand, flexibility. It is in touch with demand and has high unit costs While in the other side of the scale, the company would have a stable and predictable demand, routine, high utilisation of resources and low unit cost.

2.21   The **visibility dimension** indicates the customer's ability to track his or her order through its different stages. When it is high the customers have short waiting tolerance, satisfaction governed by customer perception, customer contact skills are needed and very important. And when it is low, the time lag between production and consumption is greater, there will be standardisation, the customer contact skills will not be very important or needed. The company must have a high staff utilisation and centralisation.

Uncertainty in supply and demand

2.22   The degree of uncertainty in demand affects the balance between planning and control. The greater the uncertainty, the more difficult it is to plan, and greater emphasis must be placed on control. This idea of uncertainty is linked with the concepts of dependent and independent demand. Dependent demand is relatively predictable because it is dependent on some known factor. Independent demand is less predictable because it depends on the changes of the market or customer behaviour.

2.23   Demand for most organisations is difficult to forecast accurately. Customer orders will fluctuate, the type of goods ordered will change as customer requirements change, maintenance and production will vary, often in a way that is not directly linked to production requirement. This relates particularly to operating supplies such as lubricants, light bulbs and stationery.

2.24   **Dependent demand** is demand that is dependent on a known factor. For example, if a motor manufacturer is about to make 100 cars, then the demand for wheels (being dependent on this production plan) is clearly 400.

2.25   **Independent demand** items are goods that are required for an operation in quantities independent of those used in the production process. These are items such as maintenance, repair and operating (MRO) supplies. Here the extent to which lubricating oil is required to maintain machines in working order does not depend on which products are being processed on the machines. It is possible to estimate that a particular amount of oil will be used each day, week or month, regardless of the production schedule.

3   The activities of operations processes

Responsibility for activities

3.1   Operations managers have responsibility for all the activities of the operation that directly or indirectly contribute to the effective production of goods and services. The direct responsibility concerns all the activities involved in the input-transformation-output process; the indirect responsibility concerns the linkages between operations and the other functional areas of the business.

3.2   As organisations have changed to meet the needs and challenges of the modern business environment, their management structures have also been altered, often to a flatter more flexible management structure that serves to encourage cross-functional teamworking between functional areas. Although not all organisations have adopted this model most have adapted it into their operations in one way or another.

Operations in the organisation

3.3   Operations has a central role within an organisation as it produces the goods and services which are central to the organisation's purpose. It is one of the three core functions that exist in any organisation. The other two are marketing (including sales) and product development. Table 3.1 summarises some of the activities of these core functions in different sectors.

Table 3.1 *The core activities in different sectors*

CORE ACTIVITY	FASHION RETAILER	RETAIL BANK	ELECTRICAL MANUFACTURER
Marketing	Promote product offering to consumers Develop website	Produce advertising and merchandising to keep customers aware of latest offerings	Develop website, trade catalogues and attend trade fairs
Product development	Design new clothing or ranges of clothing	Design new finance offering for customers	Develop new products or product variants
Operations	Manage the global sourcing operation and logistics.	Deliver retail banking services	Manage the transformation process from inputs through to outputs

3.4   The relationship between operations and the support functions is one where operations management needs to ensure that they understand the needs of operations and provide help in satisfying those needs. For example, finance should provide the money for new plant and equipment if a suitable business case is approved; human resources should provide suitable staff to operate the equipment and ensure ongoing training.

The importance of operations in all types of organisations

3.5   The function of the production and operations department in a company is to take inputs and fashion them into outputs for customer use. Inputs can be concrete physical objects, data driven, or service driven. The outputs can be intended for consumer use or for business use. The goal of production and operations is to create an end product in the most economic and efficient way possible.

3.6   In some areas of business it is easy to visualise the role of operations; in other areas it tends to take a little thought. In a straightforward manufacturing environment (such as cars, forklift trucks, televisions etc) it is easy to understand the principle of inputs-transformation-outputs. The inputs are the components; the transformation is assembling the components to transform them into the finished item; the output is, for example, the forklift truck. The forklift truck is tangible: you can see it, you can touch it.

3.7   Where it is a little more difficult to visualise is in the areas where the inputs-transformation-outputs are intangibles such as doctors, charities, and business consultants. Slack *et al* state: 'Operations management uses resources to appropriately create outputs that fulfil defined market requirements'. Resources can be people who use their knowledge and expertise in a specialised manner that adds value to what they are doing.

Chapter summary

- The role of the operations manager is well captured by the input-transformation-output model. The organisation takes inputs (human resources, materials, energy etc), processes them, and produces outputs that will be sold to customers.
- To enable the transformation process to operate to its most effective level requires a high degree of planning and control.
- A key distinction for operations managers is that between businesses producing a high variety of products or services in low volume and businesses producing more standardised products or services at high volume.
- Operations is one of the three key functions in most organisations (the other two being marketing and product development). This is as true in service organisations as in manufacturing.

Self-test questions

Numbers in brackets refer to the paragraphs above where your answers can be checked.

1   Sketch the input-transformation-output model. (Figure 3.1)

2   What types of inputs does an organisation typically work on? (1.4)

3   List the seven wastes identified by Taiichi Ohno. (1.16)

4   Describe the four activities typically involved in planning and controlling the volume and timing of operations activities. (2.6)

5   Explain the four Vs of operations management. (2.16)

6   Distinguish between dependent and independent demand. (2.24, 2.25)

7   Describe the core activities of an operations manager in a fashion retailer, a retail bank, and an electrical manufacturer. (Table 3.1)

CHAPTER 4

Process Design and Technology

Assessment criteria and indicative content

2.1 Analyse the main techniques for process design and technology

- Job design
- Scientific management and method study
- Ergonomic workplace design and behavioural approaches to job design
- Sustainability in designs and technology
- The volume-variety effect on process design and process types
- Process mapping

Section headings

1. Jobs and job design
2. Scientific management and method study
3. Behavioural approaches to job design
4. Ergonomic workplace design
5. The volume-variety effect
6. Process mapping

1   Jobs and job design

The importance of job design

1.1 The definition of a job at its simplest level is given by GA Cole in *Personnel Management* as 'a collection of tasks assigned to a position in an organisational structure'.

1.2 The allocation of tasks should be balanced to enable a reasonable workload with a variety of tasks that stimulate the worker. The blending of a natural grouping of tasks into a job may be the result of a rational exercise or as a matter of convenience. If a job is designed as the result of a rational exercise then consideration can be given to the role and content and the job can be designed to suit the needs of the individual and the organisation. If the job is formulated as a matter of convenience then it is likely to be poorly constructed, possibly repetitive and lacking in variety and challenge.

1.3 LE Davis and RR Canter, often seen as the developers of the concept of job design, defined the role as follows: 'the organisation (or structuring) of a job to satisfy the technical-organisational requirements of the work and the human requirements of the person performing the work'. Davis's later work identified a number of design issues in structuring jobs.

- Identifying job boundaries
- Identifying the factors at work in jobs
- Determining methods of estimating and controlling these factors
- Developing systematic design methods
- Developing criteria for evaluating designs

1.4 Davis went on to conclude that, in order to achieve more effective performance and greater job satisfaction on the part of the employee, it was necessary for jobs to be 'meaningful' to the individual concerned. This idea has become a dominant feature of modern approaches to job design as the concept of the 'quality of working life'.

1.5 Job design and work organisation can be defined as: 'The specification of the contents, methods and relationships of jobs to satisfy technological and organisational requirements as well as the personal needs of jobholders'. We can look in more detail at the elements of this definition.

- **The specification of the contents**. What is involved in the job? What level of skill or knowledge is required?
- **Methods**. How and where is the work to be organised and carried out?
- **Relationships of jobs**. Where does the job fit into the organisational structure? How much autonomy will the job have?
- **To satisfy technological requirements**. Technology and the use of technology is a prime consideration of organisations. Job design should reflect this.
- **To satisfy organisational requirements**. Organisational requirements will include the type of person, their suitability and how well they meet the expectations of the organisation.
- **The personal needs of jobholders**. This involves consideration of what employees want from a job, what motivates them and what will encourage them to stay.

1.6 Huczynski and Buchanan point out that 'the design of an individual's job determines both the kind of rewards that are available and what the individual has to do to get those rewards'.

1.7 Hackman and Oldham (in their **job characteristics model**) have focused on certain core job dimensions that contribute to satisfaction.

- **Skill variety**: the opportunity to exercise different skills and perform different operations, as opposed to micro-specialisation and repetition
- **Task identity**: the integration of operations into a 'whole' task (or meaningful segment of the task), as opposed to task fragmentation
- **Task significance**: the task has a role, purpose, meaning and worth within the organisational and individual value system
- **Autonomy**: the opportunity to exercise discretion or self-management in areas such as target-setting and work methods
- **Feedback**: the availability of information by which the individual can assess his progress and performance in relation to expectations and targets and the opportunity to give feedback and have a voice in performance improvement

1.8 A job which has these core dimensions will lead to the jobholder experiencing the psychological states of experienced meaningfulness and responsibility. He will produce work of high quality, will be highly satisfied with work, and will stay in his job and maintain a good attendance record.

1.9 Research by Paul Hill similarly suggests that the psychological requirements of a 'full job' for the individual are as follows.

- The content of the work should be reasonably demanding of the individual (in terms other than sheer endurance) and should have some variety.
- An individual should know what his job is, what are the standards of success and how he is performing in relation to them.
- There should be an opportunity to learn on the job and to continue learning.
- There should be some social support and recognition within the organisation.
- An individual should be able to relate their work and output to the objectives of the company and to their place in the community.
- There should be perceived potential for the job to lead to some sort of desirable future (though this does not necessarily imply promotion).

Division of labour

1.10   Division of labour becomes relevant to job design as soon as the volume of work is enough to employ more than one person. It involves dividing the task into smaller parts that can each be accomplished by a single person.

1.11   This division of work allows for each person to specialise in a certain area. Specialisation brings with it an increase in skills and improvements in efficiency and effectiveness. If the task is relatively straightforward it will be easier to learn. The repetitive nature of the task may allow for technology to be improved to meet the needs. For example, the process can become automated, as on a car production line where each operative traditionally carried out a single repetitive task with the product coming to them on an assembly line.

1.12   Division of labour does have certain disadvantages. It leads to monotony, giving rise to boredom and carelessness in workers. Absenteeism can be high as workers find their role too stifling. The repetition of the work can lead to injury. There is no interaction between the defined roles; this limits the identification of problem areas and does not encourage improvement in processes.

2   Scientific management and method study

FW Taylor

2.1   One of the most influential rationales for job design has been the need to achieve optimum output. This is the rationale of 'scientific management' where human work and effort is seen in terms of its relationship to machines and the systems created for them.

2.2   Frederick Winslow Taylor, writing in 1911, expounded principles of **scientific management**. He attempted to impose machine-like disciplines on the work carried out by factory operatives.

2.3   The movement he started, the 'scientific management' movement that reached its peak in America during 1900–1930, has had lasting effects. He was a perfectionist, always looking for the 'one best way'.

2.4   He hated the term 'soldiering', which was the term in those days for workers just doing what the informal workgroup had established as a fair day's work. He was employed as a chief superintendent or consultant in various steel factories, his most successful experience being at Bethlehem Steel, where after two years he achieved a 200% increase in productivity with only a 50% increase in wages. His techniques were as follows.

- To initiate a time study rate system. Taylor would begin by finding the fastest worker in the organisation. He then examined that person's movements on the job, suggested the elimination of unnecessary movements, and took the speediest rate at which this 'first class person' could work. Other workers were then expected to work at the same rate (with minor adjustments for newness at the job, rest periods, and unavoidable delays).
- To create functional foremen. Taylor fought against using the military model in organisations. No manager was to have disciplinary powers. The notion of 'functional' means supervision over some aspect of work, not supervision over people. This notion essentially meant the creation of specialised clerks with oversight over some aspect of the production.
- To establish cost accounting (also known as task management). This approach involves the use of instruction and routing cards and a timekeeping system where workers punched a clock when they finished a job. Labour variance could then be analysed, and management had the reporting tools they needed to identify bottlenecks. Rewards and punishments would be calculated by how the numbers looked on paper.
- To devise a system of pay for the person and not the position. Taylor instituted a system of 'piece

rates' where workers or gangs were paid according to output. There were no attempts under Taylorism at job rotation; each worker was expected to specialise in a particular task they did well.

2.5   Taylor's basic principles of job design were as follows.

- All aspects of work should be investigated on a scientific basis to establish the laws, rules and formulae governing the best methods of working.
- An investigative approach to the study of work is necessary to establish what constitutes a 'fair day's work'.
- Managers should act as the planners of work.
- Co-operation between management and workers is based on the 'maximum prosperity' of both.

2.6   His technique was basically as follows.

- Decide on the optimum degree of task fragmentation, breaking down a complex task into its most basic component parts, which would represent the whole 'job' of a worker or group of workers.
- Decide the most efficient way of performing each operation, using work study techniques and time and motion study to determine the simplest way to perform a task, eliminate wasteful motions (physical movements) and set standard times for all operations.
- Train employees to carry out their single task fragment in the most efficient way.

2.7   Jobs were therefore 'micro-designed': reduced to single, repetitive motions. The micro-division of labour was based on a production line organisation of work and offers some efficiencies for this type of work. Each task is so simple and straightforward that it can be learned with very little training. Since skill requirements are low, the effects of absenteeism and labour turnover are minimised, and workers can easily be replaced and redeployed. Tasks are closely defined, standardised and timed so that output quantity and quality are more easily predicted and controlled.

2.8   Taylor suggested that such a system was beneficial to workers as well as management.

'The man who is fit to work at any particular trade is unable to understand the science of that trade without the kindly help and co-operation of men of a totally different type of education… It is one of the principles of scientific management to ask men to do things in the right way, to learn something new, to change their ways in accordance with the science and in return to receive an increase of from 30% to 100% in pay.'

2.9   Two distinct but related fields of study developed from this thinking and will be examined in greater depth later in this chapter. Together these areas are referred to as work study.

- **Method study** focuses on determining the methods and activities that should be involved in jobs.
- **Work measurement** examines the time taken in performing a job or a series of jobs.

Frank and Lillian Gilbreth

2.10   Frank and Lillian Gilbreth analysed 17 basic movements of the hand (all based on the ability to search, grasp, load, select, hold, and transport). They also experimented with different types of factory whistle blasts, suggestion boxes, and intramural programs among employees.

2.11   In their writings from about 1915 through 1920, the Gilbreths began to talk about 15 to 16 'motion cycles', but rarely named them all and didn't allude to any comprehensive system. Indeed, it was not until the late summer of 1924, following Frank Gilbreth's death, that the 'therblig system' was presented in two articles in *Management and Administration*.

2.12   'Therbligs' are a system for analysing the motions involved in performing a task. The identification of individual motions, as well as moments of delay in the process, was designed to find unnecessary or inefficient motions and to utilise or eliminate even split seconds of wasted time. Frank and Lillian Gilbreth invented and refined this system, roughly between 1908 and 1924. (Therblig is an anagram of Gilbreth.)

2.13   The production systems employing scientific management approaches such as those of Taylor and the Gilbreths led to many improvements in efficiency and productivity at work. However, over time, it became apparent that the repetitive nature of this approach led to factors such as high absenteeism, lateness, poor attention to quality and restrictions in the flexibility of labour.

The use and techniques of work study

2.14   Work study comprises both method study and work measurement.

- Method study is concerned with establishing optimum working methods.
- Work measurement is concerned with establishing time standards for the working methods.

2.15   Method study will usually be carried out first unless there is a need to compare old and new work methods.

2.16   Work study is mainly concerned with human manual work, in particular the efficient design and execution of work and also the development of standards of performance. The principles were laid down by FW Taylor and have been applied, but not without some criticism and updating, over the subsequent years.

2.17   Work study is defined by the British Standards Institution as: 'A generic term for those techniques, particularly method study and work measurement, which are used in the examination of human work in all its contexts, and which lead systematically to the investigation of all the factors which affect the efficiency and economy of the situations being reviewed, in order to effect improvements.'

2.18   The essential aims of work study are as follows.

- To establish the most economical method of doing the work.
- To standardise this method, together with the materials and equipment involved.
- To establish the time required by a qualified or adequately trained worker, while working at a defined level of performance.
- To install this work method as standard practice.

2.19   Work study can be viewed as a comparatively low-cost way of designing work to attain high productivity or improving productivity in existing work by improving existing methods and reducing ineffective or wasted time. Improvements are sought utilising existing equipment and resources. Therefore improvement is not dependent on redesign or restructuring of products, processes or operations.

2.20   The technique is applied in circumstances where a maximum return is anticipated. The evaluation of results, whether they are increases in throughput, better utilisation of equipment or labour, reduction in waste, improvements in safety or a reduction in training time, should outweigh the cost of the investigation.

2.21   Considerations that might be applied include the following.

- The anticipated life of the job
- The contribution manual work makes to the job
- The wage rate for the job
- Utilisation of equipment, machines, tools; the costs involved, and whether the utilisation is dependent on the work method
- The importance of the job to the organisation

2.22   Does the work study exercise relate to existing jobs or to proposed or anticipated jobs? As new products and services are designed or new equipment used, jobs must be designed or re-designed. The question is to what extent work study should be used. One tool that can be applied to assess the factors involved is cost/benefit analysis.

2.23 New products will require operations managers to design and develop effective and efficient processes and procedures from the outset. Existing jobs may be re-evaluated for a number of reasons such as a change in the product or service, new equipment being utilised or changes in the wage structure. Other reasons may come from operational feedback reports or staff that may show poor utilisation, excessive overtime, poor quality or high scrap wastage rates.

Method study

2.24 Method study is 'concerned with the systematic recording and critical examination of existing and proposed ways of doing work, as a means of developing and applying easier and more effective methods and reducing cost' (BSI). Method study, when applied to an existing job, involves seven steps, which can be memorised by the mnemonic SREDDIM: select, record, examine, develop, define, install and implement, maintain. This provides a formal approach to identify and develop solutions in a structured series of steps.

- **Selection of the work to be studied**. The first stage in method study is to select jobs that are appropriate. There are numerous jobs going through an operation at any one time, so the one/s selected must have economic reasons for their selection. Factors that would be considered include return on investment and areas that are causing delays or bottlenecks in an operation where the problems add cost in related areas.

- **Recording the work method**. The objective is to obtain a record of the work method for subsequent evaluation. This is discussed in more detail later.

- **Examine the method**: The purpose of the recording stage is to examine the existing method thoroughly and meticulously with the objective of identifying areas for improvement. The aim is to evaluate the effectiveness of the operation as a whole and to identify where changes (work flow, material, design of the product or service) would be beneficial. This stage is also discussed in more detail below.

- **Develop an improved method**. By this stage there is usually a sound understanding of potential improvement areas. A process improvement formula is applied to each activity of the job. This essentially consists of four steps: eliminate, combine, sequence and simplify. Aspects such as health and safety, ergonomics and the smooth flow of work need to be incorporated to ensure that when the new method is defined and implemented it will operate successfully.

- Often outside consultants are involved at this stage; they can be more objective. The use of a quality circle improvement team can involve the organisation in the process with the eventual aim of taking ownership of the new methods. Workers should be involved in changes through teamworking, suggestion schemes and discussion on change areas.

- New methods should be thought through, planned and tested prior to implementation to ensure that the changes are workable as part of the production system.

- **Define the new method**. It will be necessary to describe the new method in detail for others to install or operate it. The definition is a statement of the new work method and can be referred to in case of any disputes or misunderstandings.

- **Install the new method**. Installation is a 'project management' exercise with initial training followed by a 'learning curve' period, then reappraisal if necessary with a target date for full implementation. New methods, after agreement and costing, must be installed. The installation and implementation will require good change management practices such as openness, discussion and information sharing, as support from all levels within the company is essential. Following successful testing, installation can be made on a phased or a one-off basis. The phased approach enables lessons to be learned but is slower. The one-off approach requires that full testing has been carried out beforehand as complete certainty is required when commencing production.

- **Maintain the new method**. Once the new method is installed a period of maintenance is required. Unnecessary changes should not be permitted but periodic checks should be carried out to see if the method is satisfactory and if anticipated performance objectives are being met. Any introduction of a new system requires different work methods and practices to be employed with every member of the team familiar and conversant with the new approach. New processes must be monitored and measured both by hard data (eg figures such as control charts or measurements for statistical process control) and soft data (eg feedback from operatives).

2.25   When recording the work method (the second of the seven steps in SREDDIM) we must consider both the procedures for obtaining data and the type of record required.

2.26   The procedure by which the information is to be obtained may be direct observation, electronic data capture, video recording or recollection (in the case of the diary being used).

2.27   Whatever method or methods are chosen they are designed either to record the sequence of activities of a job, or to record the path of movement of a job or to record the time interrelationship of the activities involved in the job.

2.28   With regard to the type of record required, a number of different tools can be applied.

- **Diary record**: a record of work method, normally constructed by the worker in the form of a diary or list of activities
- **Flow diagram**: a diagram or model substantially to scale which shows the location of specific activities carried out and the routes followed by workers, materials or equipment in their execution; also linked to string diagrams and travel charts
- **Multiple activity chart**: a chart on which the activities of one or more subjects (worker, machine or equipment) are recorded on a common timescale to show their interrelationship
- **Flow process chart**: a process chart setting out the sequence of the flow of a product or customer, or a procedure, by recording all events under review using the appropriate process chart symbols. Flow process charts are used for material; for worker and material; and for equipment.

2.29   With regard to examination of the data (the third step in SREDDIM) the mnemonic PPSPM is useful during interviews. This stands for purpose, place, sequence, person, means.

- **Purpose**. What is being done? Why is it being done? What else could be done? What should be done?
- **Place**. Where is it being done? Why there? Where else could it be done? Where should it be done?
- **Sequence**. When is it being done? Why then? When else could it be done? When should it be done?
- **Person**. Who does it? Why them? Who else could do it? Who should do it?
- **Means**. How is it done? Why that way? How else can it be done? How should it be done?

2.30   The structuring of questions in this accepted way makes it easier to identify possible alternative or more effective methods particularly when combined with supporting data.

Work measurement

2.31   Work measurement is defined as: 'The application of techniques designed to establish the time for a qualified worker to carry out a specified job at a defined level of performance.' (BS 3138). Work times are of importance to the operations manager as they are invaluable in scheduling and capacity planning where timing is an important planning tool.

2.32   Work cannot be allocated to an individual or a team without an estimate of the time involved. Standard times, once established, can be used to set labour rates, for performance measurement, to determine the effectiveness of equipment and/or to determine standard operating costs. Machine times are relatively easy to measure, but physical human work is more difficult as it will have both a physical and a mental input. The mental input is difficult to measure but good practices can be of benefit.

Time study

2.33   Time study is: 'A work measurement technique for recording the times and rates of working for the elements of a specified job carried out under specified conditions, and for analysing the data, so as to obtain the time necessary for carrying out the job at a defined level of performance.' (BS 3138).

2.34   The aim for work measurement is to determine the time required for a job to be carried out under specified conditions. The recording will require information relating to the worker or workers, machine/s, materials, layout, method, etc. Jobs will consist of a variety of repetitive tasks, occasional elements, interaction with machines, etc. For time study to be applied effectively it is necessary to divide the job being measured into elements.

- To gain a better understanding of the job
- To segment the exercise into manageable chunks
- To permit a more accurate study
- To distinguish between different types of work
- To differentiate 'machine' and 'worker' elements
- To enable time standards to be evaluated
- To enable times for certain common or important elements to be extracted and compared

2.35   A job is observed through a number of cycles. Each element (above) is timed and a subjective rating of the performance of the worker is given. Times are averaged to give the result, with consideration being given to the performance of the worker.

2.36   One important aspect of work study is the use and application of the principles of motion economy.

- Effort should not be wasted.
- Tools and materials should be placed as close as possible to the operator.
- Movements should be automatic, if possible.
- People should be supported by machines for holding and lifting tasks.
- Materials handling should be minimised.
- If possible, the operation should be done in multiples.
- Permit position changes.
- Sit, rather than stand.
- Keep movement symmetrical – make work flow.
- Ensure working areas are at the correct height for the operative.
- Where possible use both hands.
- Ensure ease of location of parts and equipment.

2.37   Work measurement has attracted many criticisms. Slack *et al* make the following observations.

- The ideas on which the concept of a standard time is based are impossible to define precisely. How can one possibly give clarity to the definition of qualified workers, or specified jobs, or (especially) a defined level of performance?
- Even if one attempts to follow these definitions, all that results is an excessively rigid job definition. Most modern jobs require some element of flexibility, which is difficult to achieve within rigidly defined jobs.
- Using stopwatches to time human beings is both degrading and usually counterproductive. At best it is intrusive; at worst it makes people into 'objects for study'.
- The rating procedure implicit in time study is subjective and usually arbitrary. It has no basis other than the opinion of the person carrying out the study.
- Time study, especially, is very easy to manipulate. It is possible for employers to 'work back' from a time which is 'required' to achieve a particular cost. Also, experienced staff can 'put on an act' to fool the person recording the times.

3 Behavioural approaches to job design

The Hawthorne effect

3.1 The Hawthorne Studies were conducted from 1927 to 1932 at the Western Electric Hawthorne Works in Cicero, Illinois where Harvard Business School professor Elton Mayo set up a series of experiments to examine productivity and work conditions. These experiments started by examining the physical and environmental influences of the workplace (brightness of the lighting, humidity, etc), and later moved into psychological aspects (eg group pressure, working hours, breaks, leadership).

3.2 Preliminary experiments looked at the effect of lighting on productivity. These experiments showed no clear connection between productivity and the amount of illumination but they did cause researchers to question what changes would influence output. Mayo wanted to find out what effect fatigue and monotony had on job productivity and how to control them through such variables as rest breaks, work hours, temperature and humidity. Various experiments were designed incorporating the above factors to differing degrees. In addition, workers were divided into teams for comparison but the significance of teamworking was also realised when the end results were evaluated.

3.3 Mayo found what he called the **Hawthorne effect**: the response of the workers appeared to be affected by their sense of being a group and of being singled out for attention. 'Management, by consultation with the female workers, by clear explanation of the proposed experiments and the reasons for them, by accepting the workers' verdicts in several instances, unwittingly scored a success in two most important human matters – the women became a self-governing team, and a team that co-operated wholeheartedly with management.'

3.4 The groups, comprising six women in each, were singled out from the rest of the factory workers. This in itself raised their self-esteem. When consulted they felt empowered. The Hawthorne effect has been described as the reward you get when you show attention to people. The mere act of showing people that you are concerned usually spurs them on to better job performance.

3.5 Mayo came to the following conclusions.

- The aptitude of individuals is an imperfect predictor of job performance. Although individual ability is important the output produced is strongly influenced by social factors.
- Informal organisation affects productivity. The researchers found a group life among workers.
- Workgroup norms affect productivity. The group themselves recognised what is 'a fair day's work for a fair day's pay'.
- The workplace is a social system made up of interdependent parts. The worker is a person whose attitudes and effectiveness are conditioned by social demands from both inside and outside the work plant.
- The need for recognition, security and a sense of belonging is more important in determining a worker's morale and productivity than the physical conditions under which they operate.

3.6 According to Huczynski and Buchanan (*Organisational Behaviour*): 'The Hawthorne studies signalled the birth of the human relations school of management'. This was an approach consciously geared to positive human relations at work, and its impact can be seen in many aspects of human resource management today such as empowered teamworking, job design and motivational programmes aimed at offering greater job satisfaction, employee involvement schemes and 'people-friendly' policies employed by some organisations.

Motivation hygiene theory

3.7 Following the Second World War emphasis was placed on the relationship between job and organisation design and productivity. As early as 1950 job rotation and job enlargement were being put forward as a means of overcoming boredom at work with its associated problems.

3.8 During the 1950s and 1960s Frederick Herzberg developed a 'two factor' theory of motivation. He interviewed Pittsburg engineers and accountants to find out what 'critical incidents' had made them feel good or bad about their work.

3.9 In his theory he distinguished between 'motivators' and 'hygiene' factors. The hygiene factors included salary, supervision, company policy and administration. These could cause dissatisfaction if workers were unhappy with them, but could never lead to positive motivation even if perfectly satisfactory. The 'motivators' included achievement, recognition, responsibility, advancement, growth and the work itself. Herzberg highlighted two basic needs of individuals.

- The need to avoid unpleasantness, satisfied by hygiene factors
- The need for personal growth, satisfied at work by motivator factors only

3.10 'When people are dissatisfied with their work it is usually because of discontent with environmental hygiene factors.' These include company policy and administration, salary, style of supervision, interpersonal relations, working conditions and job security. An individual is much more likely to be dissatisfied with his pay, for example, than satisfied with it: he may be temporarily satisfied with a pay rise, but only until he begins to take it for granted or compare it to others.

3.11 Herzberg's two factors highlighted the two types of reward that can be offered to individuals at work.

- **Intrinsic rewards** arise from the work itself, and (in a sense) from within the worker: challenge, interest, team identity, pride in the organisation, the satisfaction of achievement and so on.
- **Extrinsic rewards** do not arise from the work itself, but are within the power of others (typically management) to award or withhold: wages or salary, bonuses, prizes, promotion, improved working conditions and so on.

3.12 From his theory Herzberg developed a set of principles for the enrichment of jobs.

- Removing some controls while retaining accountability
- Increasing personal accountability for work
- Assigning each worker a complete unit of work with a clear start and end date
- Granting additional authority and freedom to workers
- Making periodic reports directly available to workers rather than to supervisors only
- The introduction of new and more difficult tasks into the job
- Encouraging the development of expertise by assigning individuals to specialised tasks

3.13 Job enrichment aims to create greater opportunities for individual achievement and recognition by expanding the task to increase not only variety but also the responsibility and accountability of the individual.

Vroom's expectancy theory

3.14 Expectancy theory basically states that the strength of an individual's motivation to do something will depend on the extent to which he expects the results of his efforts to contribute to his personal needs or goals. Victor Vroom worked out a formula by which human motivation could be assessed and measured, based on expectancy theory.

He suggested that the strength of an individual's motivation is the product of two factors.

- The strength of his preference for a certain outcome. Vroom called this 'valence': it can be represented as a positive or negative number or zero – since outcomes may be desired, avoided or regarded with indifference.
- His expectation that the outcome will in fact result from a certain behaviour. Vroom called this 'subjective probability'. As a probability, it may be represented by any number between 0 (no chance) and 1 (certainty).

3.15 In its simplest form, the expectancy equation may be stated as follows.

$F = V \times E$

Where:

F = the force or strength of the individual's motivation to behave in a particular way
V = valence: the strength of the individual's preference for a given outcome or reward
E = expectancy: the individual's perception that the behaviour will result in the outcome/reward

3.16 In this equation, the lower the values of valence or expectation, the less the individual's motivation. An employee may have a high expectation that increased productivity will result in promotion but if he is indifferent or negative towards the idea of promotion he will not be motivated to increase productivity. The same would be true if promotion was of high importance to him but he did not believe higher productivity would get him promoted.

3.17 Expectancy theory can be used to measure the likely strength of a worker's motivation to act in a desired way in response to a range of different rewards, so as to find the most effective motivational strategy.

The Porter and Lawler model

3.18 Porter and Lawler developed a more comprehensive model of motivation which they applied primarily to managers. The model suggests that the amount of effort exerted depends on the value of a reward to the individual plus the amount of energy the individual believes is required to earn the reward, and the perceived likelihood of his receiving it. The last two factors are, in turn, influenced by a number of factors, such as actual rewards received for past performance.

Figure 4.1 *The Porter-Lawler model of motivation*

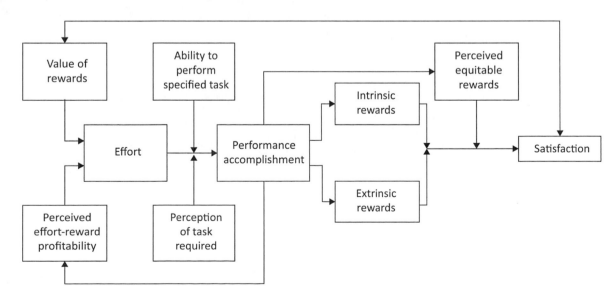

The socio-technical systems approach

3.19 The 1960s saw a move away from the idea of jobs as basic organisational units in a work system towards a wider view that saw jobs as part of a socio-technical system. Within a socio-technical systems approach management chose the most appropriate configuration of social resources (people) and technical resources (machines, computers, etc) to meet sets of conditions at a given time.

3.20 Socio-technical systems theory, according to LE Davis and Eric Trist, has two major assumptions.

- That in any work system output is achieved through the joint operation of social as well as technical systems
- That every socio-technical system is affected by the culture and values of its environment

3.21 The 'social system' (people, teams, relationships and roles) embraces both formal and informal groups such as official teams and unofficial groups based on friendship, interests etc. The 'technical system' encompasses tasks, processes, production and computer equipment.

3.22 The socio-technical approach differs from the scientific management approach in that the latter was built around machines that people have to design their work around. The socio-technical approach offers the perspective that we do not have to build jobs around machines or computers. We have the alternative of assuming that machine or computer-based systems can be adapted to meet the needs of human beings.

3.23 The socio-technical approach to designing organisations is built around the following set of guiding propositions.

- The design of the system must fit its goals.
- Employees must be actively involved in designing the structure of the organisation.
- Control of variances in production or service must be undertaken as close to their source as possible.
- Subsystems must be designed around relatively self-contained and recognisable units of work.
- Support systems must match the design requirements of the organisation.
- The design should allow for a high quality of working life.
- Changes should be made as required to meet changing environmental pressures.

Activation theory

3.24 This theory is based on the idea that to maintain productivity work must offer challenge and variety. In essence, it requires the jobholder to be 'active'.

3.25 The activation theory puts forward three principal proposals to enhance the job.

- **Job enrichment**: increasing the workers' roles and responsibilities but not necessarily their volume of work.
- **Job enlargement**: increasing the number of tasks in a given role. There is however an onus on management to ensure this enlargement is manageable by the individual.
- **Job rotation**: where applicable, moving workers between jobs to provide better variety and to develop a wider range of skills.

3.26 Results of the activation theory have been mixed. While some workers embrace and are motivated by this approach others prefer a more predictable regime and tasks.

Empowerment and self-managed systems

3.27 Considering the points we have discussed to date, what attributes of jobs contribute to the motivation of employees and can be further developed into principles for the design of jobs? Some of the following factors appear particularly relevant.

- An optimum level of variety
- An appropriate degree of repetitiveness
- An optimum level of responsibility for decisions where a degree of discretion is present
- Employee's control over their own job
- The presence of goals and regular feedback
- A perceived contribution to a socially useful product or service
- Opportunities for developing social aspects
- Opportunities for teamworking
- Perceived skills

3.28 Empowerment is one way that can be used to help achieve many of these factors. The following are definitions of the term 'empowerment' given by a number of leading human resource practitioners.

- 'What (companies) mean by empowerment varies dramatically ... Many of them are really talking about firing middle management. But companies which are really serious are talking about an orderly distribution of power and authority.'
- 'It means people using their own judgement in the interests of the organisation and the customer within a disciplined context.'
- 'The purpose of empowerment is to free someone from rigorous control by instructions and orders and give them freedom to take responsibility for their ideas and actions, to release hidden resources which would otherwise remain inaccessible.'

3.29 Empowerment has two key aspects. It involves giving workers discretion to make decisions about how to organise work in order to achieve task goals and making workers responsible for achieving production and quality targets.

3.30 Empowerment is essentially a process of decentralising control over business units, or delegating responsibility, or removing levels in the organisation to increase flexibility and initiative.

Benefits of empowerment

3.31 The argument is that empowerment (like job enrichment) is satisfying to the worker. It offers opportunities for employees to satisfy their 'higher order' needs through the work itself, by giving greater scope, challenge, interest and significance to the job.

3.32 Empowerment is also intended to enhance organisational effectiveness. It increases employee commitment and harnesses their creativity and initiative. It shortens the lines of communication and decision-making at the interface of the organisation with customers and suppliers, facilitating responsiveness.

3.33 Empowerment also takes advantage of front-line experience and expertise. 'The people lower down the organisation possess the knowledge of what is going wrong with a process but lack the authority to make changes. Those further up the structure have the authority to make changes, but lack the profound knowledge required to identify the right solutions. The only solution is to change the culture of the organisation so that everyone can become involved in the process of improvement and work together to make the changes' (Max Hand, *Management Accounting*).

3.34 Arguments against empowerment include the following.

- Empowering staff implies a loss of control. Discretion is being given to individuals who are unaccustomed to taking business decisions.
- Centralised control offers advantages of whole-organisation perspective and consistency of performance between subunits. Empowerment may lead to disintegration and inconsistent quality, as units focus on their own objectives.
- Not all employees want empowerment. They may view extra responsibility with suspicion, or may simply feel insecure about the erosion of traditional methods of working.

- Empowerment can be perceived as an attempt to manipulate employees into giving commitment – without giving them general control.
- If people feel they are being asked to take on more responsibility, they will expect to be paid more. Empowerment may be an expensive approach to motivation, rather than a 'substitute' for monetary reward.

4 Ergonomic workplace design

4.1 Ergonomics is an area that needs careful consideration and evaluation from operations managers. Ergonomics is the study of all the factors affecting the physical and psychological relationship between people and their artificial environment. Most people have heard of it in connection with seating or car dashboard design but its remit is far wider than that. It is defined by the Ergonomics Society as: *'The application of scientific information concerning humans to the design of objects, systems and environment for human use.'*

4.2 Ergonomics involves everything that interacts with people. Work systems and health and safety should all embody ergonomic principles if well designed.

Applications of ergonomics

4.3 Ergonomics has a wide application in everyday domestic situations but there are even more significant implications for efficiency, productivity and safety. The Ergonomics Society gives the following examples.

- Designing equipment and systems including computers, so that they are easier to use and less likely to lead to errors in operation – particularly important in high-stress and safety-critical situations such as control rooms.
- Designing tasks and jobs so that they are effective and take account of human needs such as rest breaks and sensible shift patterns, as well as other factors such as the intrinsic rewards of the job itself.
- Designing equipment and work arrangements to improve working posture and ease the load on the body, reducing instances of repetitive strain injury and work-related upper-limb disorder.
- Information design, to make the interpretation and use of handbooks, signs and displays easier and less error-prone.
- Design of training arrangements to cover all significant aspects of the job concerned and to take account of human learning requirements.
- Designing working environments, including lighting and heating, to suit the needs of the users and the tasks performed. Where necessary, design of personal protective equipment for work in hostile environments.

4.4 Ergonomics involves the interaction of technical and work situations with the human being. The two main objectives of ergonomics are the most productive use of human capabilities and the maintenance of health and wellbeing. Three human sciences are involved in attaining this.

- *Anatomy* involves improving the fit between people and the things they use. The science of anthropometrics provides information on the postures and dimensions of the human body and the science of biomechanics provides information on the operation of the muscles and limbs.
- *Physiology* considers two aspects: the energy requirement of the body and the setting of standards for acceptable physical workrate and workload; and energy physiology, that investigates the impact of working conditions such as temperature, humidity, noise and lighting.
- *Psychology* is concerned with human information processing and decision-making capabilities: the 'fit' between people and the things they use.

4.5 When linking ergonomics with job design the operations manager needs a broad understanding of ergonomic issues, but a number of factors are particularly relevant.

- The method used or required to accomplish the work. Work study will evaluate the most effective way of accomplishing a task but will also consider the ergonomic ramifications of the work method.
- The effort or strength required to accomplish the task. If it results in undue strain the operations manager should consider specialist lifting or holding equipment as appropriate.
- The location and position of parts and tools required to accomplish the task. These should be positioned to hand and at the correct height.
- The duration and repetition of the task. Repetitive strain injury has come to the fore in recent years with the increased use of computers and most employers are now well aware of the surrounding issues. Repetitive strain injury was first recognised in production; ergonomic design can help in reducing or eliminating the risks involved.
- The design of equipment, parts or tools. Designers will often take an ergonomic, user-centred approach to design which will include testing, appraising people using the equipment, and receiving feedback
- Environmental factors such as light, heating and noise. These factors are the subject of legislation (in the UK, for instance, by the Health and Safety at Work Act), but legislation should be viewed as the minimum acceptable standard and the operation may run more effectively if the correct ergonomic considerations are applied.

4.6   One goal of ergonomics is to design jobs to fit people. This involves taking into account differences such as size, strength and the ability to handle information for a wide range of users. The tasks, the workplace and the tools are designed to incorporate these differences. The benefits are greater efficiency, higher quality work and more job satisfaction.

5   The volume-variety effect

Jobbing, batch, flow and mass production

5.1   Production is a conversion function by which goods and services are produced. The production system is the framework within which the production activities of an organisation take place. An appropriate design of the production system ensures the co-ordination of the various production operations. There is no single pattern of production which is universally applicable to all types of production system. The systems will vary between one organisation and another.

5.2   Manufacturing operations are concerned with a process of transformation or conversion. The way in which this transformation process takes place differs from one industry to another and sometimes from one firm to another within the same industry. The main possibilities are jobbing production, batch production, flow production and mass production although projects will be included in some text books.

5.3   Jobbing production refers to situations where the output is a finished product produced to the specification of a particular customer. This is a familiar process in industries such as construction or engineering; the finished product is an office building, a bridge, a highway etc, ordered by a particular customer. Each job is a separate entity, and its production is distinct from the production of any other job. This type of jobbing is also referred to as project management.

5.4   The examples given above are large-scale, but this is not an essential feature of the jobbing approach. For example, a traditional craftsman is practising a jobbing form of production when manufacturing a chair or a cabinet to a customer's specification.

5.5   In batch production, as the name suggests, the unit of output is a batch of like products. Typically, the work involved will be divided into stages with dedicated workers and machines at each stage. All products in the batch will first pass through Stage 1 and will be worked on by the workers and machines dedicated to this stage. Once complete they will move to Stage 2, and so on until all stages of production are complete.

5.6   Batch production is a very common method – perhaps the most common method – of work organisation found in the manufacturing environment. Some specialisation of labour is evident: Stage 1 workers gain relevant skills in their particular process; Stage 2 the same; and so on. They do not, however gain the skills involved in jobbing production.

5.7   Flow production is usually taken to mean a system in which products flow from one stage of production to the next without interruption. Contrast this with batch production in which a product is not passed from one stage to the next until all products in the batch have completed the earlier stage. The aim of flow production is that any particular product will be undergoing a transformation process for every minute of its time in the production cycle. To achieve this, it is important that all stages of production are of equal length; otherwise, bottlenecks will arise at stages with longer duration. Another implication is that production is broken down into a large number of very small steps, enabling a high degree of specialisation of labour.

5.8   Mass production simply means production on a large scale. In correct usage, the term does not refer to any particular type of production – it may be organised on job, batch or flow lines – but only to the scale of production.

Factors influencing the choice of the manufacturing systems

5.9   There is no best manufacturing system for any product. The choice of the system depends on various circumstances but it must meet two basic objectives.

- It must be able to meet the specifications of the final product.
- It must be cost effective.

5.10   The product specifications can be met by choosing the right technology but that is not always an easy task. Since stricter specifications add to the cost of the product, there is always a trade-off between the desired specifications and the cost to achieve such specifications. For example, sophisticated injection moulding machines and high quality plastics can produce excellent dolls cheaply provided they are produced in volume.

5.11   However, if their demand is limited, they may not be able to compete with home made dolls produced in small quantities and sold at a fraction of the price of the moulded version.

5.12   Here are some of the factors which determine the choice of the manufacturing process.

- **Effect of volume/variety**: One of the major considerations in the process selection is the volume/ variety of the products. High product variety requires highly skilled labour, general purpose machines, detailed production planning and control systems. On the other hand low product variety (ie one or few products produced in large volumes) enables the use of low skilled labour, highly automated mass production processes using special purpose machines and simple production planning and control systems.
- **Capacity of the plant:** The projected sales volume is a major influencing factor in determining whether the firm should go in for intermittent or continuous process. Fixed costs are high for continuous process and low for intermittent process while variable costs are more for the intermittent process and less for continuous process. Intermittent process therefore will be cheaper to install and operate at low volumes and continuous process will be economical to use at high volume.
- **Flexibility:** Flexibility implies the ability of the company to satisfy varied customer requirements. Flexibility and product variety are inter-related. If more variety is to be manufactured, the manufacturing facilities will have to be commonised and depending upon the volume, the extent of commonalities will require to be justified. Greater commonalities demand intermittent manufacturing which is associated with higher inventories, large manufacturing lead times and elaborate planning and control.

- **Lead time:** Lead times expected by the customers (ie how soon the demand has to be met without losing on sales) is another major influencing factor in a competitive market. As a general rule, faster deliveries are expected in a competitive market. The product, therefore, may require to be produced to stock using principles of batch production.
- **Efficiency:** Efficiency measures the speed and the cost of the transformation process. Efficiency is greatest when the product is mass produced. But to mass produce a product, greater sales volumes are required. Therefore, depending upon the sales volume, product variety will have to be considered and the process which will give the best efficiency in terms of machine and manpower utilisation will have to be selected.
- **Environment:** Environment brings in new technologies and forces the adoption of new processes of manufacturing. For example, wooden furniture is gradually being replaced by metals and plastic. A furniture manufacturing unit will have to change its technology (eg change from one-off production to batch production) to fall in line with changing times. Similarly, as market preferences change owing to fashions or other reasons, the manufacturing process has to be changed accordingly.

6 Process mapping

6.1 A process map or process flowchart (the terms are used interchangeably) is used to describe and illustrate a process. A process is a structured set of activities that transform inputs into outputs. Processes assist in defining responsibilities, internal controls, and work standards for compliance, consistency, performance and measurement.

6.2 Flowcharts show people what their jobs are and how they should interact with one another. Everybody should be able to see from the chart what their job is and how their work fits in with the work of others in the process. Processes are simply sequences of actions designed to transform inputs into outputs. For instance, baking a cake will involve taking various ingredients (inputs) and producing the cake (output) using the recipe (process).

6.3 Process mapping is an exercise to identify all the steps and decisions in a process in diagrammatic form which fulfils the following functions.

- Describes the flow of materials, information and documents
- Displays the various tasks contained within the process
- Shows that the tasks transform inputs into outputs
- Indicates the decisions that need to be made along the chain
- Demonstrates the essential inter-relationships and interdependence between the process steps; and reminds us that the strength of a chain depends upon its weakest link

6.4 There are many different types of chart, each designed to capture particular aspects of work, such as travel charts that can record movement of people or materials in a process. The outline process map, which provides a basic 'birds eye' view of all the actions undertaken, is the most common. This chart sets out the sequence of activities and decision points. These are useful for capturing the initial detail of the process. Labels showing the grade of staff doing each step can be added if required.

6.5 Although there are many types of chart and numerous charting conventions, you should not be drawn into a technical maze. The primary objective is to make the chart as clear as possible, so that the process under review can be readily understood and improvements identified by almost anyone, even someone unfamiliar with the process.

6.6 Process mapping enables us to clearly define the current processes in chart form, identifying problem areas such as bottlenecks, capacity issues, delays or waste. Once identified, this knowledge provides a solid basis from which to develop solutions and introduce and plan new improved processes.

6.7 Process mapping enables an organisation to achieve the following results.

- Establish what is currently happening, how predictably and why
- Measure how efficiently the process is working
- Gather information to understand where waste and inefficiency exist and their impact on the customer or partners
- Develop new improved processes to reduce or eliminate inefficiency

6.8 It helps if a process map identifies a **S**upplier providing **I**nputs to a **P**rocess, which produces **O**utputs for a **C**ustomer. This basic format is a SIPOC (Supplier, Input, Process, Output, Customer) diagram. There are many variations of this SIPOC theme but it does provide a useful framework for understanding the critical elements, sources, and outputs of a process.

6.9 Standard symbols are used within a process map to describe key process elements. These symbols come from the Unified Modeling Language or UML, which is an international standard for drawing process maps.

Better understanding of a process

6.10 Process maps are used to develop a better understanding of a process, to generate ideas for process improvement or to stimulate discussion, to build stronger communication and to document a process. Often a process map will highlight problems and identify bottlenecks, duplication, delays, or gaps. Process maps can help to clarify process boundaries, process ownership, process responsibilities, and effectiveness measures or process metrics.

6.11 Process maps are not limited to a single department or function. For example, the ISO 9000 Quality Management Systems standard requires some type of process map of the organisation's quality processes. Mapping should be the first step in designing a process or in documenting a procedure. This is because to improve a process you must understand it and most of us understand a graphical picture better than a written procedure.

Chapter summary

- In organisations of even moderate size it is important to gain the benefits of specialisation. Different individuals are responsible for different tasks, typically laid out in the form of a job design.
- Early studies of job design were based on 'scientific management' principles. While this led to apparent improvements in productivity, the long-term effects were to demotivate employees.
- Later studies emphasised the importance of job satisfaction in improving employee morale and hence productivity. The pioneering work in this area was Elton Mayo's Hawthorne studies.
- Ergonomics is the application of scientific information concerning humans to the design of objects, systems and environment for human use.
- Jobbing, batch, flow and mass production systems are some of the possibilities open to operations managers. To an extent, the choice of system is influenced by the volume and variety of goods to be produced.
- For better understanding of business processes, it is possible to use various types of charts and mapping.

4

Self-test questions

Numbers in brackets refer to the paragraphs above where your answers can be checked.

1   Describe the core job dimensions identified by Hackman and Oldham. (1.7)

2   Describe the psychological requirements of a 'full job' identified by Paul Hill. (1.9)

3   List the basic principles of job design, according to FW Taylor. (2.5)

4   Describe the two different techniques that make up work study. (2.9)

5   What are the seven steps involved in method study? (2.24)

6   What were Mayo's conclusions from the Hawthorne studies? (3.5)

7   What are the two major assumptions underlying the socio-technical systems approach? (3.20)

8   List arguments against empowerment of employees. (3.34)

9   What three human sciences are involved in ergonomics? (4.4)

10   Describe factors that affect the choice of manufacturing process. (5.12)

11   What are the functions of process mapping? (6.3)

CHAPTER 5

Product and Service Design

Assessment criteria and indicative content

2.2 Analyse the main techniques for product or service design

- The product-process matrix
- The stages of creating products or services (concept generation, concept screening, preliminary product or service design, evaluation and improvement)
- Sustainability in the designs of products and services
- Computer aided design systems (CAD) and computer aided manufacturing (CAM)
- Quality function deployment
- Value engineering and value analysis
- Simultaneous engineering and simultaneous development

Section headings

1 Stages in product creation
2 Design evaluation and improvement
3 Sustainability in product design
4 Design tools
5 CAD and CAM

1 Stages in product creation

Defining 'design'

1.1 When you consider design your initial thought is probably conceptual, creative design: something new, something cutting edge, something that takes design into a new era. However, most design is a little more realistic and risk averse than that.

1.2 The dictionaries give a variety of definitions for design. 'The act of producing a drawing, plan or pattern showing details of something to be constructed', 'the arrangement of elements of a work of art' and 'a decorative pattern', are three. The term is wider than all three. It is a blend of concept, taste, style and practicality from a business perspective.

1.3 The purpose of design, in a business sense, is to satisfy the needs of customers. A product is designed to meet customer requirements. While this is of great concern to both designers and marketing, the view of operations is more pragmatic. The main operational concern is whether the product can be made to specification at an acceptable cost. To put it another way: is it designed for manufacture?

1.4 The traditional product or service development process is constrained by the functional personnel involved.

- Designers are looking for the freedom to design. They realise that the practicalities of manufacture, transformation and customer needs will impact on their design but also realise that their role involves creativity and innovation as one of their major inputs into an organisation.

- Finance staff are responsible for financing the research and development that is involved in new product introduction and for monitoring and approving the spend as the new product progresses.
- Procurement staff have an increasingly important role in new product development. If procurement is involved early in the design process they can advise on different materials, potential costs and supply problems. They can also involve potential suppliers early in the process if specialist research, involving the skills of suppliers, is called for.
- Marketing staff have responsibility for bringing the new product successfully to market. This involves an awareness of changing tastes and requirements.
- Operations staff have a central role in the new product development process. Whereas procurement has a crucial role as the external interface between an organisation and suppliers the role of operations has more of an internal focus through the development stages. The concern of operations is the integration of design into the practicalities of production.

1.5 Cross-functional teamwork brings all relevant concerns into open discussion during the formative phase of development and allows for discussion and clarification. This integrated approach helps ensure that all potential areas are discussed by the team who become increasingly familiar with the project and, in consequence, gain a wider understanding and perspective on the issues raised by other team members.

1.6 Slack *et al* refer to the four Cs of design.

- Creativity – design requires the creation of something that hasn't existed before.
- Complexity – design involves decisions on a large number of parameters and variables.
- Compromise – design requires balancing multiple and sometimes conflicting requirements.
- Choice – design requires making choices between many options.

The product-process matrix

1.7 The product-process matrix was first introduced by Robert Hayes and Steven Wheelwright in the Harvard Business Review in 1979. It helps organisations identify the type of production approach they should use for a product, based on the volumes of the product being produced, and the amount of customisation it needs.

Figure 5.1 *The product-process matrix*

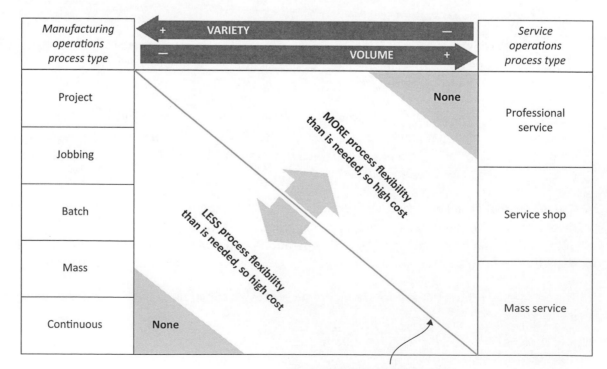

The 'natural' line of fit of process to volume/variety characteristics

Based on Hayes and Wheelwright

1.8   The diagonal of the matrix shown in Figure 5.1 represents a 'natural' lowest cost position for an operation. Operations which are on the right of the 'natural' diagonal have processes which would normally be associated with lower volumes and higher variety. This means that their processes are likely to be more flexible than seems to be warranted by their actual volume-variety position. Put another way, they are not taking advantage of their ability to standardise their processes. Because of this, their costs are likely to be higher than they would be with a process that was closer to the diagonal.

1.9   Conversely, operations that are on the left of the diagonal have adopted processes which would normally be used in a higher-volume and lower-variety situation. Their processes will therefore be 'over-standardised' and probably too inflexible for their volume-variety position. This lack of flexibility can also lead to high costs because the process will not be able to change from one activity to another as efficiently as a more flexible process.

1.10   The product-process matrix is about matching the production method to volume and product diversity – in other words, using the right process for the volume of work. As an example, suppose you have a deadline to get 500 important letters in the mail to your customers. Which of these approaches would be the more efficient?

- Scenario A: You assemble each letter one by one. You fold each piece of paper, put it in the envelope, address it, and stamp it.
- Scenario B: You work on each task in batches. First you fold the letters. Then you stuff them in envelopes. Then you address each envelope. And finally you stamp them.

1.11   While it is probably more boring, Scenario B is almost certainly more efficient because you can have the one or two items you need for that single task within easy reach, and you don't waste time switching between tasks.

1.12   In other situations when the same set of tasks must be carried out multiple times – whether you're dealing with product manufacture, administrative tasks or other types of work – it will not be as obvious how best to organise things. The product-process matrix is particularly useful when new processes are being introduced or when changes are being introduced to either the product being produced or the process being used to make it.

Phases of the design programme

1.13   Muhlemann, Oakland and Lockyer in *Production and Operations Management* state that every design programme will pass through five phases.

- **Conception**: when a draft specification is drawn up in as much detail as possible to provide a clear indication of the nature of the product or service.
- **Acceptance**: this is where the specification is shown to be achievable or not. This stage requires both cross-functional and specific area teamworking to resolve any issues.
- **Execution**: where the project has developed to the stage where trial runs or models are prepared for critical evaluation.
- **Translation**: here the role of operations management is critical. Lack of involvement between design and operations can prove costly. The translation of the design into a transformation process is an important phase.
- **Pre-operation**: Before progressing to full manufacture or release it is usual to carry out a pilot run or test marketing. Only after full evaluation of pre-operational testing should the project move to implementation.

1.14   The design activity moves through a number of stages during research and development and progresses from a concept through to a workable specification.

1.15   The development stage takes the initial research and moves the concept into something more workable. Development is involved with the improvement of concepts, ideas, existing products, services, techniques or systems into something that is better suited to meet the end objective of customer satisfaction.

1.16   The design stage has two phases.

- The first involves conceptualising the product or service and gradually refining until a specification can be drawn up. The design activity is a transformation process in itself. It takes inputs in the shape of ideas and concepts and through teamwork transforms them into a workable specification.
- The second phase is the process design. It is here that operations have an overarching role. Products and services should be designed in such a way that they can be manufactured or prepared effectively. Ideally the processes that will transform the product or service should be flexible enough that new demands can be integrated into existing systems without major changes to the operation.

Design for manufacture and assembly (DFMA)

1.17   One systematic approach to analysing a proposed design and establishing methods of saving manufacturing and assembly costs is known as **design for manufacture and assembly**. The title is largely self-explanatory. The method forces the designer and development team to consider the cost and practical implications involved in taking the design through to manufacture.

1.18   This technique has been said to achieve significant cost reductions.

- Component part reductions of 30 per cent
- Assembly cost reductions of 40 per cent
- Overall product cost reductions of up to 35 per cent

1.19   Many DFMA methods employ charting techniques where various identified measures of performance and potential manufacturing targets are established and measured against criteria such as the following.

- Design efficiency (functional analysis of each part)
- Handling analysis (relative handling cost of each part)
- Fitting analysis (assembly costs for each part)

1.20   Sequence flowcharts before and after analysis demonstrate the improvements and savings made. The process generally demonstrates a very significant change in the processes and ways in which products can be put together.

Aspects of customer satisfaction

1.21   Organisations will introduce new products and services periodically to add to the range and keep ahead of the competition or to replace unfashionable or obsolete products and services.

1.22   A product is anything that satisfies a customer need or want. We often consider products as tangible objects that a customer buys, but we need to remember that the customer is buying something to satisfy a need or want. This satisfaction might be achieved through the purchase of a service.

1.23   Muhlemann, Oakland and Lockyer (in *Production and Operations Management*) provide a number of guidelines for achieving reliability in product design. These are summarised in Table 5.1.

1.24   So what is a new product? The answer is not as obvious as it first appears. Is it something totally new, designed using cross-functional teams, tested on focus groups and designed giving the optimum performance from the operations team? Or is it something new to a particular organisation, a close copy of something else or something where the rights have been acquired from another company?

Table 5.1 *Designing reliability into products*

Use proven designs, and proven processes and operations	This is obvious – a design that is tried and tested is that much less likely to fail, and the same can be said for a manufacturing process
Use the simplest possible design	Simple components, few in number, are less likely to fail than a large number of complex components
Use components known to have high reliability	Tackling reliability at the component level is easier than at the total product level
Consider the use of redundant parts	If two identical parts are placed in parallel the second can kick in if the first fails
Design to 'fail-safe'	As noted already, nothing is completely fail-safe, but setting an ideal target is a means of achieving high standards.

1.25 A new product should be perceived in terms of customers' needs and wants. A new product can be an innovation, a major invention, an updated replacement or an imitative product. Each of these alternatives offers challenges to the operations team in terms of designing the appropriate transformation process. Totally new products will require a totally new approach whereas with replacement or imitative products lessons can be learned from what has happened before or from how other organisations arrange their transformation processes. The latter two are therefore the fastest to market in the majority of cases.

1.26 The stages in the NPD process are shown in Figure 5.2.

Figure 5.2 *The NPD process*

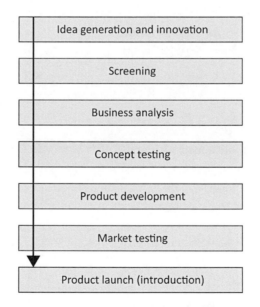

1.27 The NPD process is lengthy and thorough. Despite this, many products fail once they reach the market. Philip Kotler (*Marketing Management*) says that new products fail for many reasons.

- Shortage of important new product ideas in certain areas
- Fragmented markets
- Cost of the NPD process
- Capital shortages
- Faster development time for competitors
- Shorter product lifecycles

1.28 Achieving customer satisfaction requires a blend of good and appropriate design, an anticipation of customers' needs, and high levels of customer service. Without the first of these being achieved it is difficult to see how the other two will redeem the situation.

1.29 The design process will be ongoing. As time, technology and customer preferences evolve there is a need to monitor changes and consider adapting the product if necessary. Adaptation will only be viable if the anticipated profits from future sales exceed the cost of making the proposed design, manufacturing and marketing changes.

1.30 The technique of value analysis examines this from a manufacturing and procurement perspective, looking at cost reductions, excess product features and manufacture over time where production costs may have gone down or product features are no longer appropriate.

Understanding the full design business process

1.31 An integral part of product design and development is the role of quality in the processes and materials employed. Quality issues will be discussed later in the text but it is worthwhile at this stage to consider the perspective given on design by the Japanese quality guru Genichi Taguchi.

1.32 The Taguchi approach (often referred to as 'Taguchi methodology') requires quality to be built in to the product from the design stage. To build in quality offers considerable benefits over the life of a product; waste can be reduced, reworking will be unnecessary and customers will be satisfied with the product.

1.33 Taguchi methodology has three elements to its control of quality at the design stage.

- Systems design: achieved through careful selection and evaluation of parts, materials and equipment.
- Parameter design: according to Taguchi, performance deteriorates when the design parameters deviate from their target values. Targets must be set within specified parameters and met with minimum variation.
- Tolerance design: used to reduce variation around the target value further by tightening those tolerances that have a large impact on variation.

1.34 It is the concept of building quality in from the start, and getting it right first time, that is important. To go back and redesign products, systems and the transformation process after the product or service launch is highly expensive and should be avoidable if good management processes are used.

1.35 Another key tool used within the design process is **quality function deployment** (QFD). QFD aims to ensure that the final design actually satisfies the customer's needs. Market research is instituted both in respect of eventual customers, and also with regard to 'internal customers'. Their requirements are recorded and must be satisfied before the design can be regarded as complete. This ensures that the design is specified correctly and can be obtained in production.

1.36 The entire QFD process has been said to lead to the following benefits.

- Improved quality
- Increased customer satisfaction
- Improved company performance
- Improved time to market
- Lower cost in design and manufacture
- Reduction in design changes or problems
- Improved product reliability

1.37 In reality it is not possible to exert the same tight control over design as is possible with operations. Designs should be appropriate for their time of manufacture but as time moves on, technology advances and customer tastes change, redesign and revisiting products and services will be necessary.

1.38 Service design involves much the same considerations as product design. The role of operations in service development is through positive involvement during the development and design phases through to delivery and in designing those processes that allow for delivery to be made. Much of service design focuses on the consistent delivery of the service: the need to make the service clear and understandable, the need to ensure staff are adequately trained and knowledgeable and the design of processes to support effective delivery. Although product manufacture focuses on customers through methodology such as quality function deployment the increased interface with customers, which is a feature of most aspects of service delivery, ensures that customer needs are considered from the concept stage.

2   Design evaluation and improvement

The contribution of procurement and supply

2.1   The role of cross-functional teams in new product development has already been discussed. One of the main players in the team approach will be the procurement department. Procurement can bring a range of skills and knowledge to the process that enables a considered and realistic approach to be evaluated.

2.2   Procurement have a crucial role in that they can form the link between the internal development team and suppliers. This link role enables Procurement to investigate materials and sources of supply and advise the team of suitability. This interface role will grow in importance as the project develops.

2.3   Following the initial design and concept stage greater emphasis is placed on the practicality of design, the materials to be used and the suitability for manufacture. Procurement can investigate materials and components which can then be appraised for suitability.

2.4   New product development also gives Procurement the opportunity to design the supply chain from the start. This is an unusual opportunity as many supply chains are established over time and improved by reducing areas of waste and cost over time. With new materials and components there is an opportunity to fully consider and plan the supply chain from an early stage. Involvement in the team approach also gives Procurement the opportunity to get the views of other team members on supply chain issues in order that the design meets their needs from the earliest stage.

2.5   Procurement will often take a lead role in the design and development process as their link role between the organisation and suppliers is crucial in an organisation's ability to take the design through to production.

2.6   As the design project progresses the objective is to finalise the design specification. When working with suppliers who need to carry out development work it would be necessary to issue performance specifications. These indicate what is wanted from the material or component and allow suppliers to develop or adapt their products to meet requirements. When these are finalised they will be formalised into a conformance specification that is, in essence, the final specification that enables the product to advance to manufacture.

Product specifications

2.7   A key area for Procurement in the NPD process is the development of product specifications. Once designs have been signed off an important step is to finalise the requirements to be ordered from suppliers. Often this is accomplished by means of a formal specification although ordering by brand name may be appropriate in certain circumstances.

2.8   There are two main types of specifications: conformance specifications and performance specifications.

2.9   **Conformance specifications**: here the buyer details exactly what he expects the part or material to consist of. Conformance specifications can be difficult to draft unless the product is clearly understood and developed. If the specification is poorly drafted and the product supplied does not perform to its intended function the buyer bears the risk.

2.10   It may be that once a specification is tightly defined, there is only a small number of suppliers available. This will restrict opportunities and may endanger continuity of supply.

2.11   **Performance specifications**: here the buyer aims to describe what is expected from the part or material in terms of the functions it will perform and the level of performance expected. It is then the supplier's responsibility to furnish a product that will satisfy these requirements. A performance specification may underpin a simultaneous engineering project.

2.12   Performance specifications offer a number of advantages over conformance specifications, particularly at the design phase.

- They are easier to draft. This can be particularly important where the buyer has little technical knowledge of the product.
- They place more responsibility with the supplier. If the part supplied does not perform its function the buyer is entitled to redress.
- They widen the potential supplier base. If the task is to supply something that will perform a particular function, the ingenuity and expertise of a wide range of suppliers could potentially provide a wide range of possible solutions.

2.13   Sound specifications are a vital step in assuring the quality of the eventual product. Basic requirements of such a specification are that it should be up to date (reflecting the latest design decisions, and also the latest developments in the supplier's products) and that it should contain a detailed technical description, accompanied by a copy of the design as appropriate.

2.14   In the NPD process, the lead role in the process of preparing specifications is often taken by designers or engineers. If additional features are required there may be input from the marketing team. The role of Procurement is to collate the requirements into a formal specification that meets the needs of both internal and external users.

Areas of conflict between Procurement and Design

2.15   As we have seen, designers are often looking to make a statement with their proposed product. The cross-functional team approach is highly effective at moderating design by considering aspects such as practicality of manufacture, an appraisal of costs, establishing the costs of supply among other areas. The teamworking agenda permits detailed discussion and evaluation of the design from the practical aspects that other business functions can bring.

2.16   Procurement are looking to secure supply on a regular basis, to minimise costs, to ensure quality and, where appropriate to form a long-term or partnership relationship with suppliers. This practical aspect will often conflict with the over-ambition of design.

2.17   The conflict is between the ideal of the design and the practicalities of delivering it. An example is the design of a new car where the original concept may be quite bold but is moderated when it comes to manufacture. Issues such as building on an existing floor plan, customer acceptability, costs of materials, sources of supply etc, all serve to moderate the design into a more practical product to manufacture.

2.18   Shad Dowlatshahi, quoted by Lysons and Farrington, draws attention to the differences that may occur between Procurement and Design: see Table 5.2.

Table 5.2 *Procurement orientation vs design orientation*

PROCUREMENT ORIENTATION	DESIGN ORIENTATION
• Minimum acceptable margin of quality, safety and performance	• Wide margins of quality, safety and performance
• Use of adequate materials	• Use of ideal materials
• Lowest ultimate cost	• Limited concern for cost
• High regard for availability	• Limited regard for availability
• Practical and economic parameters, specification, features and tolerances	• Close or near perfect parameters, specifications, features and tolerances
• General view of the product	• Conceptual abstraction of product quality
• Cost elimination of materials	• Selection of materials
• Concern for JIT delivery and supplier relationship	• Concern for overall product design

2.19   The conflict Procurement have with Design is similar to the conflict areas such as operations or finance will have. Operations are looking for the design to be manufactured in a cost effective and efficient way, finance are looking to cost the ramifications of the design. The need is to obtain a balance between conflicting needs while ensuring the design retains the practical features required to meet customer needs.

Specifications online and the use of e-procurement

2.20   In many organisations Procurement is taking a more proactive role than has been the case in the past. The increased spend on component items as opposed to making in-house, the recognition of supply chain management and the move to outsourcing selected functional areas of the business are just three examples of why this is occurring.

2.21   The role of e-commerce is having a considerable impact on procurement. E-commerce encompasses e-sourcing (an upstream activity that uses the internet to make decisions and form strategies regarding how and where services or products are obtained) and e-procurement (a downstream activity using the internet to operate the transactional aspects of purchasing, authorising, ordering, receipting and payment processes for the required services or products). E-commerce goes further in procurement as it also covers the use of the internet to build more collaborative ways of working between the customer and supplier, and within organisations themselves.

2.22   E-commerce enables Procurement to:

- Find and qualify suppliers
- Issue invitations to tender
- Check real time inventory
- Receive invoices
- Access catalogued data
- Run reverse auctions
- Issue call off orders
- Monitor performance
- Make payment
- Issue specifications online

2.23   In consequence procurement has more tools and faster methods available that can be used to increase the efficiency and the effectiveness of the procurement operation.

2.24   Issuing specifications online is part of an integrated approach that enables faster, more accurate communication between purchaser and supplier. In today's business world where closer collaboration is a strategic aim the use of e-commerce tools and methods is helping to drive business forward.

2.25 One of the most effective ways that Procurement can contribute to reducing the environmental impact of products and services is to ensure that specifications are drafted in such a way as to incorporate environmental issues. Key areas such as an increase in recyclable material, reduction of packaging and reduced requirement for the inclusion of hazardous material should all become part of the specification process.

3 Sustainability in product design

Trade-offs in designing environmentally acceptable products

3.1 The design of products in such a way as to minimise their impact on the environment is becoming increasingly important. Environmental issues have traditionally focused on production processes and environmental regulation has concentrated on pollution from industry. It is recognised that people cause pollution.

3.2 Packaging is designed to be thrown away thereby adding to landfill sites. Noxious fumes can be the result of poorly designed factories or manufacturing facilities that do not use energy efficiently. Plastics require processing before their end journey to the landfill site. Pollution is a result of the throwaway society but is also a consequence of poor planning and design.

3.3 Design issues have traditionally concerned themselves with aesthetics, function and profitability. However, decisions made during the design phase have a direct impact on the materials and energy used during manufacture and the energy consumed and pollution produced during the product's lifetime.

3.4 Environmentally sensitive design has three aspects: design for environmental manufacturing, design for environmental packaging and design for disassembly.

3.5 **Design for environmental manufacturing**: this aspect of manufacture offers an attraction for many manufacturing organisations as implementation will serve to reduce cost. However, this gain will not be made without investment.

3.6 Manufacturing must be designed to minimise energy consumption, emissions and waste. For the operations manager this means a new set of considerations relating to process design (reducing energy consumption and minimising waste) and material design (to minimise waste and pollution during product manufacture and disposal).

3.7 Three drivers – increasing costs, increasing consumer awareness on environmental issues and increasing legislation – look set to make environmental manufacturing a subject of higher level debate in the future.

3.8 **Design for environmental packaging**: environmental packaging has been subject to European legislation for some years and centres around four main areas.

- Minimising the use of packaging materials. This is increasingly being enforced by making the manufacturer liable for disposal costs.
- Encouraging the use of reusable pallets, totes and packaging. This is made possible by adopting unitised sizes throughout an industry, coupled with a returns capability.
- The use of biodegradable packaging materials is growing in consumer acceptance and provides companies with an additional selling point.
- The use of recyclable packaging materials involves a number of design considerations. Initially the right material should be used to last the intended lifetime. Filler materials should be carefully selected for disposability and the packaging should be designed for disassembly.

3.9 **Design for disassembly**: the 1991 BMW Z1 Roadster was conceived and designed for disassembly and recycling. The side and other panels were designed to come apart. The use of glues was limited and replaced with fasteners to enable areas such as the bumpers and the dashboard to be removed and disassembled more easily. At design, the portion of the car to be recycled was 80 per cent. BMW now aims for 95 per cent.

3.10 W Beitz ('Designing for ease of recycling', *Journal of Engineering Design*, 1993) identifies the following considerations.

- Designing for ease of disassembly, to enable removal of parts without damage
- Designing for ease of purifying, to ensure that the purifying process does not damage the environment
- Design for ease of testing and classifying, to make it clear as to the condition of parts which can be reused and to enable easy classification of parts through proper marking
- Designing for ease of reconditioning – this supports the reprocessing of parts by providing additional material as well as gripping and adjusting features
- Designing for ease of re-assembly, to provide easy assembly for reconditioned and new parts.

3.11 Beitz goes on to argue that when a product reaches the end of its life it should be able to be dealt with in such a way that it has future use.

3.12 Design for the environment (DFE) is becoming increasingly important. J Fiskel defines DFE as 'a systematic consideration of design issues related to environmental and human health over the lifecycle of a product'. This definition highlights the key areas of a systematic approach that reflects the whole life of the product, not just the design and development stages.

3.13 Increasing environmental awareness will mean that design will change. Slack *et al* highlight the following reasons for this.

- Source of materials used in a product
- Quantities and sources of energy consumed in a process
- The amount and type of waste material created during the manufacturing process
- The life of the product itself
- The end of life of the product – can the product be disposed of safely? Can it be recycled?

3.14 The above list causes numerous issues for the operations manager. To balance the factors relevant for making the right decision, in a given set of circumstances, involves compromise. One approach is to apply a lifecycle analysis to the product. This will involve balancing the above environmental issues over the whole life of the product in order to arrive at an environmentally aware decision.

3.15 This decision will then require justification in a business situation.

Lifecycle analysis

3.16 Buyers must consider a wide range of factors relating to their procurement activities. Environmental impact is one of them but areas such as cost, quality and delivery are always important too.

3.17 CIPS consider whole life costing (lifecycle costing) as a best practice tool for evaluating options for any substantial procurement. Whole life costing (WLC) is a technique used to establish the total cost of ownership over the entire life of the product. The WLC approach addresses all the elements of cost and can be developed to produce a spend profile over the product's anticipated lifespan. WLC can be developed further to consider disposal costs, therefore establishing the WLC over the entire life of the product.

3.18 CIPS explain the technique as follows.

In whole life costing, all costs over the life of goods and services are taken into account. This enables savings in running costs to offset any increase in capital costs. The savings are calculated for each year of the equipment or service contract life. It shows either a simple payback time or the payback during the life of the equipment or service contract. It can be applied to most situations to justify extra expenditure.

3.19 Whole life costing requires an evaluation of the costs of ownership. These can be categorised under six main headings.

- **Pre-acquisition costs**: such as research, sourcing, preparation of tenders and structural changes to allow for the product.
- **Acquisition costs**: including the purchase price, delivery, installation and commissioning etc.
- **Operating costs**: embracing labour, materials, consumables, electricity usage, environmental costs etc.
- **Maintenance costs**: such as spares and replacement parts, servicing, reducing output with age etc.
- **Downtime costs**: lost profit, extra labour costs, costs resulting from non-performance and claims resulting from non-performance.
- **End of life costs**: disposal, ongoing liabilities, decommissioning, sale for scrap, resale etc.

End of life issues

3.20 Whole life costing involves considering the entire life of a product from the design stage through to disposal. As we have seen this approach is becoming increasingly embedded in business processes from the design stage.

3.21 One area that is difficult to quantify at the time of purchase is the end of life costs. Legislation in this area is likely to be far tougher at the time of decommissioning than it is now and this should be factored into any calculations. The uncertainty about legal regulation should be balanced against an organisation's stance on corporate social responsibility issues where good practice may enable a company to be ahead of merely fulfilling its legal obligations.

3.22 For example, European legislation places considerable emphasis on environmental issues surrounding the product lifecycle and this is being enacted into English law. The EC Directive on Waste Electrical and Electronic Equipment (WEEE Directive) places responsibilities on both manufacturers and users in relation to design, recycling and disposal. The UK Waste Electrical and Electronic Equipment (WEEE) Regulations 2006, which implement the Producer Responsibility aspects of the WEEE Directive, came into force on 2 January 2007. Other aspects of the Regulations have since been rolled out: the requirement to mark EEE products with a producer identifier and crossed-out wheelie bin 'do not recycle' symbol) came into force in April 2007; and the VCA (Vehicle Certification Agency) became the enforcing body, to make sure that retailers and distributors of electrical equipment play their part in helping household users, in July 2007.

3.23 Other environmental legislation concerns packaging and waste (EC Packaging and Waste Directive 94/62/EC). This concerns identification of the 'waste stream' and covers all aspects of waste, recycling and disposal. A further example is the proposed legislation on end of life vehicles (ELVs) in relation to the composition of vehicles going on to the market and the levels to which they should be recycled. The legislation aims to reduce, or prevent, the amount of waste produced from ELVs and increase recovery of usable materials and recycling

3.24 In 2003 the European Commission published the Integrated Product Policy (IPP) outlining its strategy for reducing the environmental impact caused by products throughout their lifecycle. The IPP is based on five key principles.

- **Lifecycle thinking**: aims to reduce a product's environmental impact from the cradle to the grave. In doing so it also aims to prevent individual parts of the lifecycle from being addressed in a way that results in the environmental burden being shifted to another part.
- **Working with the market**: establishing incentives in order that the market moves in a more sustainable direction and rewarding companies that are innovative, forward-thinking and committed to sustainable development

- **Stakeholder involvement**: aims to encourage all those who come into contact with the product (industry, consumers and the government) to act across their sphere of influence and encourage the purchase of more environmentally aware products and how they can better use and dispose of them
- **Continuous improvement**: the IPP seeks to encourage improvements that can be made to decrease a product's environmental impacts across its lifecycle.
- **Policy instruments**: the IPP approach requires a number of different initiatives and regulations to be enacted. The initial emphasis will be placed on voluntary initiatives although mandatory measures may be required.

3.25   The Eco-Management and Audit Scheme (EMAS) will be made more product focused and organisations will be encouraged to adopt the systemised and recognised approach embedded within it.

3.26   End of life issues are increasingly becoming an integrated aspect of product management. Organisations need to balance directives and legislation, stakeholder views and corporate social responsibility issues in a proactive and positive manner to ensure good practice is followed.

Environmentally preferred materials

3.27   The environmental impact of a material can occur at all stages of the material's lifecycle, from extraction and processing through its useful operating cycle to disposal or recycling. These impacts are not always apparent and require an environmental risk appraisal in order to ascertain the issues involved.

3.28   The use of environmentally preferred materials is being adopted by many procurement departments who are increasingly developing strategies and policies with regard to environmental purchasing. The procurement department has a key role to play: as the interface between the organisation and suppliers it can apply environmental supply chain issues that can be filtered down the supply chain.

3.29   Environmental purchasing focuses on the ideal of waste reduction. Environmentally preferred products or services are those that have a lesser or reduced effect on human health and the environment when compared with competing products or services that fulfil the same function. Preferred products or services may include, but are not limited to, those that contain recycled content, minimise waste, conserve energy or water and reduce the amount of toxic material disposed of or consumed.

Guidance by ISO

3.30   Environmental standards under ISO 14000 are a series of international standards on environmental management. These standards provide a framework for the development of the system and the supporting audit programme.

3.31   ISO 14001 was first published in 1996 and specifies the actual requirements for an environmental management system. It specifies a framework of control against which an organisation can be audited by a third party. It applies to those environmental aspects that the organisation can control and over which it can be expected to have influence.

3.32   ISO 14001 is an international standard that specifies a process for controlling and improving an organisation's environmental performance. Detailing the specification of an environmental management system, it is also the standard against which an organisation can be audited and certified.

3.33   ISO 14001 enables companies to identify elements of their business that impact on the environment and produce objectives for improvement supported by regular review for continuous improvement.

3.34 Other standards in the ISO 14000 series are guidelines. These include the following:

- ISO 14004 provides guidance on the development and implementation of environmental management systems
- ISO 14011 provides guidance on the audit of an environmental management system (now superseded by ISO 19011)
- ISO 14020 provides guidance on labelling issues
- ISO 14040 provides guidance on lifecycle issues

3.35 Auditing can be carried out against generic ISO 14000 criteria. However different approaches are permitted to meet local, national or industry specific requirements.

- **Type 1 (ISO 14024)**. Environmental claims are based on criteria set by a third party being based on the product's lifecycle impacts. The awarding body can be governmental or private. Examples include the EU Eco-label, the German Blue Angel and the Nordic Swan.
- **Type 2 (ISO 14021)**. Environmental claims are self-declared by suppliers, eg 'made of x% recycled material'.
- **Type 3 (ISO 14025)**. These environmental claims give quantified product information based on a full lifecycle analysis. Car companies such as BMW and Volvo are currently leading the way.

4 Design tools

Standardisation

4.1 The British Standards Institution (BSI) describes a standard as 'a published specification that establishes a common language, and contains a technical specification or other precise criteria, and is designed to be used, consistently, as a rule, a guideline, or a definition'.

4.2 Standards define many commonly accepted products, services and safety levels etc. Standards may be internal or external.

Internal standards

4.3 Internal standards may be developed by an organisation for inventory management purposes. Management of the stock range is often coupled with the need to standardise components or assembly items particularly if the items are frequent purchases. The need to manage stock effectively has been identified as a key business issue. The waste from obsolete or redundant stock can be severely detrimental to profitability and the need to buy effectively requires a committed approach to stock management. Aided by effective coding and IT systems organisations will seek to manage stock in such a way as to reduce stock holding where possible and to ensure that sound policies are pursued in relation to stock management.

4.4 Standardisation involves reaching agreement in areas such as size, shape, colour, properties, performance etc. Organisations frequently purchase a greater variety of products or services than is necessary. Here are some reasons why this may occur.

- Specifiers prefer to design their own items.
- Specifiers do not check whether similar items already exist.
- The organisation does not have an inventory control system that vets new products.
- The organisation's information systems make it difficult to establish what items are already in use.

Management of the stock range

4.5   The introduction of new products coupled with the new components or parts required for assembly can increase the overall number of parts on the order book of an organisation. Management of the stock range requires organisations to monitor the introduction of new components and parts by asking questions about how necessary the part is and whether the requirement can be met with an existing component and part.

4.6   Proliferation of stock items can be a common occurrence if the introduction of new stock is not managed well or if the product coding system is deficient. New items should require authorisation before being entered onto the system, with responsibility given to one individual or department.

4.7   Variety reduction programmes are an integral part of good inventory management. Holding inventory is expensive; holding duplicated or unnecessary stock is an area that deserves regular review. Variety reduction will cause an organisation to ask a number of questions. The first is a move to standardisation on areas such as product sizes, suitability of new products to use existing registered components and reduced offerings on colours and finishes. Variety reduction programmes will often involve cross-functional teamworking with the procurement department who will often have similar standardisation objectives.

4.8   Approval for new items requires a formal approach from those involved. This will involve an examination of why new stock items are being entered on to the system and ensure the relevant questions are asked.

- Why is the item required?
- What is the potential future demand?
- Can the need be met by a current stock item?
- Can the new item replace any item currently held on the existing inventory?
- Is it essential to stock this item? Can the supplier deliver on a just-in-time basis?

4.9   Variety reduction or adoption of standardised parts serves to ensure that procurement can be better managed and controlled and instils a discipline on an organisation in relation to the introduction of new parts and components. Unnecessary duplication will often lead to redundant or obsolete stocks that contribute greatly to waste within organisations. In today's trading environment this should not be acceptable.

External standards

4.10   External standards are defined by outside organisations. There are a number of different sources of standards.

- Industry standards, often developed by trade associations in specific industry or service sectors, eg car manufacture, local government and banking
- National standards, which are those established and agreed within a country such as the British Standards Institution (BSI) standards or DIN standards in Germany. BSI is the oldest standards body in the world. Formed in 1901 it publishes over 20,000 standards and operates in over 100 countries.
- International standards such as those of the International Standards Organisation (ISO). ISO is a federation of national standards bodies from over 150 countries and promotes the development of standardisation with the objective of facilitating international trade.
- European standards, the most familiar being the CE marking which defines certain requirements for a wide variety of products.

4.11   Purchasers should be familiar with the standards that exist for the products and/or services within their remit. Each standards body will publish indexes of these standards by hard copy, CD-ROM or on the internet. IT enables rapid searching for particular standards. Purchasers of a new item should identify whether any appropriate standards exist before spending time and money developing an in-house specification.

4.12   Many standards can be complex and buyers must establish the suppliers' depth of knowledge in relation to them. If their experience is not considered sufficient the purchaser can, if applicable, work with the supplier to ensure that the product or service to be provided meets the required specification standard.

4.13   The principal advantages and disadvantages of standards are summarised in Table 5.3.

Table 5.3 *Advantages and disadvantages of standards*

ADVANTAGES OF STANDARDS	DISADVANTAGES OF STANDARDS
They simplify suppliers' quotes, because if all suppliers are quoting to the same standards then other decision criteria can be applied.	Any standard represents a compromise agreed by the various parties that prepared it. Meeting it may not necessarily satisfy all the purchaser's requirements.
They promote competition as suppliers have a common benchmark to quote against.	The standard will reflect the point in time when it was produced. Standards may not reflect the latest technology or practices.
They are increasingly important in international trade as they form a basis for a common understanding between trading partners.	
They help remove uncertainty as to what is required.	
The purchaser does not have to write a specification for items covered by standards.	
They promote standardisation, and, in consequence, reduction of inventory.	
They can reassure customers, who often see conformance with a standard as an indication of quality and safety.	

Modularisation

4.14   A modular approach to assembly has become increasingly common over recent years. Common in the construction industry for many years the approach allows for multi-functional assembly items to be integrated into product design and delivery. Examples can be seen in areas such as car assembly where the modular unit is integrated with the car's IT system. This enables diagnostic fault finding and replacement of the module in a fast and convenient manner. The same technique is seen in computer manufacture where a number of multi-functional modules are combined together to form the end product.

Value analysis

4.15   Value analysis presents a role for Procurement following the product launch. As time passes customers' tastes change and technology advances. As a consequence a product may fail to meet customers' current expectations and may not be making the best use of new materials and design. As R&D and initial production costs have been recouped there is a chance to consider price reductions.

4.16   Value analysis has been defined as 'the organised, systematic study of the function of a material, part, component or system to identify areas of unnecessary cost. It begins with the question "What is it worth?" and proceeds to an analysis of value in terms of the function the item performs'. (Gary J Zenz, *Purchasing and the Management of Materials*)

4.17   The origin of the technique lies in the Second World War when it was developed by Larry Miles of General Electric in the USA as a response to wartime shortages of materials. His idea was that careful attention to the make-up of products would lead to changes that would save money. At the same time, he believed that quality would not suffer; indeed a more critical investigation of what was included in a product, and why, would lead to improvements in quality.

4.18   These days the concept has been adopted in a large number of manufacturing firms. Alongside it there is a technique referred to as value engineering (closely linked with simultaneous engineering), which considers design from the conceptual stage. Value analysis involves looking afresh at a product already in existence.

4.19   This is the distinction adopted in this text, but you should be aware that other authors distinguish the terms differently. For example, in some accounts you will find that the distinction lies in who initiates and manages the process. If it is the engineering department, then the term used is **value engineering**; on the other hand, it tends to be procurement personnel in charge of **value analysis** exercises. Clearly, this method of distinguishing the terms overlaps with the previous one. Unless it is important to distinguish the two in a particular context, we will usually refer simply to value analysis and leave the reader to infer that the same applies to value engineering.

4.20   A possible problem with value analysis in the sense used above is that the changes in the configuration of a part or assembly may make it difficult to use in other products of which it forms one element. Another shortcoming is that each value analysis exercise, to the extent that it leads to change, is in effect shortening the lifecycle of the product that is being changed. The effect may be to cancel out the benefit that was supposed to arise.

4.21   For these reasons, among others, there is merit in the value engineering approach because, in effect, it gets things right from the beginning and minimises the need for later change. Many organisations now place considerable emphasis on value engineering all new products to the extent that this is feasible. However where the process was not used at the design and engineering stage, there may be increased scope for the application of value analysis at a future date.

4.22   Whichever term is used, the process is the same. The idea is to establish what function a particular part is fulfilling; then to consider the various design options for achieving this function to the desired standard; and finally, to analyse the cost of alternatives.

4.23   This approach is summarised in the five 'tests for value' that were developed in General Electric's pioneering use of the technique.

- Does use of the material, part or process contribute value?
- Is the cost of the material, part or process proportionate to its usefulness?
- Are all the product features actually needed?
- Can a lower-cost method be used while retaining the features and functions that add value?
- Is anyone paying less for this part?

4.24   A more detailed checklist is quoted by Dobler and Burt (*Purchasing and Supply Chain Management*).

- Can the item be eliminated?
- If the item is not standard, can a standard item be used?
- If it is a standard item, does it completely fit the application or is it a misfit?
- Does the item have greater capacity than required?
- Can the weight be reduced?
- Is there a similar item in inventory that could be substituted?
- Are closer tolerances specified than are necessary?
- Is unnecessary machining performed on this item?
- Are unnecessarily fine finishes specified?
- Is 'commercial quality' (ie the most economical quality) specified?
- Can the item be made more cheaply? Can it be bought more cheaply?
- Is the item properly classified for customs and shipping purposes to obtain the lowest transportation costs?
- Can the cost of packing be reduced?
- Are suppliers being asked for suggestions to reduce cost?

4.25 The specific outcomes of a value analysis exercise may be reduced costs and/or improved quality, but this is not the only benefit to the organisation. Individuals involved in this kind of exercise find that they look at their work in a different way, no longer regarding previous decisions and engineering as binding, but taking a fresh approach. The whole process of value analysis therefore fosters a positive approach towards innovation and overcomes the entrenched resistance to change that may otherwise be encountered.

Value engineering

4.26 Value engineering is the application of value analysis from the development stage onwards. A simultaneous engineering approach can be instigated where suppliers can be involved and offer research and development using their specialist skills in their supply area.

4.27 An example is the simultaneous approach used by Ford and Pilkington Glass where the Ford car design and Pilkington car windscreen and windows are developed collaboratively. If the car design does not work in concert with the thickness and structural integrity required of the windscreen and windows then both organisations can work together to make design improvements and modifications until a suitable product is engineered.

4.28 Value engineering attempts to organise the design and development of new products by deploying cross-functional teams, including specialists from all the functions that can contribute to overall objectives, as well as external suppliers. The aims of this approach are as follows.

- To ensure quality is built in from inception, not merely 'inspected in' later. (Estimates suggest that from 60 per cent to 80 per cent of costs are committed at the design stage.)
- To reduce the need for engineering changes at a later stage.
- To reduce time to market – the lead time between inception and launch.
- To reduce development and production costs.
- To improve sensitivity to customer needs.

4.29 Value analysis, value engineering and the other methodologies discussed demonstrate the thought and commitment that organisations put into bringing products from the design stage into production in a way that meets customer needs cost effectively.

5 CAD and CAM

5.1 The use of technology in both the design and manufacturing process has led to rapid improvements in recent years. Computer-aided design (CAD) and computer-aided manufacture (CAM) enable organisations to link their CAD/CAM systems directly with the communications and manufacturing systems. This assists both in speeding up the approval time for design and in designing tooling and operations processes.

5.2 Computer-aided design (CAD) is a technology that allows interactive design and testing of a manufacturing component on a computer. This allows 3-D visualisation of the object that can then be tested, coloured or analysed as appropriate with the objective of removing as many design flaws or issues as possible at this early stage. This serves to reduce overall cost and speeds time to launch.

5.3 Computer-aided design has advanced rapidly in recent years as computer hardware and software have become faster and more refined. Design drawings and specifications can be evaluated and developed without the need for expensive prototypes. Using CAD enables products and components to be created, dimensions changed, robustness considered and features added or removed.

5.4 CAD databases and software can store substantial amounts of information and knowledge that can be managed to enable an integrated approach that considers design through to production as well as for disassembly, if appropriate. This storage of knowledge, often referred to as expert systems technology (EST) enables better decisions to be made, new materials to be evaluated and integrated, emphasis placed on safety and quality aspects and reductions in costs to be achieved.

5.5   The benefits that CAD/CAM systems can bring are as follows.

- Reduced costs with product testing enabled in digital rather than tangible form
- Reduced costs in more productive use of staff time
- Greater understanding during the teamwork phase of product development and design
- Fewer problems in translating designs into the final product
- The possibility (with integrated stock control systems such as just in time) of interfacing with suppliers to enable product modification if required

5.6   A simultaneous engineering approach where there is close collaboration between supplier and purchaser or partner and partner, often involves an integrated approach to CAD throughout the product development process.

5.7   Computer-aided design enables companies to take a global approach to product development. Specialists, either in-house or outsourced, can comment on designs within tight time frames and crossing international boundaries. The use of virtual teams is now established for many organisations and can be particularly relevant for multi-functional design projects.

5.8   Computer-aided engineering (CAE) enables designers to test whether their design can be manufactured on the available machines, and to ascertain the costs of doing so. Both CAD and CAE contribute to systems of computer-aided manufacture (CAM), in which technology permits the programming and control of production equipment in performing manufacturing processes.

5.9   CAM develops CAD further in that it takes CAD-generated design and evaluates the manufacturing implications of the design. This enables a detailed appraisal of manufacturing issues prior to investment being made.

Figure 5.3 *Computer control of design, engineering and manufacturing*

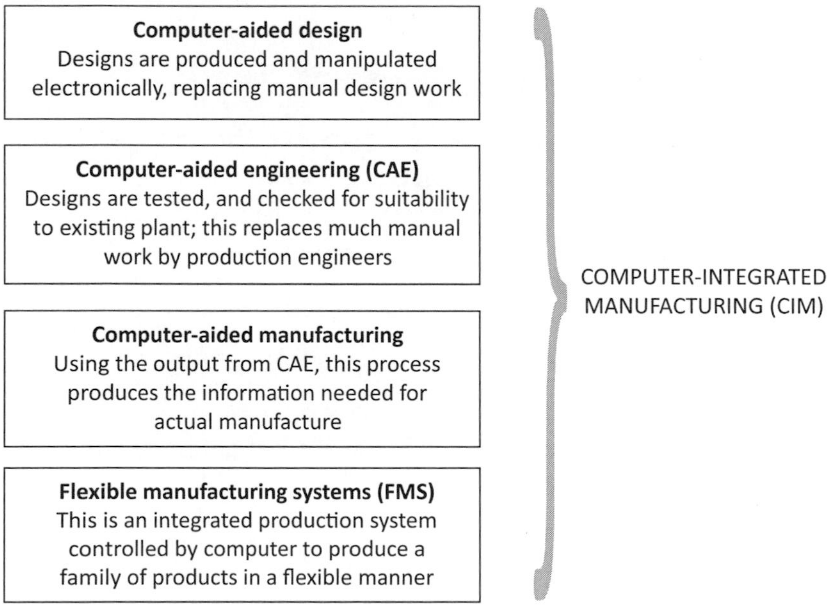

Computer-aided design
Designs are produced and manipulated
electronically, replacing manual design work

Computer-aided engineering (CAE)
Designs are tested, and checked for suitability
to existing plant; this replaces much manual
work by production engineers

Computer-aided manufacturing
Using the output from CAE, this process
produces the information needed for
actual manufacture

Flexible manufacturing systems (FMS)
This is an integrated production system
controlled by computer to produce a
family of products in a flexible manner

COMPUTER-INTEGRATED
MANUFACTURING (CIM)

5.10   The whole complex of computer-controlled activities is often referred to under the global title of computer-integrated manufacturing (CIM). These systems also bring a professional approach to an organisation. Employees see the commitment to invest and see their own role empowered and enhanced by attaining new skills and developing new work practices.

5.11 It is becoming increasingly common that organisations will use web-based collaboration where appropriate, within the organisation or with business partners, to develop design ideas and concepts. Collaboration allows for the use of international specialists if required to refine design issues. Web-based collaboration allows:

- File sharing across departments and organisations
- Quicker, more responsive and accurate design
- The ability to develop electronic supply chains from the concept stage.

5.12 The supply chain is the network of customers and suppliers that an organisation does business with. Early customer and supplier involvement allows full consideration to be given to supply chain issues as the design project progresses. The role of procurement is important in product development projects because buyers are the link between organisations and suppliers and, as such, form an important interface function. Their role in early design of an effective supply chain is equally relevant in allowing for good practice in supply chain management to be integrated from an early stage.

Computer-integrated manufacturing (CIM)

5.13 The integrated approach of individual developments in manufacturing can be developed further. Areas such as computer-aided design, computer-aided manufacture, the use of automatic guided vehicles and modern approaches to inventory management (examined later in the text) can be brought together under the umbrella of computer-integrated manufacturing (CIM).

5.14 CIM co-ordinates the entire process of design to the manufacture of a part, component or product through to the manufacture itself.

5.15 CIM offers fast throughput times and flexibility when compared to other, more traditional systems. It offers large-scale unsupervised operations but is constrained by high investment and capital costs. There is a fear that over reliance may cause issues related to system breakdowns and errors and production line breakdown. It is however being adopted as the way forward by leading manufacturers and looks set to grow in importance in the future.

Simultaneous development

5.16 Increased competition together with the rapid pace of technological development has driven organisations to develop a more cross-functional approach to product design and development. The simultaneous development approach (also referred to as simultaneous engineering) encourages the development of multi-functional teams operating with suppliers or providers in order to improve the design and the speed of the process.

5.17 The benefits can be summarised as follows.

- Getting products to market in a shorter time
- Incorporating more features or variety in the product at less cost
- Producing more new products more often

Chapter summary

- The process of new product development can be mapped systematically as a number of defined stages. Operations management has an important role to play at many of these stages.
- New product development is a cross-functional process, in which procurement and supply has an important role to play. There is often a tension between procurement and design specialists.
- Increasingly, organisations are seeking to ensure sustainability in their products. This issue is best tackled at the earliest possible stage of the design process.
- One of the most effective ways that procurement can contribute to reducing the environmental impact of products and services is to ensure that specifications are drafted in such a way as to incorporate environmental issues.
- Important design tools include the use of standards, variety reduction, modularisation, value analysis and value engineering.
- A CAD/CAM system may form part of a more integrated computer integrated manufacturing (CIM) system where design, planning and manufacturing are linked via computer systems.

Self-test questions

Numbers in brackets refer to the paragraphs above where your answers can be checked.

1 Describe the different priorities of internal functions in the process of product design. (1.4)

2 What are the five phases that every design programme will pass through according to Muhlemann, Oakland and Lockyer? (1.13)

3 What three resultant savings are claimed for design for manufacture and assembly (DFMA)? (1.18)

4 What are the stages of the new product development process? (Figure 5.2)

5 List advantages of performance specifications over conformance specifications at the design stage. (2.12)

6 List potential areas of conflict between procurement and design specialists. (Table 5.2)

7 What are the three aspects of environmentally sensitive design? (3.4)

8 List the six categories of costs in whole life costing. (3.19)

9 What are the advantages and disadvantages of using standards? (Table 5.3)

10 Define 'value analysis'. (4.16)

11 List benefits of CAD/CAM systems. (5.5)

12 List benefits of simultaneous development. (5.17)

CHAPTER 6

Design of Networks and Layouts

Assessment criteria and indicative content

2.3 Analyse the main techniques for supply network design

- The supply network perspective
- Configuring the supply network
- Aspects of vertical integration – outsourcing versus insourcing
- Location decisions in supply network design

2.3 Critically compare layout and flow designs in operations management

- The types of layout (such as fixed position, functional, cellular and product) for products and services
- Selecting a layout type
- Computer aided functional layout design
- Cycle times of product layouts

Section headings

1 Supply network design
2 Configuring the supply network
3 Location decisions
4 Types of process layout
5 Selecting a layout type
6 Product and process design

1   Supply network design

The supply network perspective

1.1   Integrated management of the supply chain (the 'network' that links suppliers, your organisation and customers) is increasingly recognised as a core competitive strategy. Organisations can no longer operate alone but need to operate on a co-operative basis with the best organisations in their supply chain in order to succeed. Supply chain management is the integration of these activities through improved supply chain relationships, to achieve sustainable competitive advantage.

1.2   The supply chain includes the management of information, procurement activities, inventory management, order processing, production scheduling, logistics, and customer service through to disposal of packaging and materials. With modern developments the reach can be extended to include product recycling and disposal.

1.3   The supplier network encompasses all organisations that provide inputs, either directly or indirectly, to the focal company. Each 'first-tier' supplier (the supplier to the focal company) has its own suppliers (second-tier suppliers) who, in turn have their third-tier suppliers etc. Supply chains are essentially a linked network of suppliers and customers with every customer a supplier to the next downstream organisation.

1.4   Internal functions within an organisation drive the network. The operations function includes control of the different processes used in transforming the inputs provided by the supplier network. The co-ordination and planning of these work flows can be challenging, particularly in diverse manufacturing environments, and need effective management in order to minimise waste and maximise productivity.

Strategic decisions in developing a network

1.5   The strategic plan forms the basis for the direction of the organisation and, in consequence, the investment decisions that will need to be made in order to meet the planned aims. In the vast majority of situations organisations are looking to adapt existing processes and facilities in the most appropriate way to meet any changes in direction rather than invest in new ones.

1.6   Ideally the processes that will transform the product or service should be flexible enough that new demands can be integrated into existing systems without major changes to the operation. Network design is not only about the most efficient and effective system, it is also about flexibility: flexibility to meet strategic changes, flexibility to adapt to future needs, as well as flexibility to respond to changes in the business environment.

1.7   To assess the design of the operations network the organisation must visualise the entire network. The organisation can then take a strategic view as to how best to use the operations network to compete effectively in the long term. This viewpoint also enables operations management to take a step back from their normal working environment and identify any links in the network that are particularly significant.

1.8   The operations role has the transformation process at its core but the entire network encompasses both the inputs and the outputs of the organisation. The inputs are the supply side of the operation: the materials, components, people, ideas, data and information that flow into the transformation process. The outputs interface with the demand side of the organisation (the customers).

1.9   The supply side of the operation consists of a number of suppliers who directly supply the organisation. These 'first-tier' suppliers are so-called as they deliver directly to the organisation. It is with these suppliers that we have the most contact and may look to form longer-term business relationships. The 'second tier' represents the suppliers who supply to our suppliers. These are of interest to us (although not often directly), as our demands on areas such as quality, price and delivery need to be met by these suppliers in order that the supply chain functions effectively. These second-tier suppliers are the first-tier suppliers to our own first-tier suppliers.

1.10   On the demand side of the operation there may be a number of intermediaries between the ultimate customer and ourselves. To our organisation our customer may be a warehouse or distributor. These are our direct customers and form the 'first tier' on the demand side. The warehouse or distributor may feed into a retail network. The retailer is a 'second-tier' customer. The eventual consumer is a 'first-tier' customer to the retailer but a 'third-tier' customer to us. That is not to say we disregard their views. It is after all these final consumers that we are trying to 'delight'.

1.11   From an organisation standpoint the immediate concern is the first tier that you are dealing with. Organisational emphasis is on ensuring supplies of the right quality delivered to the right place at the right time and on transforming these supplies to meet the demands of the first-tier customers.

1.12   Quality issues, environmental concerns, ethical sourcing and competitive considerations can all be made clear in discussions and agreements with suppliers. To enforce these demands they will be passed along the supply chain to the suppliers' suppliers. Suppliers will be required to meet and/or evidence agreed criteria in areas such as service quality (evidenced by ISO standards such as the ISO 9001 group of standards) or environmental standards (evidenced by the ISO 14001 group of standards) and so on. Our suppliers then make similar demands on their suppliers.

1.13 The link with suppliers is often referred to as 'upstream' operations. Equally the link with customers is known as 'downstream'. This is all illustrated in Figure 6.1.

Figure 6.1 *Tiering*

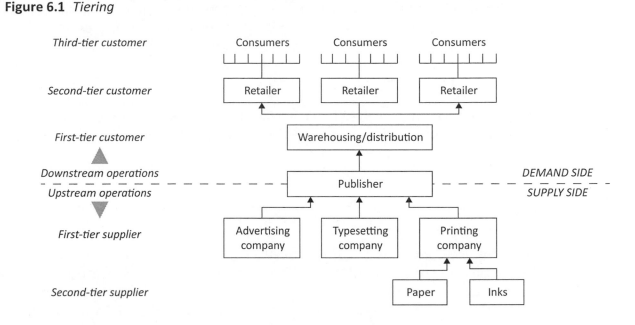

The supply network

1.14 The supply network is a number of supply chains that together describe the flow of goods and services from their original sources to their end users. Interdependent networks such as these have been described by Martin Christopher as 'a confederation of mutually complementary competencies and capabilities which compete as an integrated supply chain against other supply chains'.

1.15 Network design and management requires a modern view of business relationships to be considered and developed. Supply chain thinking emphasises 'win-win' scenarios, rather than the more conventional adversarial approach. Identified gains and improvements must be shared so that all members of the supply chain benefit. Improvements identified by the use or implementation of shared information technology, analysis of storage and distribution requirements and reductions possible through identified areas of 'waste' are all examples of how a 'partnering' approach can bring cost savings and efficiency improvements to the supply chain.

1.16 Marshall Fisher distinguishes between 'innovative' and 'functional' products.

- 'Functional' products include items such as stationery or basic foodstuffs with long product lifecycles and stable, predictable demand. Profit margins are low; therefore the emphasis of the network is on cost minimisation by long production runs, efficient distribution and storage, and low inventories.
- 'Innovative' products have unpredictable demand and shorter product lifecycles. Profitability will be higher than with 'functional' products over a shorter time frame. The supply network will need to be quick from design to market and also flexible and responsive to market demand.

1.17 The network for 'functional' products will focus on cost and being lean (taking areas of waste out of the supply chain) while the 'innovative' network requires speed, flexibility and the ability to adapt to market changes.

Downstream networks

1.18 Downstream management equally requires careful consideration. Different customers may have different needs, all of which must be satisfied. As an example, the warehouse or distributor may require regular deliveries in 40-foot containers with seasonal variations. Retailers may want smaller quantities from the warehouse but placing emphasis on regular supplies. The eventual consumer wants the goods to be readily available on demand. The needs of the demand tiers must be fully understood and also regularly updated when designing the transformation-output link of operations.

1.19 The objective of downstream management is to meet not only the needs of first-tier or second-tier customers (if appropriate) but also to meet the needs of the end customer or user.

2 Configuring the supply network

2.1 Slack *et al* highlight the overall network perspective as important because it helps to highlight three important design decisions.

- How should the network be configured? How can the organisation shape the network to best meet its own needs? Can better control be achieved by supplier reduction, removing tiers (eg by encouraging merging of suppliers), by moving responsibility or by an innovative approach? Should the organisation own more of the supply chain (ie take over a first-tier supplier – known as vertical integration) or will this detract from concentration on core activities?
- Where should each part of the network owned by the organisation be located? Near suppliers, overseas, near motorway links, near a readily available labour force?
- What physical capability should each part of the network owned by the company have? Decisions in this area require considerable foresight and planning. Long-term capacity management decisions form a crucial aspect of operations management and will be considered further as this text progresses.

2.2 Reconfiguring the supply network may be required in order to change the scope of the activities performed by operations in the network. This process can involve parts of the network being merged or removed. However the most common reason is the trend towards reducing the number of direct suppliers. The larger the supply base, the more distant the relationship with the supplier and the more difficult the network is to manage.

Disintermediation

2.3 The process of disintermediation is a growing feature of supply networks. In essence it means doing away with the middleman and dealing directly with suppliers' suppliers or customers' customers. The fashion industry has used this approach to a greater degree when sourcing. It gives the advantage of greater transparency in the supply network, particularly when considering corporate social responsibility issues.

2.4 The internet and the way people purchase has also driven changes. When booking a holiday many of us will bypass travel agents and book flights and accommodation online. Buying from Amazon or eBay online uses these services as consumer portals to suppliers. The supply network needs to constantly monitor all the trends that may affect the way it operates.

Co-opetition

2.5 Co-opetition is a recent term that relates to all the players in and surrounding the supply network as both friends and enemies at different times. Supply networks can be viewed as being surrounded by four types of players: suppliers, customers, competitors and complementors. Complementors are products or services that when sold with your product add value in the eyes of the customer. Competitors are the direct opposite in that they serve to make the value of your product less in the eyes of the customer.

2.6 However competitors can also be complementors. In the theatre area of a major city such as London or New York there will be a number of competing theatres. However, the grouping of them in a single area means that they complement one another by broadening the overall offering. The same principle can be applied to restaurants and shopping malls, as examples.

2.7 The role of suppliers within the supply network changes over time. Pressurising suppliers will not necessarily add value to the network. Savings gained in one area may lead to increased costs in others. Over the longer term it creates additional value to the network to find ways of increasing value for both suppliers and customers.

Financial factors

2.8 All the above considerations about network configuration involve investment decisions. These decisions relate to the allocation or reallocation of spend or resources to identified areas that have been strategically considered. These areas may be premises, projects, machinery, products or service centres amongst others.

2.9 Investment decisions are influenced by a number of changing situations that organisations will constantly face.

- **Expansion**: the decision facing an organisation when considering expansion is that investment in building, plant and machinery is both capital intensive and long-term in nature. Decisions must be well thought through and thoroughly costed. Alternatives such as make-or-buy decisions, outsourcing and leasing may be appropriate.
- **Diversification**: where decisions are made to invest in new products or services. This strategy causes operations to re-evaluate their current resources as new networks and transformation processes may become appropriate.
- **Changing technology**: this is one of the most fast-moving areas of business and one of the most difficult to visualise into the future. Technology investments are crucial to design and development and play a key role in both stock management and customer service. Investment decisions must be carefully evaluated and appropriate to meet current and future needs.
- **Replacement**: of existing plant, machinery etc. Options such as leasing, outsourcing, and hiring may be appropriate and should be evaluated.
- **Changes in the business environment**: increasing emphasis is being placed on areas such as corporate social responsibility (CSR), environmental and ethical issues and supply chain management. These and other issues require an organisation to consider both external and internal issues when evaluating investment decisions.

Feasibility factors

2.10 The feasibility of network design centres around the ability to find suitable supply chain partners and the location or locations of the operation. Supply chain partnerships involve a closer degree of integration between organisations with the procurement emphasis moving to developing a more strategic relationship.

2.11 Organisations will increasingly evaluate a supply chain partner's willingness to develop longer-term or strategic relationships. One major misconception in the supply chain scenario is the idea that all organisations will want to develop closer relationships. This is not always the case. A number of questions for organisations wishing to establish long-term business relationships were given by Robert Spekman in *Strategic Supplier Selection: Understanding Long-Term Business Relationships*.

- Has the organisation signalled a willingness or commitment to a partnership-type arrangement?
- Is the organisation willing to commit resources that it cannot use in other relationships?
- How early in the product design stage is the organisation willing or able to participate?

- What does the organisation bring to the relationship that is unique?
- Will the organisation have a genuine interest in joint problem solving and a win-win agreement?
- Is the organisation's senior management committed to the process inherent in strategic partnerships?
- Will there be free and open exchange of information across functional areas between companies?
- Does the organisation have the infrastructure to support such cross-functional interdependence?
- How much future planning is the organisation willing to share with us?
- Is the need for confidential treatment taken seriously?
- What is the general level of comfort between companies?
- How well does the organisation know our business?
- Will the organisation share cost data?
- What will be the organisation's commitment to understanding our problems and concerns?
- Will we be special to the organisation or just another customer/supplier?

Benefit factors

2.12 The benefit from closer relationships comes from gaining satisfactory answers to the above questions. The closer integration leads to an improved understanding of a mutual business situation where partners can combine to contribute above their individual weight.

2.13 Internal supply chains are that part of a supply chain that occurs within an individual organisation. With the multi-divisional and global organisational structures found in many large businesses it is likely that these internal links will be quite involved and complex. An understanding of the internal supply chain is important in understanding the overall impact and contribution that the supply chain concept can bring.

2.14 The development of supply chain maps (flowcharts) for major supply chains is a useful discipline. Process map development is usually accomplished through the use of cross-functional teams as part of a supply chain review. Operations must have a central role in this process and in understanding the supply chain because the flow from the supply chain evidences itself as the inputs coming into the organisation.

2.15 Once an understanding of the internal supply chain is gained the logical extension is to analyse the external aspect of the supply chain, again using process mapping and cross-functional teams. Once the key supply chains have been identified then the main supply chain members can be weighted as the most critical to the organisation's supply chain management goals. Strategies can then be developed to maximise the benefits of the supply chain approach with these providers.

Outsourcing versus insourcing

2.16 Organisations must be fully aware of the optimum capacity level of their operations. The need is to maximise the use of manufacturing facilities in order to gain economies of scale in production and maximum profitability.

2.17 To operate at the optimum capacity level requires planning and foresight from operations management. Make-or-buy decisions are fundamental to any business, either manufacturing or service. Do we make in-house? Do we invest in machinery and/or technology? Do we staff the operation? Do we provide for the overhead costs of the operation? Do we need to control the operation internally as core to our business? Have we the skills to manufacture in-house? Or do we buy in from outside?

2.18 Make-or-buy decisions face all organisations. From the concept stage organisations can look to make everything (ie only buy raw materials) or to minimise everything (ie buy everything from external suppliers). The decisions are based on a number of factors.

- Strategic planning
- Manufacturing capacity

- Suitable external suppliers
- Relationships with suppliers
- Effects on the manufacturing workforce
- Labour market conditions
- Sales forecasts

2.19 Managing the make-or-buy decision while ensuring optimum capacity utilisation is a difficult balance for the operations manager to achieve. It requires excellent business knowledge of all strategic, tactical and operational levels of the organisation to implement effectively.

2.20 Outsourcing is a strategic use of outside resources to perform activities previously handled by internal staff. Organisations began outsourcing the physical activities of a business such as facilities management, logistics and production to a large degree from the 1980s onwards. In addition the outsourcing of IT is increasingly common. However, all 'non-core' activities can be seen as possible candidates for outsourcing.

2.21 Outsourcing is addressed at a strategic level in operations as investment decisions can be substantial in terms of cost and commitment and in consequence carry a high degree of risk if proved unsustainable. The role of the finance function during the design and capital equipment procurement processes is to question all potential investment decisions. One question that will be asked will be: 'do we need to make this ourselves (with the investment that entails) or can we outsource the work to a supplier or business partner?' It is only when that argument has been fully discussed and evaluated that any go ahead will be given.

Core competencies

2.22 Competencies are 'the activities or processes through which the organisation deploys its resources effectively' (*Johnson & Scholes*).

- **Threshold competencies** are the basic capabilities necessary to support a particular strategy or to enable the organisation to compete in a given market. (The effective use of IT systems, or fast idea-to-market innovation cycles, would now be considered a threshold competency in most markets.)
- **Core competencies** are distinctive value-creating skills, capabilities and resources which (according to Hamel and Prahalad) add value in the eyes of the customer; are scarce and difficult for competitors to imitate; and are flexible for future needs. They offer sustainable competitive advantage: for example, by enabling differentiation or cost leadership, or putting up barriers to competitor entry into an industry. Hamel and Prahalad argue that 'senior managers must conceive of their companies as a portfolio of core competencies, rather than just a portfolio of businesses and products'.

2.23 The concept of core competencies is used in make/do or buy (or strategic outsourcing) decisions. Strategic outsourcing should only be applied to:

(a) **Non-core** competencies, which if outsourced will benefit from the expertise, technology or cost efficiency of a specialist supplier **without** disadvantaging the organisation with loss of in-house capability or vulnerability to market risks; and

(b) Activities for which external contractors have the required competence, capability and capacity.

2.24 The make/do or buy options can thus be depicted as follows: Figure 6.2.

Figure 6.2 *Competencies and contractor competence*

		COMPETENCE OF CONTRACTORS	
		High	*Low*
CORE IMPORTANCE	*Low*	Outsource/buy in	Develop contracting
	High	Collaboration	In-house

Repositioning strategies

2.25   The concept of repositioning an organisation within the supply or value chain implies the extension of its operations or control to a wider range of upstream or downstream activities – and a greater share of responsibility for creating and adding value.

2.26   Repositioning strategies include: organic or internal development and diversification into activities one step up or down the chain; acquisition of, or merger with, organisations one step up or down the chain; and/or strategic collaboration and integration with organisations one step up or down the chain. These are growth strategies. Repositioning may also, however, include withdrawal or contraction: outsourcing or subcontracting activities, say, or divesting from activities, in order to narrow the organisation's focus to its core competencies.

2.27   **Vertical integration** refers to strategies by which an enterprise gains control over the processes involved in supply or distribution.

- **Backward** integration occurs when an organisation becomes its own supplier of raw materials, components or services: in other words, it controls the inputs to its business. For example, a bakery might set up its own flour mill – or acquire an existing flour-milling business. This has the key advantage of providing secure supply and greater control over input quality and cost – as well as claiming a share of the profits obtainable in the supply market.
- **Forward** integration occurs when an organisation enters areas concerned with the outputs of its business. A manufacturer, for example, might open or acquire a chain of retail outlets, franchise dealerships or a direct marketing business. This has the key advantage of strengthening relationships and contacts with end-users – as well as claiming a share of the profits obtainable in the distribution market.

2.28   Repositioning in either direction may help an organisation to extend its core competencies and capacity, and commentators identify a major trend towards the increasing 'verticalisation' of supply chain management activities. At the same time, the concept of core competence suggests that any given organisation will also want to 'stick to the knitting' to some extent: in other words, to leverage its resources by doing what it is best at – and outsourcing to others what they are best at and can perform more efficiently on its behalf.

3   Location decisions

3.1   Location is one of the most important decisions to be made as it impacts across many areas of the business and the supply network that it forms part of. If the location is wrong it can have a profound, long-term impact on profits and levels of service. Many company locations are legacies of the past and the result of decisions made many years ago. It may not be practical or feasible to move location now as the cost and disruption to the business may outweigh any gains made.

3.2   There are two main reasons for organisations wanting to change location.

- Changes in demand. The globalisation of business has had serious implications for location decisions. As business moves toward low-cost areas so does the demand for support services. As the garment industry moved to Asia so did the need for zips, sewing machines etc. It made sense for many companies to relocate or at the very least establish a presence in the overseas market. If business grows it may be that current premises are no longer large enough.
- Changes in supply. As resources become more scarce it will affect the supply of inputs into the operation. If a mining company closes in one location and moves to another then the supply network designed when the mining company was in its original location may no longer be viable. One of the growth factors of Silicon Valley in California was the supply of skilled labour. As more companies located to the area more skilled people migrated causing the supply base to expand therefore attracting more companies.

3.3   The objective of the location decision is to find a balance between three objectives.

- The spatially variable costs of the operation
- The provision of service to customers
- The revenue potential

3.4   The last two factors in particular are inter-related in that the better the service provision, the better the revenue generated. For not-for-profit and public sector organisations these may not be relevant criteria. Not-for-profit organisations may look for low-cost premises with good transport infrastructure links and many public sector organisations look to provide employment in identified areas and will take a different perspective on location decisions.

3.5   Location may not affect an operation's revenues significantly but the cost of the operation can be greatly affected. The provision of services can however be impacted severely if the wrong decision is made. The delivery of the required or anticipated improved level of service can often be one of the key factors when making the location decision.

Supply-side influences

3.6   Supply-side influences on location decisions are concerned with the various inputs required for the organisation to carry out its operations. We look at some of these inputs here.

3.7   Clearly **labour costs** have been a significant factor in location decisions, particularly internationally. Less developed countries have often offered lower labour costs which can be attractive where the labour input cost is high in relation to the value of the goods or services.

3.8   **Land costs** are another influence. Land costs vary between countries and between regions within countries. Rental costs may look attractive but may be offset by the legal implications that surround the decision. However, in some industries it is expected to pay a premium to rent in high-end and more prestigious locations.

3.9   **Energy costs** are a major factor for operations that are energy intensive. Heavy industry, such as steel manufacture, will often be sited near sources of power, particularly if they are able to secure inexpensive and guaranteed supplies of power.

3.10   **Transportation costs** from the site to the customer can also be important. In international trade the journey may involve road, sea and/or rail transport and storage. Organisations will need to factor in the costs, time and other issues such as risk, security and insurance associated with locating overseas. Within a country it may be an issue to be located near road and rail hubs in order to provide the required levels of service. Proximity to facilities such as milling in agriculture can prove important.

3.11   Appropriate **labour skills** must be locally available. The attraction of Silicon Valley in California to the computer industry, the design capabilities of Milan and the engineering skills in the North of England all have provided reasons for location in these areas. Slack *et al* also cite the science parks which surround universities, attracting companies that are interested in using the skills available at the university.

Demand-side influences

3.12   The major factor here is the convenience of the customer. For many service sector companies (doctors, hospitals, retailers, hotels etc) the location of the operation is crucial to the organisation. The need is to be within the catchment area for customers or clients. This is essential particularly for operations delivering personal services.

4 Types of process layout

The importance of layout

4.1 The layout of an operation refers to the physical location and positioning of the transforming resources. The layout includes the physical appearance and characteristics of the operation and will affect the organisation of the facilities, the technology used to support the operation and the flow of work through the unit.

4.2 Layout is important as it defines the 'shape' of the operation and the flow of work through the unit. The speedy and even flow of work through the unit is fundamental to achieving success. Decisions relating to workflow, methods to be used and the organisation of the unit should be made prior to the facilities being laid out. Relatively small changes can cause disruption to the intended plan and may cause disproportionate problems.

4.3 The objectives of good facilities layout include the following.

- Maximising the return on the fixed investment by enabling optimum production levels to be achieved and by minimising the amount of floor space required.
- Minimising materials handling and transportation requirements
- Ensuring that labour is utilised effectively and efficiently
- Reducing the hazards in the production operation that may affect production workers and products
- Allowing for flexibility for changes that may come from new products, processes or growth in demand
- Enabling a smooth, logical flow of product or customers through the processes

4.4 Muhlemann, Oakland and Lockyer detail considerations relating to layout: Table 6.1.

Table 6.1 *Criteria for good layout*

Maximum flexibility	Can be rapidly modified to changing circumstances. Particular attention to ease of access for services (more easily addressed at design stage than later on)
Maximum co-ordination	Entry and exit should be designed in a manner that suits both issuing and receiving departments. The layout as a whole needs to consider other areas of the organisation's business and customers.
Maximum use of volume	Facilities should utilise the full available volume of premises. Cables, conveyors, racking, storage of tools etc can all be planned in such a way as to minimise the use of floor space.
Maximum visibility	All people and materials should be observable at all times.
Maximum accessibility	All servicing and maintenance points should be readily accessible. Legislative requirements such as the UK's Health and Safety at Work Act and the Equality Act also place the onus of clear and unfettered access on employers.
Minimum distance	All movements should be necessary and direct. Unnecessary movement adds cost not value (Taiichi Ohno).
Minimum handling	Ideally no handling but where it is required it should be reduced to a minimum by the use of appropriate devices such as forklifts, conveyor trucks etc.
Minimum discomfort	Adequate heating and lighting. Noise pollution, smells and excessive sunlight can cause problems.
Inherent safety	All layouts should be inherently safe, and no person should be exposed to danger.
Maximum security	Safeguards against fire, moisture, theft etc, should be considered in the original layout rather than by the addition of doors and cages at a later point.
Efficient process flow	Work and transport flow should not cross. The flow of work should be even, with no bottlenecks that may cause excess stocks to be stored on a temporary basis. The flow of paperwork should complement the physical transformation of the product.
Identification	Wherever possible, working groups should be provided with their own 'working space'. This helps in team building and aids productivity.

The four basic layouts

4.5   There are four basic types of layout. These are not mutually exclusive and often overlap each other.

4.6   **Fixed position layout**. The transforming, rather than the transformed, resources move. In other words, the product remains in one position and the workers, materials and tools move to it. The reason is that the transformed resources may:

- Object to being moved
- Be too delicate to be moved
- Be too big to be moved

4.7   An example would be shipbuilding. As the ship is too big to move, the transforming resources come to it. Other examples are construction sites (too big to be moved), surgery (too delicate to be moved) and high-class restaurants (would object to being moved).

4.8   The main issue with the fixed position layout is one of accessibility to the location, storage and control of the movement surrounding the fixed position. This leaves the fixed position vulnerable to disruptions in planning and control as different contractors may require access to the same point at the same time. A common adaptation of the fixed position layout is an assembly line where the product remains in a fixed position but is moved to the workers and materials by conveyor belt or overhead cranes.

4.9   **Process layout**. Here the layout is designed to suit the needs of the transforming resources. Related processes are grouped together. Products, information and customers flow from process to process according to their needs. The problem is that different products, information and customers have differing needs.

4.10   An example would be a supermarket where some processes are grouped together both for marketing and convenience reasons: tea, coffee, hot chocolate drinks; tinned fruits, pet food. The grouping together also makes stock replenishment easier. More specialist areas such as freezer cabinets require technology; fresh fruit and vegetables require more frequent stock replenishment. A manufacturing example would be machine components that need to undergo different processes during manufacture (eg machining, heat treatment and finishing). The item moves from one process to the next.

4.11   The process layout is often used where volume is low, several products are made and flexibility is required (eg one product may require drilling, milling, trimming and painting while another may require sawing, milling, trimming and polishing). Often general purpose low-cost machines are used, enabling work to be shifted to another machine in case of breakdown. As equipment used in a process layout does not require to be in a particular sequence machines that produce excessive noise, fumes or vibration etc, can be situated in isolated areas.

4.12   To the operations manager the process layout involves complexity in planning and control as routing and scheduling can be involved. The process layout will lead to costlier materials handling, larger work in progress inventory, increased storage and floor area requirements, increased costs for skilled labour, more frequent inspection and greater supervision.

4.13   **Product (or line) layout.** Transforming resources are located entirely for the benefit of transformed resources. Product layout is frequently used in a repetitive production system where the number of end products is small, and the parts or components used are highly standardised or interchangeable (eg the manufacture of computers). Layout by product is appropriate for the production of a small range of products in large quantities. This leads to a simple flow that is easy to control, but requires standardised products. Each product, customer or item of information follows a prearranged route in which the sequence matches the sequence in which the processes have been set.

4.14   The product layout arranges the equipment according to the progressive steps involved in the manufacturing process. This layout enables the use of specialised and/or high volume equipment supported by materials handling by conveyors or automated guided vehicles. For the operations manager quality is more consistent, production and job control are easier and smaller aisles are required making the floor area more productive. Disadvantages may include the high initial investment cost, increased vulnerability to work stoppage, the repetitive nature of the work and a lessening in flexibility.

4.15   A service example would be a customer being served along a counter at a self-service restaurant. Start with the menu, move to the starter server, move to the main course server, move to the dessert server, move to the drink server, and finally pay.

4.16   **Cell (group) layout**. This layout is indicated when a product is manufactured by means of group technology, ie equipment and operations have a common sequence that can be effectively grouped together. This enables economic production of small lots, minimising work in progress, space requirements and production lead times. The layout is arranged so that similar groups of resources to be transformed are processed in a single area. After being processed in one area, the transformed resources move to another area for further processing. The cell layout tries to bring an ordered state to the complexity of flow that is often a feature of process layouts.

4.17   Cell layouts differ from layouts by product as they are used for the manufacture of similar (but not the same) items required for the batch manufacture of the final product. Cell work will often involve groups of workers, working as a team. This approach fits in well with modern quality orientated production organisations where teamworking and a team approach have proven invaluable.

5   Selecting a layout type

5.1   The choice of the appropriate layout type will be influenced by the nature of the product and/or service to be provided together with the volume and variety characteristics of the operation. The objectives of the operation will also influence the decision. Is it to minimise cost or is it to be flexible or to attract the most customers? Whatever decision is arrived at, we must consider a range of operational factors relating to minimising movement, adhering to health and safety legislation and ensuring a suitable flow of work or customers through the process without bottlenecks or queues.

5.2   The advantages and disadvantages of each layout are summarised in Table 6.2.

Table 6.2 *Advantages and disadvantages of layout types*

TYPE OF LAYOUT	ADVANTAGES	DISADVANTAGES
Fixed position	Very high mix and product flexibility Product or customers not moved or disturbed Wide variety of tasks for staff	High unit costs Scheduling of activities and space can be difficult May mean considerable movement of plant and staff
Process layout	High mix and product flexibility Robust system in the case of disruptions Reasonably easy supervision of plant or equipment	Low facilities utilisation Can have very high level of work in progress or customer queuing Complex flow can be difficult to manage
Product layout	Low unit costs for high volume Allows for specialisation of equipment Materials or customer movement is convenient	Can have a low mix and limited flexibility Not very robust if disrupted Work can be very repetitive
Cell layout	Can offer a good compromise between cost and flexibility Fast throughput Group work can result in good motivation	Can be expensive to rearrange the existing layout May require more plant and equipment Can give lower plant utilisation

Computer-aided functional layout design

5.3   Once the basic layout type has been decided, the next step is to decide on the detailed design of the layout to determine:

- The exact location of all facilities, plant, equipment and staff that constitute the 'work centres' of the operation
- The space to be devoted to each work centre
- The tasks that will be undertaken by each work centre.

5.4   A model is described which can be used to assist in the design of a facility, where the facilities design includes the selection of the materials handling system and the placement of departments within the facility. The model is entitled COFAD, an acronym representing **computerised facilities design**. COFAD selects the facilities design which approaches the minimal materials handling system cost.

5.5   The detailed design of process layouts is complex, because of the complex workflow patterns that are associated with this layout to ensure a very wide variety of products can be made. The techniques employed in designing a layout are based on many years of experience and, in recent years, supported by IT design systems such as PLANET (planned layout analysis and evaluation technique), CORELAP (computerised relationship layout planning) and COFAD (computerised facility design).

5.6   Optimal solutions are difficult to achieve and many process layouts are designed through intuition, common sense and systematic trial and error.

Cycle times of product layouts

5.7   The cycle time of a product layout is the time between completed products emerging from the operation. Cycle time is a vital factor in the design of product layouts and influences most other detailed design decisions. It is calculated by considering the likely demand for the products over a period and the amount of production time available in that period. For example, suppose a factory is to process wooden doors. The number of doors to be processed is 160 per week and the time available to process the doors is 40 hours per week.

Cycle time for the layout = time available/number to be processed

In this case, cycle time = $\frac{40}{160}$ = ¼ hour = 15 minutes. Therefore the factory layout must be capable of processing one completed wooden door every 15 minutes.

5.8   The next decision concerns the number of processing stages, where a processing stage is a distinct period of time to carry out part of the door manufacture. The number of such stages can be anything between one and several hundred, depending on the cycle time required and the quantity of work involved in making the product. The latter quantity is called the **total work content** of the product. The larger the total work content and the smaller the required cycle time, the more stages will be necessary.

5.9   At the moment we can imagine a line of four stages, each contributing a quarter of the total work content in processing the door. In practice of course, the flow would not be so regular. Each stage might on average take 15 minutes, but this time would vary for each door processed for the following reasons.

- Products being processed along the line might be a little different, for example different models of the same basic door.
- Products might require slightly different treatment, for example it may take longer to plane the surface of one door than another because of the quality of the wood.
- There are usually slight variations in the physical co-ordination and effort of the person, or the performance of the machine undertaking the task.

5.10   This variation can make the flow of work along the line irregular, which in turn can lead to work in progress queues and lost processing time. This reduces efficiency and may require additional resources (such as more staff time or more storage space) at additional cost to compensate for this variation.

5.11   The most problematic, detailed design decision in product layout is ensuring the equal allocation of tasks to each stage in the line. This is called **line balancing**. In the door-processing example, we have assumed that 15 minutes of work content has been allocated equally to the four stations. This is nearly always impossible to achieve in practice and some imbalance in the work allocation between stages will inevitably result. This will increase the effective cycle time of the line.

6   Product and process design

6.1   Process design involves the sequence of operations together with the appropriate use of technology involved in transforming products from the design stage into actual goods or services. An example would be a visit to the dentist: Figure 6.3.

Figure 6.3 *Process design: visiting the dentist*

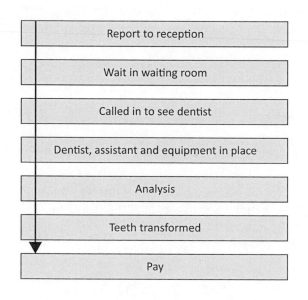

Report to reception

Wait in waiting room

Called in to see dentist

Dentist, assistant and equipment in place

Analysis

Teeth transformed

Pay

6.2   This is a sequence of events or operations (inputs) leading to the transformation process: teeth transformed and payment secured.

6.3   The more complex aspect of the visit to the dentist involves the time spent with the dentist. General equipment will be required for all patients (dental lighting, reclining chair, and mouthwash). Specialist equipment will be required to account for a number of different permutations (eg X-rays, extractions, descaling). To add to this the specialist skills of the dentist are required at the agreed time.

Timetabling

6.4   The timetabling of activities is a feature of repetitive service functions. Examples include bus, train and air services, dentists, cinemas, teaching, etc. These are all 'customer push' systems where customers need to take advantage of the timetabled operation at the required time.

6.5   We are all aware of the issues surrounding timetabling as a function. Buses run late, appointments are subject to delays and staff delivering a specialist service are late or are taken ill. Communication is a key customer service aspect here. Many bus stops in large cities now have travel information on the current situation regarding the arrival of a bus route at a given stop. Customers or clients who fail to arrive without notification also cause problems as service specialists (such as doctors or dentists) may not have a client at the given time, leading to waste.

6.6   Timetables are arrived at by weighing a number of factors such as past experience, potential bottleneck or pinch points, preferred order or sequence and customer feedback. They are ideally designed to suit the needs of both the service provider and the customer but often fall somewhere in the middle.

6.7   Process design has two aspects.

- The technical aspect that involves the sequencing of operations, the application of technology and the methods used for the transformation process. Sequencing involves determining priorities. In the case of the dentist advance booking and the use of timetables achieve this. In manufacturing, sequencing may be influenced by the physical nature of the transformation equipment being used or the timing of work arriving where the complementary mix of work may determine the priority given to particular jobs.
- The economic aspect caused by commercial and competitive factors, leading to process improvements over time. Hayes and Wheelwright argue that operations managers are not only involved with the economic aspects but also need to consider limitations and constraints placed on the organisation such as skills requirements, legal implications and existing facilities.

Hayes and Wheelwright

6.8   Hayes and Wheelwright list a number of considerations when evaluating process technologies and the roles of technical specialists and operations managers: Table 6.3.

Table 6.3 *Analysis of processes*

Mechanics	How does the process work? What physically happens and how does it happen?
Economics	How much does it cost in the short and long term?
Time-span	What is the set-up time? How long does it take per unit once set up?
Constraints	What can't be done? What is very difficult to do in an acceptable time/cost frame?
Uncertainties	What can go wrong? What do people worry about? What is predictable and what isn't?
Skills	What isn't done automatically? How long will it take to learn the processes?
Flexibility	How does the process react to changes? Which changes are easy and which are not?
Reliability	What tolerances does the process meet? How repeatable are those tolerances?

6.9   The Hayes and Wheelwright list relates to the design of manufacturing processes but how can it be applied to the service sector? In essence few changes need to be made. Time-spans may need to be linked with IT processes rather than set-up times and reliability measured in terms of customer service levels but everything else applies.

6.10   The operations processes are highly important in delivering the service provision. Although operations management is frequently criticised for its production origins and its alleged lack of application to service industries there is an increasing correlation in the thinking behind both sectors.

Chapter summary

- Integrated supply chain management (the 'network' that links suppliers, your organisation and customers) is increasingly recognised as a core competitive strategy.
- The supply side of the operation consists of a number of suppliers who directly supply the organisation. On the demand side of the operation there may be a number of intermediaries between the ultimate customer and ourselves.
- The link with suppliers is often referred to as 'upstream' operations. Equally the link with customers is known as 'downstream'.
- Configuration of the network is influenced by financial factors, feasibility factors, benefit factors, and the organisation's core competencies. Organisations are increasingly prepared to outsource non-core competencies.
- Supply side influences on the location decision include labour costs, land costs, energy costs, transportation costs, and availability of labour skills.
- Layout is important as it defines the 'shape' of the operation and the flow of work through the unit. Four basic types of layout are fixed position layout, process layout, product (or line) layout, and cell (or group) layout.
- Layout decisions are nowadays often taken with assistance from computerised programs.
- Process design involves the sequence of operations together with appropriate use of technology.

 ## Self-test questions

Numbers in brackets refer to the paragraphs above where your answers can be checked.

1   Define a supply network. (1.14)

2   What are the objectives of downstream management? (1.19)

3   What is meant by co-opetition? (2.5)

4   List as many as you can of the relationship questions asked by Robert Spekman in *Strategic Supplier Selection: Understanding Long-Term Business Relationships*. (2.11)

5   Distinguish between threshold competencies and core competencies. (2.22)

6   Give two reasons why organisations may wish to change location. (3.2)

7   What are the objectives of effective facilities layout? (4.3)

8   Briefly describe each of the four types of layout. (4.6, 4.9, 4.13, 4.16)

9   What is meant by the cycle time of a product layout? (5.7)

10 List the considerations identified by Hayes and Wheelwright in relation to evaluation of process technologies. (Table 6.3)

CHAPTER 7

Planning and Control in Operations Management

Assessment criteria and indicative content

3.1 Analyse the main techniques that can be applied to planning and control in operations management

- The difference between planning and control
- Achieving balance between planning and control
- Responding to demand
- Loading, sequencing and scheduling

3.2 Explain the main techniques that can be applied to capacity management

- Defining capacity
- Capacity constraints
- Planning and controlling capacity
- Forecasting demand fluctuations
- Measuring capacity
- Capacity planning through level capacity plans, chase demand plans or demand management

Section headings

1 Operations planning and control
2 Planning and controlling capacity
3 Methods of forecasting demand
4 Loading, scheduling and sequencing

1 Operations planning and control

The difference between planning and control

1.1 The central role of operations management is the transformation process. Enabling the transformation process to operate to its most effective level requires a high degree of planning and control of an organisation's activities. The role of planning and control in operations is to manage the continuing operational activities while still satisfying customer demand.

1.2 Planning can be defined as 'the setting of the intention for what is supposed to happen' while control is 'the process of coping with changes in variables' (Slack *et al*). Control is the practical actions that can be taken to bring the plan back on track. To accomplish this requires that options are available such as additional shift work, outsourced manufacture or temporary staff etc. Without practical options control cannot be exercised.

1.3 The plan is a mechanism enabling management to visualise the future and to evaluate whether it has sufficient critical resources (resources that could limit the organisation's ability to accept orders now or in the future). All organisations face cost constraints and no organisation has infinite resources. Planning and control decisions must be made about the effective deployment of those resources.

1.4   Drawing up a plan can be a difficult and complex process and it is an area of business that occupies a considerable amount of management time. A plan is a set of expectations based on the aims of corporate strategy and placed into an operational context in order to deliver those expectations.

SMART objectives

1.5   An operational plan will involve setting a number of objectives to ensure that the plan has been met. An objective is something you want to achieve and will often be outlined using the SMART framework.

- **Specific**. Objectives should be succinct, precise and understandable.
- **Measurable**. Objectives should clearly state tangible targets that can be measured in the future. The targets should be compatible with both internal and external constraint factors and be flexible enough to react to a change situation.
- **Achievable**. Objectives should be challenging but also achievable. They should act as a motivational spur.
- **Realistic**. Objectives should be based on sound market research and analysis. The plan should be agreed, understood and accepted by all those concerned as a practical and workable way forward.
- **Timebound**. A timescale should be established against the achievement of each objective in order that project or cross-functional teams are aware of the need for completion by a certain date.

1.6   The strength of SMART objectives is that they are simple to understand, quantifiable and in consequence easier to measure, monitor and control.

The time frames of planning and control

1.7   Planning and control within operations will exist over three (often overlapping) time frames.

- Long-term planning and control will often have a primarily financial perspective. Long-term planning is by necessity based on forecasts about future developments and events and as such will be based on many assumptions that may or may not occur as predicted. The longer the forecasting timeframe the more difficult it is to attain accuracy.
- Medium-term planning and control will involve addressing issues in order to bring long-term planning back on track or modifying it to meet a changed or changing situation. It involves setting targets and objectives that form the basis for many aspects of operations management. Planning at this level also requires taking a future perspective and, as a result, contingency planning (a 'what if?' scenario) can be considered ahead of time if it is felt that a planning assumption or situation change may impact on the plans in place. Contingency plans offer the organisation a considered and prompt response in case of planning changes.
- Short-term planning and control is usually at the weekly or daily operational planning and control level and is often about responding quickly to operational or unforeseen problems and rectifying and remedying them in order to meet both medium-term and long-term plans and controls.

1.8   Ray Wild defines operations planning as 'concerned with the determination, acquisition and arrangement of all the facilities necessary for future operations'. Planning involves matching the supply of an operation's products and services with the expected demand for them and putting in place the infrastructure to enable delivery.

- **Determination**: involves effective forecasting and/or demand management techniques to accurately predict future requirements, the planning of capacity availability, and scheduling of that capacity to meet and effectively deliver those requirements.
- **Acquisition**: resources will need to be available to meet the planned requirements. Acquisition may refer not only to owned, leased or hired machinery but also (by extension) to outsourced areas of an organisation's operational requirement (storage, maintenance, security etc), where the skills or availability of services are acquired in order to deliver the objective.
- **Arrangement**: the design of the operation determines the capability. Planning serves to determine what the operation actually does and how it does it.

- **Future operations**: the definition also considers the ability to be flexible and have adequate facilities to meet the future operational needs either in-house or by effectively outsourcing the requirement.

Achieving balance between planning and control

1.9 Planning and control involves matching the operation's ability to supply goods and services to the demands of its customers.

1.10 A plan is the formalisation of what is intended to happen in the future (eg production of 5,000 units by a set date) while control is the process of rectifying changes to the plan while causing as little disruption as possible.

1.11 The balance between planning and control will change over time. Planning will dominate over the long term, usually on an aggregated basis, while in the short term control operates within the resource constraints of the operation adjusting to short-term changes in circumstances.

1.12 Having created a plan to manage the operation through loading, sequencing and scheduling, each individual part of the operation must be monitored and controlled to ensure the planned activities are being met. Deviation from the plans can then be examined, analysed and rectified. The output from the work centre is being monitored and control activities are being actioned over the short term.

1.13 Control becomes easier when:

- An operation's performance can be measured against clear objectives
- Where measurable output means that the anticipated level of performance or output is known
- Where the consequences of any interventions or changes to the operation are predictable
- Where doing a repetitive task facilitates improved skills and learning

Responding to demand

1.14 Strategic plans are established in advance of operations. In the case of production these plans form the basis for deciding operational requirements in terms of machinery, capacity, layout etc that will be needed to meet the strategic objectives. Aggregate plans and operations planning seek to bring those advance strategic decisions in line with the actual requirements for manufacture.

1.15 Aggregate planning will include the forecast demand and the capacity. Aggregate planning looks at the long- to medium-term production need and how this need is to be met. Aggregate planning will examine areas that allow the more short-term materials and capacity requirements planning to be implemented more effectively. Questions considered at this level include the following.

- Should areas of manufacturing be outsourced or subcontracted?
- Should production levels be kept constant or respond to demand?
- Should stock be used to alleviate fluctuations in demand (ie produce excess stock in periods of low demand and use stock in periods of high demand)?
- How can work patterns be changed to respond to changing demand?
- Can the size and skills of the workforce be changed with demand?
- Can demand be smoothed?
- What level of customer service, in terms of orders correctly fulfilled at the projected time, is the target?

Actions necessary to control operations

1.16   Wild goes on to define operations control as 'concerned with the implementation of a predetermined operations plan or policy and the control of all aspects of operations according to such a plan or policy'.

1.17   Control means ensuring that the plan is on track and coping with unforeseen circumstances as they arise; remedying them and bringing the plan back on track. Control is the process where plans are modified or adapted so that they can still meet their objectives, even though the initial assumptions made when drawing up the plan may no longer be valid.

1.18   Tocher (as quoted in Muhlemann, Oakland and Lockyer) gives four conditions that are necessary for the existence of a control function.

- There must be a specified set of times at which a choice of action is possible.
- At each time there must be a specified set of actions from which to choose.
- A model must exist which can predict the future of the system under every possible choice.
- There must be a criterion or objective on which a choice of action is based by a comparison of predicted behaviour of the system with the objective.

1.19   An evaluation of possible actions should be made and their outcomes assessed. Control can only be applied if a choice can be made.

1.20   Operations control systems are highly dependent on information. The flow of goods into, through and out of the organisation can all be monitored by the use of IT. Where the physical movement of goods is controlled through linking ordering, delivery, storage, internal transport, transformation, end storage, despatch and delivery to the customer, the control is exerted by the recording, measuring and monitoring of the effectiveness of this movement.

1.21   The flow is predominantly monitored through the inventory management system and the activity scheduling system. These should interface effectively to give a smooth 'information flow' of operations information.

1.22   Control systems require definition of the requirement or objectives, the adequate level of detail and information, the ability to choose options and a system that can identify and react to issues. The majority of operational control systems are 'closed systems' (in that outputs feed back into the system) where outputs are monitored in order that control may be exercised. The system must be able to record output, compare actuals with intended results and highlight to operations managers any areas of discrepancy that require action to be taken.

1.23   Operations planning and operations control are closely linked and highly dependent on each other. Planning can be seen as a course of action undertaken prior to the commencement of operations while control occurs during and immediately after production.

Stages in operations planning and control

1.24   Wild details the main stages in operations planning and control and identifies the area of responsibility of capacity management that will be examined further in the following section of this chapter.

- **Demand estimation or measurement**. An essential requirement of planning is a statement of the demand to be met. This will require accurate forecasting and/or demand management to ensure a high degree of correlation between estimates and actuals.
- **Aggregate capacity planning**. The objective of aggregate capacity planning is to develop a medium- to long-term plan examining the facilities and resources needed in order to satisfy anticipated demand. The term aggregate in capacity terms is concerned with the total demand.

- **Master operations schedule.** The master operations schedule develops in response to the aggregate capacity plan and is a breakdown of the main operations required for each expected item of demand. The master operations schedule translates the aggregate capacity plan into a workable operations format.
- **Rough-cut capacity planning**: involves the analysis of the master operations schedule in order to identify time-phased capacity requirements. Rough-cut capacity planning concentrates on the abilities of operations and resources to meet anticipated capacity requirements. It serves as a method of testing the master operations schedule and its ability to meet the demands expected of it.
- **Detailed operations schedule.** If the master operations schedule proves robust following the application of rough-cut capacity planning the next requirement is the development of a detailed, time-phased operational schedule that can be translated into actual production.
- **Short-term rescheduling and prioritising and control.** An essential feature of any operations schedule is the ability to be flexible as capacity demands change. The operations control system will monitor the changes and update the detailed operations schedule as appropriate.

1.25 For OPC to be effective the plan must lie within reach of the operation (ie it must be workable). The role of the control aspect is to ensure that the requirements of the plan are met.

2 Planning and controlling capacity

Defining capacity

2.1 Capacity management involves matching the operating system with the demand placed on the system. Capacity management is a key requirement of operations management as all other operations plans and actions are dependent on the availability of capacity. Capacity is the ability to produce work in a given time.

2.2 Effective system capacity and system efficiency are measures of an organisation's ability to meet customer requirements.

Forecasting fluctuations in demand

2.3 Capacity management requires medium- and long-term forecasts in order to plan ahead. Resources must be in place to meet anticipated demand. However, forecasts may be unreliable. Concentrated effort must be invested to ensure that forecasts are based on sound business projections and are as accurate as circumstances permit. Investment and related decisions will be made on the basis of these forecasts so they will need to be updated as appropriate.

2.4 The design of operations networks is highly dependent on the accuracy of long-term forecasts. Strategic decisions are made about the long-term direction of the organisation and it is the role of the operations function to enable the strategic goals to be met.

2.5 Accurate long-term forecasts are essential to operations management as they dictate the manufacturing or service provision requirement that needs to be met. The development of long-term operational plans is based on the organisation's strategic plan. Operations managers must then make decisions relating to resources, system design and capacity management strategies in order to deliver the projected requirement in the most effective and efficient manner.

2.6 Demand is difficult to predict, particularly over the longer term. However, decisions made at this stage (including capacity decisions) will have a major impact on an organisation's ability to meet the demands placed on it in the future.

2.7 Capacity to meet that demand establishes a limit on possible productivity. The organisation will evaluate possible strategic options (at this stage, as well as at the later operational stage) such as outsourcing, subcontracting, partnering, co-destiny business relationships, joint ventures, increased horizontal and/or vertical integration. These options may limit the investment required or introduce gains in cost sharing, technological input or wider market spread that may enhance the organisation's strategic and operational capability.

2.8   Forecasting has an important role to play at all levels of operations management. Accurate strategic forecasting allows for investment and related decisions to be taken with a degree of certainty. For the operations manager this confidence in strategic forecasts can translate into a more effective and efficient system as considered long-term decisions have been made and are implemented within an appropriate timeframe.

2.9   Unfortunately this is not often the case. Strategic forecasting involves a number of assumptions relating to competitors, prices, availability of supplies, the economic environment and a host of other related factors, all of which are subject to change. Forecasting is a continuous process where changes are common. The key is that updates are passed to those concerned in order that remedial action can be considered and taken as appropriate.

Capacity constraints

2.10   As a general rule many organisations will not operate at optimum capacity. There are two main reasons for this. The first is that orders are inconsistent and there is not enough overall demand to maximise capacity. The second is that operating below capacity enables an operation room to manoeuvre when additional demands are placed on the operation such as urgent orders or reworking of below standard items.

2.11   Demand may not be consistent and as a result some parts of the operation may be working at or near full capacity while other parts may not. The area where the operation is working to maximum capacity is referred to as the **capacity ceiling** which places a capacity constraint on the entire operation. If all operations are working to their maximum extent then the whole operation is working at maximum capacity and is constrained from doing more given the current process and operation.

2.12   Reaching capacity in one area can affect other areas as it may cause a bottleneck in the overall operation. Examples can include high seasonal demand or high level of sales for a particular variant of the product. Unless additional resources are made available to cover this surge in activity then the entire operation is constrained by one area's inability to meet overall demand.

2.13   Capacity planning and control is the setting of effective capacity of the operation in order that it can respond to the demands placed upon it. Key to decisions made is how the operation should respond when additional demands are placed upon it. Capacity decisions of this type are made within the current constraints of an operation and are largely short-term in nature.

2.14   Long-term capacity planning is by its nature prone to error. Planning five years or more ahead can never be totally accurate. Therefore short-term and medium-term capacity issues will occur and it is the role of operations management to ensure manufacturing or service commitments are met. Few forecasts will be totally accurate so it is common to need to respond to capacity issues – both over-capacity and under-capacity – at short notice.

Measuring capacity

2.15   Muhlemann, Oakland and Lockyer distinguish between three different capacity levels.

- **Potential capacity**: is the capacity that can be made available within the time frame detailed in the strategic plan. This aspect requires accurate forecasting linked to a resource analysis that will allow for plans to be developed in order that anticipated demand will be met.

- **Immediate capacity**: is the capacity available within the current budget period. Immediate capacity is constrained by a number of factors such as the availability of cash, manpower, skills and equipment; the ability to outsource or subcontract; and the technical complexity of the task and the number of tasks. Muhlemann, Oakland and Lockyer give a simple example: the capacity of a restaurant is limited by the size of the eating area, or the number of tables.
- **Effective capacity**: is the capacity used during the existing budget period. Effective capacity measures the effectiveness of the ongoing operation and can be influenced by a range of factors such as technical abilities in the planning stages, implementation of activities, flexibility and skills of the workforce, and procurement, outsourcing and subcontracting skills.

2.16 Capacity planning and control decisions require operations managers to take a sequential approach to assessing their ability to meet demand. As forecasts will largely prove inaccurate to differing degrees the role of the operations manager is to work within the existing operational framework to deliver the organisation's requirement.

2.17 The stages in capacity planning and control are as follows.

- Measure aggregate or overall demand and capacity over a specific timeframe (units produced, revenue received or tonnes produced).
- Identify alternatives or changes that can be made to capacity plans.
- Choose the most appropriate capacity plan.

2.18 The decisions taken by operations managers when developing capacity plans will affect different aspects of performance. Slack *et al* list the following considerations.

- **Costs**: will be affected by the trade-off between capacity and demand. Under-utilisation of capacity will be reflected in higher unit costs.
- **Revenues**: require the trade-off to be considered in the opposite way. High capacity should result in a commensurate revenue yield.
- **Working capital**: will be affected by the approach to inventory control. If the organisation effectively implements systems such as MRP, MRPII, JIT etc then capital held in stock can be kept to a workable minimum.
- **Quality**: of both goods and services may be affected by peaks and troughs in demand. As an example concentration could be placed on quantity manufactured at the cost of quality.
- **Speed of response**: can be aided by holding additional inventory or finished goods but at the cost of working capital tied up.
- **Dependability**: will be affected by an organisation operating to maximum capacity as it may be more prone to suffer from the effects of disruptions to the production schedule.
- **Flexibility**: is enhanced by surplus capacity. If demand and capacity are balanced or demand is exceeding capacity then it is more difficult to have a level of flexibility.

2.19 Time may be a constraint on capacity management where a customer has a specific delivery date. In this situation operations managers may 'plan backwards', ie they allocate the final stage of the production operation to the period where delivery is required, and this is then passed down the production process stages in reverse of normal practice. This process identifies whether there is adequate time to meet the production demands or whether capacity needs to be increased on a temporary basis if available.

System efficiency

2.20 Capacity, being the ability to produce work in a given time, is measured in the **unit of work**. For example, a factory that has a capacity of 10,000 'machine hours' in each 40-hour week should be capable of producing 10,000 'standard hours of work' during a 40-hour week. Whether the factory can actually produce this will depend on several factors.

- The amount of work involved in the production (does it require 1, 3, 9 standard hours?)

- What time is required in production (including set-up time and maintenance)?
- The design and productivity of the factory and its effectiveness at delivering operational requirements.

2.21   The nature and mix of most operations makes measuring capacity difficult. It is only where the product or service repeats that it is relatively easy to measure. Mass production (where items repeat in a similar manufacturing format) allows for accurate measurement; however, when a variety of items are manufactured then the task becomes more complex.

2.22   The variety of products means that machines have to be changed or reconfigured, maintenance may need to be carried out during any changeover and the machines may not be totally compatible with each other (for example, the output quantity in a given hour may be different). Quantities produced may be smaller, losing the gains that could be made from lengthy production runs. Measurement is consequently more involved with a greater number of variables.

2.23   Goldratt and Fox put forward the argument that the capacity of the system is governed by its weakest link, ie the bottleneck. If Machine 1 produces 500 units an hour while Machine 2 (that refines the output from Machine 1) works at 400 units per hour, the true capacity is 400 units per hour despite the higher efficiency of Machine 1.

2.24   A high level of control must be exercised by operations managers in order that bottlenecks do not occur. Differing production rates cause additional problems such as temporary storage, reduction in the effectiveness of capital employed and an overall reduction in the efficiency of the transformation operation.

2.25   The capacity of an operation that was envisaged at the design stage may not be evident in practice. Capacity planning may look at the theoretical design capacity but the practical capacity may be different. Different products than anticipated, machine breakdowns, maintenance and bottlenecks all reduce the capacity of the operation. The term **effective capacity** is often used to give a true picture of the production capability of an operation.

2.26   The late 1970s and early 1980s saw a rapid period of growth in capacity planning tools. The use of computers allowed the integration of procurement, inventory management and production/operations to a degree that had not been possible before. Systems such as materials requirements planning (MRP) allow for this integrated approach to go ahead and also incorporate forecasts as well as actual orders on hand.

2.27   Such systems allow for production scheduling and capacity management to be linked with the operations that supply to it in such a way as to minimise inventory and have stock on hand when required for the transformation process – in essence, matching inputs with outputs. The benefit for capacity management is an increased degree of predictability that allows operations managers to plan ahead and by doing that to maximise capacity.

Adjusting capacity

2.28   Adjusting capacity is usually a consideration when the operation cannot meet the demands being placed on it. These issues are often considered at a strategic level when the need for a production operation is being justified and are built in to the strategic and operational plans. Often though, this is not the case. Some of the methods open to operations managers are as follows.

- **Increasing operating times**: change from a two-shift to a three-shift system (eg instead of operating two eight-hour shifts increase to three eight-hour shifts). This is easier said than done. In practice the workforce may object, residents nearby may object and trade unions may object. If, however, this approach can be implemented it will often increase the effectiveness of the operation by maximising existing resources.

- **Overtime**: this is often the most responsive method of increasing capacity. The extension of the working day allows labour to be available when required to meet increased capacity requirements.
- **Use of part-time staff**: by hiring temporary staff at peak times. Operational issues such as insufficient training, security clearance and third-party costs (using an agency) may arise. This approach is coming under increased scrutiny as organisations consider their stance on corporate social responsibility issues and evaluate whether this 'hire and fire' approach is ethically correct in today's business environment.
- **Subcontracting**: if considered during the strategic stage the organisation may have established long-term links with subcontractors. The subcontracting issue is often an operational concern. There are often issues regarding the profit margin of the subcontractor, quality standards and ethical and environmental concerns that must all be fully considered before entering into any contractual business relationship of this type.

Measurement

2.29 Measurement must be in an accepted and meaningful format to the operation. In the example above there is the input measure of capacity (machine hours available) and the output measure of capacity (the number of units manufactured in a given time period).

2.30 Complexity with inputs and outputs will often mean that operations will choose to use one only as a main measure. In the case of a college, for example, managers can categorise inputs as the number of students who enrolled compared to the number who successfully passed.

2.31 With hospitals it is more complex. **Inputs** could be the number of patients requiring treatment, but consideration should be given to the **level** of treatment required. Outputs depend on the variety of services offered by the hospital. If the hospital specialises in a certain area then more meaningful measurements can be obtained, while if it offers a general mixed service output figures may mean little.

2.32 With colleges there is the problem of the academic level of students, the past academic record and the commitment of each student. Social considerations are relevant (eg would you expect a higher retention rate in an inner city college or a small-town college?) When benchmarking performance measures against other colleges are you comparing like with like?

Capacity management strategies

2.33 Capacity management is concerned with ensuring that the capacity of the operation matches the evolving demands of the business in the most effective and time efficient manner. The aim of capacity management is to balance various factors.

- **Cost and capacity**: to ensure that any processing capacity purchased is justifiable in terms of both business need and the efficient use of resources.
- **Supply against demand**: making sure that the availability of goods or services matches the demands made on the business.

2.34 Capacity management deals with the identification of present and future business requirements in order to ensure that demand needs are met cost effectively.

2.35 There are two main strategies for capacity management.

- **Capacity leading demand**: here capacity is designed to be able to produce more goods or services than the forecast demand. The operation should then have enough capacity to meet anticipated demand. This ensures that revenue is maximised and that customer satisfaction standards are high. This approach also means that the operation will operate with a certain amount of 'slack' built in to meet increases in demand and as a result the utilisation of the operational capability may be low.

- **Capacity lagging demand**: here capacity will not meet the demand anticipated of it. This ensures that resources will have a high degree of utilisation but may still be insufficient to meet anticipated demand, causing customer dissatisfaction.

Smoothing capacity

2.36 Where possible organisations will endeavour to have demand fluctuations smoothed out or eliminated altogether. There are various techniques to achieve this.

2.37 Offering inducements to customers (such as price reductions, additional quantities etc) may advance demand. Although profit margins may be affected, the exercise may be cost effective as the operation keeps running and the product being manufactured may offer the least reduction in profit margin.

2.38 Encouraging customers to wait for completion of their orders will clearly affect customer service levels and the reputation of the organisation and requires careful handling and management.

2.39 Subcontracted manufacture may be utilised to meet peaks in demand. However, the process is time-intensive for operations management, as contractual agreements will be entered into, specifications agreed and quality standards established and monitored among a range of other related issues.

2.40 Spare capacity may be used to build up stock that can be used or sold at a later date. Finished stock bears not only the delivery price of the component parts but also the cost of the transformation process that goes into the finished item. Holding finished inventory ties up capital and also a major risk is that the stock may deteriorate or become obsolete.

2.41 Reducing downtime of machines by preventive maintenance can minimise problems caused by demand peaks. The same idea lies behind more effective work practices, enhanced mechanisation or automation, offering inducements to employees or increasing work shift patterns (eg increasing from two eight-hour shifts to a 24-hour operation incorporating three eight-hour shifts).

2.42 Re-evaluating and improving product design may attain customer service and productivity gains.

2.43 Re-examining the flow of work through the transformation process, particularly if bottlenecks are apparent, may also help to smooth production.

2.44 Smoothing of the capacity system is considered at all levels of the organisation. Smoothing is the matching of orders to capacity over an identifiable timeframe and brings considerable benefits in terms of planning and structure to the operations manager.

2.45 Production scheduling attempts to smooth demand in order to produce a stable manufacturing plan. This may involve increasing production runs beyond immediate requirements in anticipation of future orders. This will, of course, mean that excess finished stock will be held for a period of time. This goes against the idea of producing what the customer wants when they want it; however, the need for effective and efficient use of capacity will in certain situations take precedence. The efficient use of the production set-up, perceived future production demands and customer forecast projections would all be used to justify why seemingly excess stock will be made. The argument is about capacity but also needs to justify itself financially.

2.46 A feature of many organisations is how they cope with seasonal fluctuations to their business. Seasonality of demand is very common for a wide variety of reasons such as climate, social, festive, religious and political factors.

2.47   Customer service is a major contributor to an organisation's view of demand and capacity management strategies. If customer satisfaction is high on the agenda then a strategy of capacity leading may be adopted; and by contrast, if cost constraints dominate, a capacity lag approach may be employed.

2.48   Decisions relating to demand and capacity strategies are made at all levels of the organisation as it is accepted that strategic decisions based on forecasts will, to differing degrees, prove inaccurate calling for remedial action to be taken at lower levels of the management hierarchy.

Techniques of capacity planning

2.49   Much in the way that a person adjusts taps to achieve a desired temperature, the individual in charge of this type of planning adjusts the workforce and process flow to obtain a regular use of company resources with minimal downtime, minimal bottlenecks and some level of output consistent with all the resources being put in the process.

2.50   There are two pure planning strategies available to the capacity planner: a level strategy and a chase strategy. Organisations may choose to utilise one of the pure strategies in isolation, or they may opt for a strategy that combines the two.

2.51   A **level capacity plan** seeks to produce an aggregate plan that maintains a steady production rate and/or a steady level of resource usage. In order to satisfy changes in customer demand, the firm must raise or lower inventory levels in anticipation of increased or decreased levels of forecast demand.

2.52   The firm maintains a level workforce and a steady rate of output when demand is somewhat low. This allows the firm to establish higher inventory levels than are currently needed. As demand increases, the firm is able to continue a steady production rate and steady use of resources, while allowing the inventory surplus to absorb the increased demand.

2.53   A second alternative would be to use a backlog or backorder. A backorder is simply a promise to deliver the product at a later date when it is more readily available, usually when capacity begins to catch up with diminishing demand. In essence, the backorder is a device for moving demand from one period to another, preferably one in which demand is lower, thereby smoothing demand requirements over time.

2.54   A level capacity plan allows a firm to maintain a constant level of output and still meet demand. This is desirable from an employee relations standpoint. Negative results of the level strategy would include the cost of excess inventory, subcontracting or overtime costs, and backorder costs, which typically are the cost of expediting orders and the loss of customer goodwill.

2.55   A **chase demand plan** implies matching demand and capacity period by period. This could result in a considerable amount of hiring, firing or laying off of employees; insecure and unhappy employees; problems with labour unions; and erratic utilisation of plant and equipment. It also implies a great deal of flexibility on the firm's part. The major advantage of a chase strategy is that it allows inventory to be held to the lowest level possible, and for some firms this is a considerable saving. Most firms embracing the just in time production concept utilise a chase strategy approach to aggregate planning.

2.56   Most organisations find it advantageous to utilise a combination of the level and chase strategy. A combination strategy (sometimes called a hybrid or mixed strategy) can be found to better meet organisational goals and policies and achieve lower costs than either of the pure strategies used independently.

3 Methods of forecasting demand

Introduction

3.1 Forecasting is an essential part of all planning and decision-making and is of fundamental importance to many areas of operations management. It forms a key element in the long-term management process and the accuracy of long-term forecasts can have a considerable impact on the activities of operations managers at a later date.

3.2 Accurate forecasting can mean that the right resources are available as required. Inaccurate forecasting can mean different degrees of remedying operational activities to bring them in line with strategic plans.

3.3 Forecasts will rarely be 100 per cent accurate as they are based on projections and assumptions. Forecasts involve a number of considerations.

- **What is the forecast for?** As with any project the objectives should be clear from the outset.
- **What is the projected timescale?** Traditionally forecasts are categorised as long-term (two to five years or more), medium-term (six months to two years) or short-term (less than six months).
- **On what data should the forecast be based?** Forecasting is often a combination of 'hard data' ie facts and figures (such as prices, trends, sales, etc) and 'soft data', eg customer feedback, market knowledge, etc.
- **What forecasting techniques should be applied?** These can be divided into two approaches: quantitative (hard data, using figures with the application of statistical analysis) and qualitative (using such techniques as the Delphi method and test marketing that will be discussed below).
- **How accurate is the forecast?** A key requirement of forecasting is to monitor the accuracy achieved.

3.4 Characteristics of a good forecast include:

- **Timely**: have a horizon with time to implement possible changes
- **Accurate**: state the degree of accuracy
- **Reliable**: be reliable and work consistently
- **Meaningful**: be expressed in meaningful units
- **Written**: be expressed in writing
- **Easy to use**: simple to understand and use
- **Consistent**: be consistent with historical data

Simple moving average

3.5 As the name suggests, this is a simple technique. All we do is to look at the demand for recent periods, and assume that demand for the coming period will be the average of that experienced in the past. There is no particular rule about how many past periods we should take into account. If we are trying to estimate demand during July we might, for example, look at the actual demand experienced during January to June, and take the average of those six months.

3.6 Suppose that usage of an independent demand material was as follows in the months of January to June.

Month	Usage in litres
January	450
February	190
March	600
April	600
May	420
June	380
Total usage January to June	2,640

3.7 Using a simple moving average we would simply take the average of these six months: $^{2,640}\!/_6$ = 440 litres. This would be our estimate of usage in July.

3.8 The reason for the term 'moving' average is that each month we move along by one step. Thus in estimating usage for August, we discard the January figure above and replace it with the figure for actual usage in July. Our estimate for August is therefore based on the six months preceding August, namely February to July.

3.9 Of course, this procedure is really a bit too simple. It is clear from the figures that demand for this material fluctuates quite markedly. The figures for January to June show a low of 190 litres, and a high of 600 litres. The simple average of such figures does not inspire confidence. The actual figure in July might turn out to be either of these extremes, in which case our estimate of 440 litres will prove wide of the mark. The next method tries to inject greater sophistication into the estimates.

Weighted average method, or exponential smoothing

3.10 The simple moving average gives equal weight to each of the figures recorded in previous periods. In the example, the figure for January contributed exactly as much to the averaging calculation as did that for June. This does not take account of a fact which is very commonly observed in practice, namely that older figures are a less reliable guide to the future than more recent figures. If there is any gradual change taking place in our pattern of usage of the item, it is more likely that the change will be reflected in our usage for June than in the figure for January six months ago.

3.11 To take account of this, the technique of exponential smoothing can be used. This is designed to give greater weight to the figures experienced in recent months, and to reduce the weight given to older figures. Our first step is to settle on a number between 0 and 1 – say 0.2. We then perform the following calculation, using the figures from the example above.

$$
\begin{aligned}
\text{July usage} &= 0.2 \times 380 + (0.2 \times 0.8) \times 420 + (0.2 \times 0.8^2) \times 600 + \ldots + (0.2 \times 0.8^5) \times 450 \\
&= 0.2 \times 380 + 0.16 \times 420 + 0.128 \times 600 + \ldots + 0.066 \times 450 \\
&= 76 + 67.2 + 76.8 + 61.4 + 15.6 + 29.5 \\
&= \underline{\underline{326.5}}
\end{aligned}
$$

3.12 The factor 0.8 is simply 1 minus our chosen factor of 0.2. How we chose the value of 0.2 – rather than 0.1, say, or 0.95 – is a matter of experience. We look back on known values from the past and we work out what factor would have given the best estimates if we had used it in the basic formula. We deduce that this is the value which best encapsulates the nature of the historical trend, and so we apply it for the future in the hope that it will continue to give good results.

3.13 Notice that this has given a lower estimate for demand in July than the simple moving average. This is because the high values of March and April, being some months ago, have little weight in the calculations above, but were given full weight in the simple average calculation.

3.14 It is very easy to calculate the value of the weighted average from one month to the next, once the initial calculation has been done. This is because the arithmetic of the situation leads to a simple formula. The estimate (E) for the coming period is given by the formula:

$E = (0.2 \times D) + (0.8 \times A)$

where **D** is the actual demand experienced in the most recent month (June in our example), and **A** is the average which we calculated last month (when we were trying to estimate the figure for June).

3.15 Of course, this formula uses the value 0.2 that we decided on in the case of this particular material. In the case of another material, we might have settled on a different value and the formula above would have to be amended accordingly.

Time series trend analysis

3.16 A time series is a sequential arrangement of selected statistical data according to their occurrence in time. The objective of a time series trend analysis is to measure the variation of a data set about the average, often for the purpose of data comparison.

3.17 In assessing trends, you can also make meaningful comparisons with comparable organisations in the same industry or related overall industrial averages, the general industrial economy, gross national product, population, and so on. Current data may be compared with past data in the same series, such as sales volume or product costs. Using this approach you can anticipate future trends with greater certainty.

3.18 Projecting the time series into the future is a form of statistical forecasting. Time series analysis is therefore very important to analysts who apply statistics to business activity and economics. An economy's or company's dynamic nature makes the time factor a vital element in analysing sales, product costs, production etc. A time series represents economic data moving through time, and its analysis provides the basis for reviewing the statistics in motion.

3.19 The factors to be taken into account in time series analysis are as follows.

- Trend
- Seasonal variation
- Cyclical changes
- Irregular (random) fluctuations

3.20 A trend is a long-term movement, either upward or downward. Time series trends can be attributed to a number of factors, such as the introduction of mass production, technological changes, variations in population growth, development of new products, revisions in product mix, war, inflation, and so on.

3.21 Seasonal variations represent period movements that occur at regular time intervals, particularly during the calendar year. For example, consumer expenditures in retail stores increase at Christmas, and costs for utilities go up during the winter season.

3.22 Cyclical variations are usually influenced by prosperity, recession, and depression. In periods of prosperity, sales, production, income, and employment are accelerated, whereas the opposite effect applies in periods of depression. The cycles of economic activity show no regularity with respect to their occurrence or duration. History has shown that predicting future cycles with any degree of accuracy could be extremely difficult.

3.23 Irregular fluctuations are exactly what the term suggests: no amount of statistical analysis can account for every variation in demand patterns. There will always be random variations that are not predicted by the analysis.

Regression analysis

3.24 Regression is a technique for deriving a mathematical relationship between two variables that are thought to be connected with each other. For example, managers might suspect that the level of sales achieved each month is related to the advertising spend in the previous month.

3.25 To investigate this idea scientifically, managers might use one axis of a graph to represent the value of sales achieved each month. The other axis of the graph would represent the amount of advertising spend in the previous month. The actual values might be plotted for each month in a period of, say, a year. Managers would then look at the pattern disclosed by the graph and examine whether it revealed a relationship.

3.26 The mathematical technique involved is called regression analysis. For any two variables – such as sales levels and advertising spend – a relationship can be calculated mathematically. Managers would use the information by predicting the amount of extra sales they might achieve by increasing the advertising spend to a particular level, or the amount of sales they might lose by a defined reduction in advertising spend.

3.27 Time series trend analysis (discussed above) is a variation of this technique. It can be used to predict sales levels over time (which is relevant to calculating usage of dependent demand items). The trick is to treat time itself as the variable to be related to sales levels. The manager can then derive a relationship between sales on one hand and months of the year on the other.

3.28 The mathematics of regression analysis is fairly complex and unlikely to be tested in the examination but you should be aware of the general approach outlined above.

Qualitative approaches to forecasting

3.29 Qualitative (judgemental) approaches to forecasting fall under two broad headings: marketing research and expert opinion.

3.30 **Marketing research** is a common marketing tool used to ascertain potential interest and demand particularly in new products or to help identify trends in sales and the reasons behind them. Processes include focus groups, questionnaires, test marketing and interviewing. Research in the operations environment can mirror these methods and comparable results in terms of applicability to the specific operation may be obtained from suggestion boxes, quality circles, discussion groups, exit interviews etc.

3.31 **Expert opinion** is the gathering and collation of views, judgements and opinions from people regarded as knowledgeable in specific business areas (directors, consultants and business area specialists). The value of the contributors and the judgement made can be called into question, but knowledge and experience will usually provide a sound basis on which to develop a forecast.

The Delphi method

3.32 The method of using experts is frequently criticised. The 'Delphi' method (originally developed in 1944), in essence seeks to impose a statistical rigour and counter the argument of bias that frequently accompanies the gathering and use of 'expert opinion'.

3.33 The term Delphi refers to the site of the most revered oracle in ancient Greece. The objective of the Delphi method is the reliable and creative development of ideas or the production of suitable information to aid decision-making.

3.34 The Delphi method involves group communication by experts who are geographically dispersed. Questionnaires are sent to the selected experts by post or email and are designed to elicit and develop individual responses to the problems posed. The responses are considered and refined with subsequent questionnaires to develop a group response.

3.35 A main consideration of the Delphi method is to overcome the disadvantages of conventional committee action where individuals may dominate, bias may develop or groups polarise in their thinking. The group interaction in Delphi is anonymous, as comments made are not identified to their originator. A panel director or monitor, whose role is to focus the group on the stated objectives, controls the interaction between group members.

3.36 To operate successfully the participants should understand the process and aim of the exercise although there is some debate on the level of expertise required from the 'sages'. Armstrong and Welty suggest that a high degree of expertise is not necessary while Hanson and Ramani state that the respondents should be well informed in the appropriate area.

3.37 Fowles describes the following ten steps for developing and applying the Delphi method.

- Formation of a team to undertake and monitor the exercise on a given subject
- Selection of one or more panels to participate in the exercise – customarily, the panellists are experts in the area to be investigated
- Development of the first round Delphi questionnaire
- Testing the questionnaire for proper wording (ambiguities, vagueness etc)
- Transmission of the first questionnaire to the panellists
- Analysis of first round responses
- Preparation of second round questionnaires (and possible testing)
- Transmission of the second round questionnaires to the panellists
- Analysis of second round responses (these steps are reiterated as long as desired or necessary to achieve stability in the results)
- Preparation of the report by the analysis team to present the conclusions of the exercise

3.38 The Delphi method has proved useful in answering specific, single-dimension questions. There is less support for its use to determine more complex forecasts that involve multiple factors.

4 Loading, scheduling and sequencing

The nature of scheduling

4.1 A schedule is a representation of the time necessary to carry out a particular task. Scheduling is one of the more complex tasks facing operations managers, as they need to balance a range of resources to achieve the best overall result.

4.2 Machines have varied capacities and capabilities and staff will have a wide range of skills and degrees of specialisation. Scheduling requires operations managers to develop a 'timetable' approach to production or service delivery (with commencement dates, progression dates and completion dates) to ensure that the required resources are available at each stage of the operation.

4.3 A job schedule shows the plan for the manufacture of a particular job or the sequence of service operations. It is created through 'work/study' reviews that determine the method and times required or (often in the case of service delivery) through experience and refining what has been done before.

4.4 The job schedule is a small 'project' that requires tasks to be completed in a certain order in order to effectively deliver the desired outcome.

4.5 Most operations will carry out a range of production tasks simultaneously. This will entail amalgamating several job schedules into a workable and productive plan of action. This process is known as 'scheduling' and the result is known as the production schedule or the factory schedule for the operation as a whole.

4.6 There are two key issues with production scheduling.

- The measurement of performance. This is often a battle between financial performance requirements (minimise stockholding) and marketing performance requirements (produce enough to meet customer demand).
- The large number and complexity of production schedules. Most operations are running a large number of production processes and runs simultaneously.

4.7 There are a number of variables that must be taken into account in order to deliver an effective production schedule.

- Delivery dates
- Job schedules for each relevant production task

- Capacities of the production sections
- The efficiency of these production sections
- Planned holidays
- Anticipated sickness
- Projected absenteeism
- Projected training
- Availability of required materials

Loading

4.8 Loading describes the amount of work allocated to a machine or work centre. For example a unit operates two eight-hour shifts for six days a week. It is apparently available for 96 hours a week. However, a number of factors must be considered as they can impact on the availability of the work unit.

- Statutory holidays
- Weekends
- Maintenance
- Machine reliability
- Absenteeism

4.9 **Finite loading** allocates work to a machine, unit, person or group of people up to a set limit. This limit is based on an estimate of the capacity available and is not exceeded. Finite loading can prove suitable in a number of situations.

- Where it is possible to place a limit on the load (eg by using an appointment or timetabling system)
- Where it is a requirement to limit the load (eg for safety reasons)
- Where the cost of limiting the load is not considered too expensive (where for marketing reasons in particular limiting production offers exclusivity to customers)

4.10 Finite capacity scheduling systems have developed considerably in recent years. There are now few, if any, manufacturing and services areas where finite loading cannot be used practically. It has been used in jobbing manufacture for many years but is now equally practical in more complex batch manufacture operations. The use of finite loading will often be seen in continuous production, as even this method will have some batch production aspects within it.

4.11 **Infinite loading** does not limit the amount of work accepted. It is a system that will try to cope with the loading placed upon it. This can happen in the following situations.

- Where it is not possible or practical to limit the load (eg the Accident & Emergency operation of a hospital). To address the possible fluctuation in loading, doctors and nurses are 'on-call' should the need arise.
- Where it is not necessary to limit the load. At times the 'loading' in a restaurant will be low and at other 'peak' times high. Initially people will queue and eventually some may go elsewhere. If a finite system approach were used there would be a need to book and a possible limit at the time you can spend at a table.
- Where the costs or issues involved in limiting the load are prohibitive (eg customers turned away from a January sale as the store is considered full).

Sequencing

4.12 Sequencing determines the best order for progressing demands through an operation. Whether the demand sequence is finite or infinite, decisions must be taken with regard to the order in which the work will be undertaken.

4.13 This can present the operations manager with many complex and interrelated decisions. Later in the text we will examine critical path analysis. In essence, certain things must be achieved before progression can be made to the next step. There is a 'critical path' or sequence that is essential to progress from one stage to another. That does not stop preparation in advance but it will mean that the operations manager must be fully aware of the critical stages in the operation.

4.14 For example, a car being resprayed must be rubbed down, prepared and primed to accept the paint, then sprayed and dried. Materials can be readied in advance and staff can be readied but the sequence is set by the nature of the job.

4.15 Sequencing is often governed by priority rules, which take the elements of a particular scheduling problem and, using an applicable procedure, aid in working out the plan. The plan can be further influenced by the organisation's own priorities such as customer preferencing or the interdependence of machines or people in the process.

4.16 The rules include the following.

- FCFS: **First come, first served** where jobs are sequenced as they arrive (eg buying a railway ticket). This is also referred to as FIFO: first in, first out.
- LIFO: **Last in, first out** which is not often used in operations. An example would be people getting in and out of a lift. However, the method will often have an adverse effect on service particularly where customers are involved.
- LPT: **Longest processing time** goes first which can be particularly relevant when set-up times are long or where gains can be made from economies of scale in production.
- SPT: **Shortest processing time** goes first where jobs are allocated according to the shortest time they will have at a workstation. This enables a greater number of customers' needs to be satisfied.
- EDD: **Earliest due date** where jobs are allocated on the basis of their completion date with the earliest one first.

Gantt charts

4.17 Developed by Henry L Gantt, Gantt charts are a visual tool that has widespread acceptance in scheduling. The Gantt chart represents time as a bar on a chart.

Figure 7.1 *Gantt chart*

STOCK CHECK ITEMS SIGNED OFF					
	MONDAY	*TUESDAY*	*WEDNESDAY*	*THURSDAY*	*FRIDAY*
Target Actual	150 100	100 125	150 150	150 150	75 100
Notes	*Working with trainee*	*One hour overtime*			*Devlpt mtg cancelled*

4.18 Charts are now usually constructed and amended on computers but this can restrict their visual impact. Where a number of operatives are involved in the manufacturing process it is still common to display on a whiteboard chart. If Gantt charts are computer-based then different levels of entry are required for those who are authorised to amend details and for those who merely need to view the chart.

4.19 Gantt charts can be used to plan alternative schedules in advance. Computer programmes will assess various options presented and gauge the operational outcome which can then assist in choosing the optimum scheduling route for a given operation or set of operations.

4.20   Variations on the Gantt chart theme include the following.

- Load charts that show the loading and idle time for machines or operators
- Flow charts that display orders or jobs in progress in order to show how work is progressing against a schedule

4.21   These variations are often incorporated into one chart.

Line balancing

4.22   Line balancing is a technique to ensure that resources are deployed effectively among the workstations. Each stage of the production line should be designed to operate at the same rate (ie the capacity of each of the sequenced workstations should be the same). This requires not only planning of the capacity loading but also consideration of both idle and maintenance time.

4.23   The objective is to maximise productivity by using the machines or people to their total practical capability. To achieve this requires planning, particularly relating to the timing of operations and the problems that can be caused by bottlenecks within the process. Line balancing, despite the best advance planning, can be very difficult. It is estimated that it will take over three months of operation in car manufacture to balance the line effectively.

4.24   It is usually not possible to operate at 100 per cent efficiency. The operations manager needs to consider the following questions.

- What is the maximum output of the production line?
- What labour is required?
- What will be the efficiency of labour with this proposed layout?

4.25   To assist with these considerations a precedence diagram can be developed which seeks to maximise the operation. As with Gantt charts much of the calculation work and analysis is now handled by IT systems but the operations manager is still required to bring practical experience to bear on the resultant computer output.

Figure 7.2 *Precedence diagram*

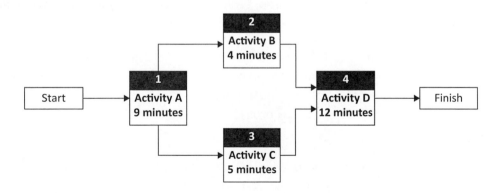

4.26   The precedence diagram gives a visual display of the tasks to be performed together with the sequence they will be performed in.

4.27   The balancing of assembly or manufacturing lines is clearly a complex and involved task with many considerations and variables to be evaluated and possibly re-evaluated. Precedence diagrams are one tool that can be used and they will normally be integrated within a computer-based system. The most accepted is known as COMSOAL (Computer Method of Sequencing Operations for Assembly Lines) which generates various solutions in response to the parameters set but will still require the operations manager to make the final operating sequence decision.

4.28   Work cycle times establish the rate of output for the production or assembly line. Calculation of cycle times is important as it serves to establish the maximum time required to perform the given operation, usually on one machine or for a defined operation.

$$\text{Output capacity} = \frac{\text{Daily working (operating) time}}{\text{Cycle time}}$$

Scheduling in low-volume systems

4.29   Earlier in this Course Book we looked at process types in manufacturing and service industries. We described process, product and cell layout operations and their applicability for different types of operation. The type of operation or mix of these methods of operations has a high impact on the ability and flexibility of any operation and its ability to deliver effective and efficient product or service.

4.30   Scheduling in low-volume or 'job shop' systems is often more complex and involved than more predictable mid-volume or high-volume systems. Job shops such as garages, bespoke furniture manufacture or even hospitals or any manufacture or service operation where production or service is carried out to customers' order requirements or needs, each differing in their wants, requires an increased degree of planning and monitoring for the needs to be satisfied effectively.

4.31   As a result each order must be planned to maximise resources and availability, often at short notice, and monitored as it progresses through an organisation's operational structure.

4.32   As an example, take the operation of a garage. Customers are encouraged to book ahead (this permits a 'timetabling' approach). Each element of the work cycle (such as 20 minutes to change oil, 60 minutes to change brakes etc) has already been calculated, based on industry norms and past experience.

4.33   This allows the operations manager to plan and schedule work after consideration of staff and available resources. Some jobs will take longer than anticipated and some may be quicker.

4.34   New demands will be made as customers suffer breakdowns or faults with their cars that must be scheduled in or delayed until a suitable 'slot' can be found. Delays may result in lost business. Diagnosis may take an unpredictable amount of time. Customers may need to be contacted before repair work can be started. Spares may need to be delivered. Resources required may already have been allocated so there may be a delay in commencement of the remedial work.

4.35   Planning by means of Gantt charts offers a visible and flexible approach for the low-volume operation where not only the scheduler but also the operatives require to view the plan for the day. The Gantt chart provides a visible representation of the plan and workload and so enables discussion and revision in a flexible and responsive manner. This may prove a suitable and effective planning and scheduling tool in these particular circumstances.

4.36   More complex operations (whether in manufacturing, assembly or service) may be more reliant on computer based assessment and scheduling. However, the principle and approach remain fundamentally the same.

4.37   The garage operation often requires that cars pass from one 'work station' to another (eg diagnosis of the problem, holding area, maintenance bay, tuning operation before completion). Work stations must be scheduled, staff available when required to carry out their particular role at the work station, timings planned and communicated to avoid bottlenecks and possible alternatives considered in case of delays and 'slack' in another area (eg valeting the car).

4.38   Job shops or similar operations with many work centres provide a high degree of complexity particularly with regard to scheduling. To effectively accomplish their workload a number of factors must be considered and monitored on an ongoing basis.

- Rough planning and sequencing at the front-line or office
- Rough prioritisation that refines over time
- Flexible staff
- Decentralisation of certain detailed sequencing decisions to operatives
- Progress chasing in real time
- Regular review of operational activities with a view to the continuous improvement of the operation.

4.39 The job shop operation is one where planning can only be proactive to a certain degree. Much of the planning is reactive in the sense that it responds to fast moving and changing circumstances. Often the size and complexity of the job means that investment in more sophisticated capacity and scheduling tools and methods would not be cost effective and may prove too complex in operation.

Scheduling in intermediate-volume systems

4.40 Intermediate or batch systems are designed to take advantage of the relative size of each order and the repetition of the manufacturing or assembly process. Batch systems could operate in the same way as job shop operations, but this would not maximise the economies of scale that can be gained in manufacture or assembly or the reduction in variety offered that permits an increased degree of specialisation.

4.41 Batch systems (eg a production run of 10,000 units of product A followed by a production run of 20,000 units of product B) enable a **master production schedule** (MPS) to be developed. This MPS enables machines to be allocated in the most effective manner.

4.42 The development of the MPS is dependent on a number of associated factors.

- **Aggregate sales and operations plan**. This covers medium-term projections, without detailing individual orders, and identifies the range of products that are expected to be manufactured. The plan will be broken down to detail batch sizes, estimated delivery dates and estimated production dates and times.
- **Materials requirements planning** (MRP). The MPS can be broken down into requirements for each batch production run under a materials requirements plan. The material requirements plan enables ordering of the right net quantity of items at the right time to enable the manufacturing process to go ahead in the anticipated manner while minimising stockholding to a practical level.
- **Capacity requirements planning** (CRP). This examines (over a planning period – often a day or a few days) the availability and capacity of machines to meet projected manufacturing demands. The aggregate sales and operations plan enables 'rough cut' planning; the capacity requirements plan refines this into operational practicality.

4.43 Aggregate planning tries to find ways of meeting demand while maintaining production at a stable level and satisfying any other specific constraints and/or objectives. It enables operations managers to fully consider issues in advance so that they can plan accordingly when implementing the MPS for work to be carried out over a short timeframe and will be considered and evaluated in greater depth in the following chapter.

Scheduling in high-volume systems

4.44 High-volume systems should be easier to manage than job shop or batch systems owing to the repetitive manufacture involved. The organisations involved in high-volume production are usually large multinationals that gain from economies of scale in production. The concentration of effort is focused around the elimination of waste, improved throughput times and maximisation of resources.

4.45 The assembly line is one of the most visual representations of a high-volume system. The idea when first introduced was an adaptation of the system used in meat processing and grain mills, where conveyor belts moved goods and overhead cranes to the workers.

4.46   Owing to the predictable nature of mass manufacturing, scheduling becomes less of an issue. Greater issues arise in relation to line balancing in order to maximise the benefits to be gained.

4.47   Modern views of the assembly line are focused around the application of JIT systems and continuous flow manufacturing (CFM). Continuous flow focuses on producing one item at a time (or a small and consistent batch of items) through a series of processing steps as continuously as possible, with each step making just what is requested by the next step.

4.48   Parts are built as they are needed while maintaining efficient use of operators and machines. Flexibility is used as a substitute for work in progress inventory. A 'product focus' is established in all areas of the operation and all non-value added activities of the operation are eliminated.

4.49   Continuous flow can be achieved in a number of ways, ranging from moving assembly lines to integrated manual cells. The continuous flow approach is also known as **one-piece flow**, **single-piece flow**, and **make one, move one**.

4.50   CFM focuses on lowering the work in progress inventory and replacing it with flexibility and increased labour productivity. CFM can bring the following benefits.

- Simplify the manufacturing operation into product or process flows.
- Organise manufacturing operations so that one day resembles the next.
- Establish flow or cycle times that are consistent with total man hours.
- Use activity based costing methods to analyse in detail potential areas of cost savings.

Chapter summary

- Planning and control within operations will exist over three (often overlapping) time frames.
- Planning involves matching supply with expected demand. Control is the practical actions that can be taken to bring the plan back on track.
- Capacity management involves matching the operating system with the demand placed on the system.
- Forecasting demand may be approached by means of quantitative techniques, qualitative techniques, or a mixture of both.
- Scheduling is the effective timing of the use of resources to meet organisational requirements and is a common feature of all organisations. Scheduling requires a route or sequence to be followed in order to complete the task at hand.
- Loading describes the amount of work allocated to a machine or work centre. Finite loading allocates work to a machine, unit, person or group of people up to a set limit. Infinite loading does not limit the amount of work accepted on a machine or work centre.
- Line balancing ensures that resources are deployed effectively among the work stations.
- Scheduling in low-volume or 'job shop' systems is often more complex and involved than more predictable mid- or high-volume systems.
- Planning by means of Gantt charts offers a visible and flexible approach for the low-volume operation where not only the scheduler but also the operatives need to view the plan for the day.

Self-test questions

Numbers in brackets refer to the paragraphs above where your answers can be checked.

1   Define planning. (1.2)

2   Explain SMART objectives. (1.5)

3   How does Ray Wild define operations planning? (1.8)

4   What is meant by capacity management? (2.1)

5   Muhlemann, Oakland and Lockyer distinguish between three different capacity levels. What are they? (2.15)

6   What methods are open to operations managers when adjusting capacity? (2.28)

7   What are the two main strategies for capacity management? (2.35)

8   List characteristics of a good forecast. (3.4)

9   Describe how the Delphi method of forecasting works. (3.32–3.38)

10   What is the purpose of 'sequencing'? (4.12)

11   What is meant by line balancing? (4.22)

12   What are the benefits of continuous flow manufacturing? (4.50)

1.4 The situation is easier in the case of items subject to independent demand. For example, the amount of oil required to maintain a manufacturing machine in working order does not depend on which products are being processed on that machine. It is possible to estimate that a particular amount of oil will be used each day, week or month, regardless of the exact detail of the production schedule.

1.5 As a further example, what items are bought out in a typical service organisation? This will depend on the exact nature of the organisation, but the following are likely answers. Notice that in all cases the items are characterised by independent demand; they are not related to the exact volume and nature of the service organisation's outputs. Clearly these purchases are not limited to service companies but they serve to illustrate the difference between dependent and independent demand.

- Office equipment and supplies such as stationery
- Computer hardware and software
- Motor vehicles
- Advertising and design services
- Maintenance services

1.6 The distinction between dependent and independent demand is important because some inventory control systems (such as materials requirements planning or MRP) take into account the peculiar difficulties of dependent demand, while other methods are more suited to independent demand items. Both methods require good inventory management as the optimum goal is to operate effectively carrying as little stock as possible.

Introducing materials requirements planning

1.7 Materials requirements planning (MRP) developed during the 1970s but is equally applicable today. It operates as an integrated information management, production planning and stock management system that has been enhanced in practicality in recent years as the speed and power of IT systems have increased.

1.8 MRP is also known as MRPI. This differentiates it from manufacturing resources planning (MRPII) which will be addressed later in the chapter.

1.9 MRP enables the advance planning of materials required for manufacture. The system utilises a bill of materials (BOM), in essence a breakdown of all the materials and components that go to make a finished product. The BOM serves to inform Procurement that goods must be ordered to meet an anticipated manufacturing date. Procurement will then order, taking into account suppliers' lead times and a 'safety margin' (it is not a just in time system but works to allow a practical margin for error, ie an agreed number of days in advance of production). The objective is to ensure that when production commences the goods are available as required and that inventory levels are minimised.

1.10 MRP is defined as 'a set of logically related procedures, decision rules, and records designed to translate a master production schedule (MPS) into time-phased 'net requirements', and the planned coverage of such requirements for each component inventory item needed to implement this schedule'. The elements of this definition are examined below.

- **A set of logically related procedures**: MRP systems follow a logical sequence that incorporates decision rules relating to existing stock held, forecasting etc.
- **Translate an MPS into time-phased 'net requirements'**: time-phased because not everything is required at the same time. If the manufacturing run is extending over six days it may not be until the final day that you require a particular component. By getting delivery later than when the run commenced inventory cost savings can be made. We refer to 'net requirements' because the MRP system takes into account that you may already hold some of the required items in stock and will reduce the ordered quantity accordingly.

CHAPTER 8

MRP, MRPII and ERP

Assessment criteria and indicative content

3.3 Analyse the use of materials requirements planning (MRP) and manufacturing resource planning (MRPII) systems technology for planning and control in operations management

- Master production scheduling
- Bills of materials
- Inventory data
- MRP calculations
- The limitations of MRP systems

3.3 Analyse the use of enterprise resource planning (ERP) systems technology for planning and control in operations management

- Defining ERP
- The origins of ERP
- The structure of a common ERP system
- Web integrated and supply chain integrated ERP systems

Section headings

1 Materials requirements planning
2 Manufacturing resource planning
3 Enterprise resource planning

1 Materials requirements planning

Dependent and independent demand

1.1 The need to accurately assess demand is crucial in today's business environment. Accuracy in forecasting brings with it the opportunities to maximise resources and minimise spend and waste. The increased business emphasis in forecasting and demand management marks it out as an identified aspect of business operations where substantial gains can be made and competitive advantage enhanced.

1.2 Confidence in the predictability of demand enables better decisions at the operational level. When linked to effective inventory management the two areas combine to be greater than the sum of their parts.

The distinction between dependent and independent demand

1.3 Many stock items are subject to dependent demand – that is, the extent to which the item is used depends on the production schedule for a larger item of which it forms part. To estimate the demand such items requires detailed examination of the product breakdown. For example, if 1,000 units are b manufactured and each unit requires 5 modules, then the production requirement is for 5,000 modu The number of modules ordered is dependent on the number of units being produced.

- **The planned coverage of such requirements for each component inventory item needed to implement this schedule**: ensuring that each item required, taking into account suppliers' lead times, is ordered correctly.

Principles of MRP

1.11 An MRP system is a **dependent demand** system. For example, suppose you are making 5,000 square-framed prints. You require four pieces of wood cut to the same length and shape for each frame – a total of 20,000 pieces of wood. You require 5,000 pieces of glass to fit the frame, etc. The number of parts you require is dependent on the number of finished units to be produced.

1.12 The approach of materials requirements planning to dependent demand is to start from the end and work backwards. The first step is to estimate customer demand for a finished product, and then to calculate a production schedule to meet that demand. Customer demand will usually include orders received together with forecast estimates of additional customer demand.

1.13 Forecasting is important as it enables longer production runs to be undertaken, thereby gaining in reduced set-up time and economies of scale, where either future sales are predicted or where a justifiable case of manufacturing for stock has been accepted.

1.14 The main elements of the MRP process are shown in Figure 8.1.

Figure 8.1 *The main elements of an MRP system*

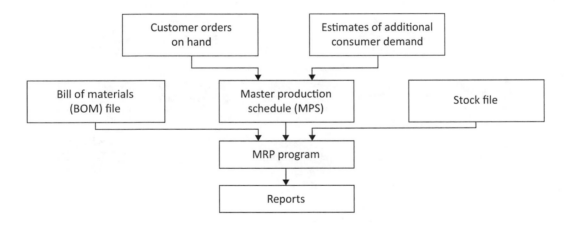

The master production schedule

1.15 Both forecast demand and actual orders on hand are combined in the MPS to decide the quantity to be produced. The role of the MPS is crucial in the MRP system. It provides the specification of the work to be progressed. Linking with the manufacturing availability in the capacity requirements plan (CRP) it brings together what is to be made, assembled or bought in within a specific timeframe.

1.16 The MPS enables us to plan the utilisation of both labour and equipment. In turn this identifies to the procurement department when delivery is required from suppliers to meet production run requirements.

1.17 The MPS is in effect a summary of customer demand. The MRP program acts on the MPS as follows.

- By reference to the BOM file the program translates details of finished products required into details of materials and components required.
- By reference to the stock file the program compares what is required with what is in stock.

1.18   The outputs from the program specify not just the amounts required in this process but also the time by which each is required. They also highlight the need for any special action, such as a possible need to reschedule or expedite orders.

1.19   Detailed outputs of the system will include any or all of the following.

- Order releases to Procurement for the current period, including the dates when required.
- Planned order releases to Procurement for future periods, based on current stocks, orders in progress, scheduled requirements and known lead times.
- Order releases for items to be produced in-house, with due dates for completion.
- Feedback on problems such as bottlenecks or lack of availability. This allows schedulers to make adjustments that can then be incorporated in a revised program run.

The bill of materials

1.20   The BOM is a list showing all the raw materials and components required to make a particular product. It specifies which parts go into which product and in what quantity. The structure of a typical BOM is shown in Figure 8.2.

Figure 8.2 *Structure of a bill of materials*

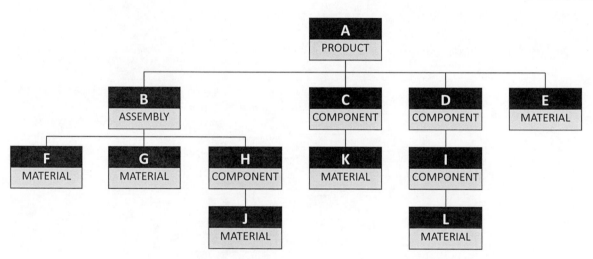

1.21   The diagram illustrates a bill of materials for Product A. Product A is made of Assembly B, Components C and D, and Material E. Assembly B is made from Materials F and G, and Component H (as well as other assemblies or products). This analysis is continued until it captures all of the materials, components etc that are used in manufacture of Product A.

1.22   A typical BOM will contain the following items of information.

- Quantity required. The quantity is one of the most important parts of the BOM because it tells us how many parts are needed for a product.
- Item identification number. This tells us which part to order. It can be a catalogue number, unique product code, or any other identification number.
- Description of item. This provides a check that the correct item is being ordered.
- Cost. This is included to show how much each part is per item and the total cost of all like parts.
- Total product cost

1.23   The BOM is a detailed breakdown of all the component parts that comprise the final product. For components this is usually in the form of part numbers or unique identifiers. The breakdown enables Procurement to place orders for the exact quantity required.

CHAPTER 8

MRP, MRPII and ERP

Assessment criteria and indicative content

3.3 Analyse the use of materials requirements planning (MRP) and manufacturing resource planning (MRPII) systems technology for planning and control in operations management

- Master production scheduling
- Bills of materials
- Inventory data
- MRP calculations
- The limitations of MRP systems

3.3 Analyse the use of enterprise resource planning (ERP) systems technology for planning and control in operations management

- Defining ERP
- The origins of ERP
- The structure of a common ERP system
- Web integrated and supply chain integrated ERP systems

Section headings

1 Materials requirements planning
2 Manufacturing resource planning
3 Enterprise resource planning

1 Materials requirements planning

Dependent and independent demand

1.1 The need to accurately assess demand is crucial in today's business environment. Accuracy in forecasting brings with it the opportunities to maximise resources and minimise spend and waste. The increased business emphasis in forecasting and demand management marks it out as an identified aspect of business operations where substantial gains can be made and competitive advantage enhanced.

1.2 Confidence in the predictability of demand enables better decisions at the operational level. When linked to effective inventory management the two areas combine to be greater than the sum of their parts.

The distinction between dependent and independent demand

1.3 Many stock items are subject to dependent demand – that is, the extent to which the item is used depends on the production schedule for a larger item of which it forms part. To estimate the demand for such items requires detailed examination of the product breakdown. For example, if 1,000 units are being manufactured and each unit requires 5 modules, then the production requirement is for 5,000 modules. The number of modules ordered is dependent on the number of units being produced.

1.4   The situation is easier in the case of items subject to independent demand. For example, the amount of oil required to maintain a manufacturing machine in working order does not depend on which products are being processed on that machine. It is possible to estimate that a particular amount of oil will be used each day, week or month, regardless of the exact detail of the production schedule.

1.5   As a further example, what items are bought out in a typical service organisation? This will depend on the exact nature of the organisation, but the following are likely answers. Notice that in all cases the items are characterised by independent demand; they are not related to the exact volume and nature of the service organisation's outputs. Clearly these purchases are not limited to service companies but they serve to illustrate the difference between dependent and independent demand.

- Office equipment and supplies such as stationery
- Computer hardware and software
- Motor vehicles
- Advertising and design services
- Maintenance services

1.6   The distinction between dependent and independent demand is important because some inventory control systems (such as materials requirements planning or MRP) take into account the peculiar difficulties of dependent demand, while other methods are more suited to independent demand items. Both methods require good inventory management as the optimum goal is to operate effectively carrying as little stock as possible.

Introducing materials requirements planning

1.7   Materials requirements planning (MRP) developed during the 1970s but is equally applicable today. It operates as an integrated information management, production planning and stock management system that has been enhanced in practicality in recent years as the speed and power of IT systems have increased.

1.8   MRP is also known as MRPI. This differentiates it from manufacturing resources planning (MRPII) which will be addressed later in the chapter.

1.9   MRP enables the advance planning of materials required for manufacture. The system utilises a bill of materials (BOM), in essence a breakdown of all the materials and components that go to make a finished product. The BOM serves to inform Procurement that goods must be ordered to meet an anticipated manufacturing date. Procurement will then order, taking into account suppliers' lead times and a 'safety margin' (it is not a just in time system but works to allow a practical margin for error, ie an agreed number of days in advance of production). The objective is to ensure that when production commences the goods are available as required and that inventory levels are minimised.

1.10   MRP is defined as 'a set of logically related procedures, decision rules, and records designed to translate a master production schedule (MPS) into time-phased 'net requirements', and the planned coverage of such requirements for each component inventory item needed to implement this schedule'. The elements of this definition are examined below.

- **A set of logically related procedures**: MRP systems follow a logical sequence that incorporates decision rules relating to existing stock held, forecasting etc.
- **Translate an MPS into time-phased 'net requirements'**: time-phased because not everything is required at the same time. If the manufacturing run is extending over six days it may not be until the final day that you require a particular component. By getting delivery later than when the run commenced inventory cost savings can be made. We refer to 'net requirements' because the MRP system takes into account that you may already hold some of the required items in stock and will reduce the ordered quantity accordingly.

- **The planned coverage of such requirements for each component inventory item needed to implement this schedule**: ensuring that each item required, taking into account suppliers' lead times, is ordered correctly.

Principles of MRP

1.11 An MRP system is a **dependent demand** system. For example, suppose you are making 5,000 square-framed prints. You require four pieces of wood cut to the same length and shape for each frame – a total of 20,000 pieces of wood. You require 5,000 pieces of glass to fit the frame, etc. The number of parts you require is dependent on the number of finished units to be produced.

1.12 The approach of materials requirements planning to dependent demand is to start from the end and work backwards. The first step is to estimate customer demand for a finished product, and then to calculate a production schedule to meet that demand. Customer demand will usually include orders received together with forecast estimates of additional customer demand.

1.13 Forecasting is important as it enables longer production runs to be undertaken, thereby gaining in reduced set-up time and economies of scale, where either future sales are predicted or where a justifiable case of manufacturing for stock has been accepted.

1.14 The main elements of the MRP process are shown in Figure 8.1.

Figure 8.1 *The main elements of an MRP system*

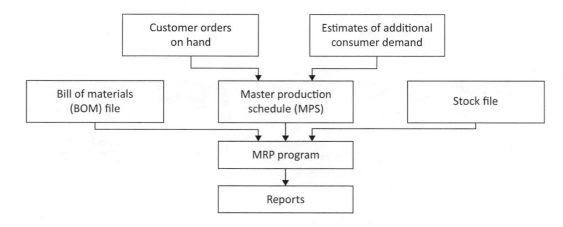

The master production schedule

1.15 Both forecast demand and actual orders on hand are combined in the MPS to decide the quantity to be produced. The role of the MPS is crucial in the MRP system. It provides the specification of the work to be progressed. Linking with the manufacturing availability in the capacity requirements plan (CRP) it brings together what is to be made, assembled or bought in within a specific timeframe.

1.16 The MPS enables us to plan the utilisation of both labour and equipment. In turn this identifies to the procurement department when delivery is required from suppliers to meet production run requirements.

1.17 The MPS is in effect a summary of customer demand. The MRP program acts on the MPS as follows.

- By reference to the BOM file the program translates details of finished products required into details of materials and components required.
- By reference to the stock file the program compares what is required with what is in stock.

1.18   The outputs from the program specify not just the amounts required in this process but also the time by which each is required. They also highlight the need for any special action, such as a possible need to reschedule or expedite orders.

1.19   Detailed outputs of the system will include any or all of the following.

- Order releases to Procurement for the current period, including the dates when required.
- Planned order releases to Procurement for future periods, based on current stocks, orders in progress, scheduled requirements and known lead times.
- Order releases for items to be produced in-house, with due dates for completion.
- Feedback on problems such as bottlenecks or lack of availability. This allows schedulers to make adjustments that can then be incorporated in a revised program run.

The bill of materials

1.20   The BOM is a list showing all the raw materials and components required to make a particular product. It specifies which parts go into which product and in what quantity. The structure of a typical BOM is shown in Figure 8.2.

Figure 8.2 *Structure of a bill of materials*

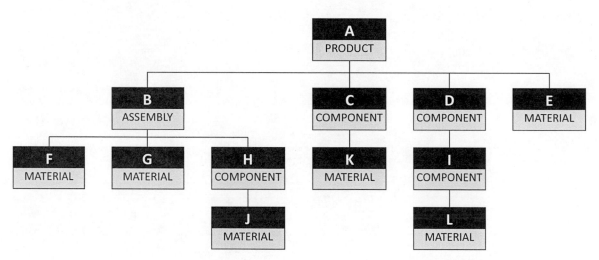

1.21   The diagram illustrates a bill of materials for Product A. Product A is made of Assembly B, Components C and D, and Material E. Assembly B is made from Materials F and G, and Component H (as well as other assemblies or products). This analysis is continued until it captures all of the materials, components etc that are used in manufacture of Product A.

1.22   A typical BOM will contain the following items of information.

- Quantity required. The quantity is one of the most important parts of the BOM because it tells us how many parts are needed for a product.
- Item identification number. This tells us which part to order. It can be a catalogue number, unique product code, or any other identification number.
- Description of item. This provides a check that the correct item is being ordered.
- Cost. This is included to show how much each part is per item and the total cost of all like parts.
- Total product cost

1.23   The BOM is a detailed breakdown of all the component parts that comprise the final product. For components this is usually in the form of part numbers or unique identifiers. The breakdown enables Procurement to place orders for the exact quantity required.

Inventory data

1.24 Accurate inventory records are a fundamental requirement of an MRP system. We need to know our 'net requirements'. For example, if we need 1,000 units of X, and we hold 300 units in stock, our 'net requirement' is 700 units.

1.25 It may be that for practical purposes we have decided to hold a minimum stock of 100 units. Our 'net requirement' would be 800 units, allowing for the agreed 'safety stock'.

1.26 MRP requires inventory records that describe:

- Each item of stock (part number, part description, supplier's lead time for supply). The information is held on the item master file and requires regular review particularly with regard to supplier lead times.
- Stock location, which is normally held on a location file following delivery. This will often form part of an integrated system covering storage and distribution in this instance.
- Transaction records relating to each stock item. This information is stored on a transaction file and may be linked to a procurement management system such as SAP or ORACLE.

Capacity requirements planning

1.27 The capacity requirements plan (CRP) estimates the workload of each department or machine in the plant. Its purpose is to anticipate problems in advance to ensure that short-term adjustments can be made in order to meet capacity requirements. The CRP can operate at monthly, fortnightly or daily levels (for example) and can feed back to the MPS to bring forward or delay orders as appropriate.

1.28 CRP will look initially at aggregate plans and seek to meet those needs in a manner consistent with operational protocols. On a shorter timeframe it will look at planned orders and schedule accordingly. Finally, it looks at released orders particularly with regard to short-term remedies and issues such as overtime or idle time to ensure production objectives can be met

1.29 The MPS controls both the MRP and the CRP with the objective of bringing all considerations together to maximise efficiency and effectiveness.

MRP and inventory control

1.30 The MRP program works by 'exploding' the BOM by reference to the production schedule. What this means is that for each finished product on the MPS, the program scrutinises the BOM file and calculates how much of each material will be needed in the manufacture of the required number of finished units. This process is repeated for each finished product.

1.31 The result of this calculation is the gross requirement for each material. This is translated into a net requirement by referring to the stock file for details of stock already on hand or on order. The net requirement is time-phased, ie the program determines when each material must be to hand and consequently when it must be ordered from a supplier or alternatively when internal production must commence.

1.32 This process of time-phasing is crucial to the inventory control process. By using the detailed calculations prepared by the program, buyers can delay ordering until the materials are really required. For example, a seven-day production run may not require a particular item until Day 6. This serves to cut down the amount of stock in the overall system.

1.33 In this respect MRP produces similar benefits to those arising under a just in time system. However MRP is not primarily aimed at eliminating stock and it is common in practice to find that a safety margin is

8

allowed. The safety margin accepts that delays and problems will occur (eg suppliers will deliver late, deliver faulty goods or suffer manufacturing problems of their own). This is not to say that these issues are accepted by the procurement department, who will always seek improvements from their suppliers, but is more practical in the sense that being unable to start a production run as scheduled will be very costly in both financial and customer service terms.

1.34   The safety margin will vary between organisations. The aim will always be to reduce it to the minimum acceptable time. MRP can be viewed as an inventory minimisation process rather than a just in time approach.

MRP calculations

1.35   MRP is a planning tool geared specifically to assembly operations. The aim is to allow each manufacturing unit to tell its supplier what parts it requires and when it requires them. The supplier may be the upstream process within the plant or an outside supplier. MRP was created to tackle the problem of 'dependent demand' – determining how many units of a particular component are required from knowledge of the number of finished products. Advances in computer technology made the calculation possible.

1.36   The process starts at the top level with a master production schedule (MPS). This is an amalgam of known demand, forecasts and product to be made for finished stock. The phasing of the demand may reflect the availability of the plant to respond. The remainder of the schedule is derived from the MPS.

1.37   Two key considerations in setting up the MPS are the size of time buckets and the planning horizons. A time bucket is the unit of time on which the schedule is constructed and is typically daily or weekly. The planning horizon is how far to plan forward, and is determined by how far ahead demand is known and by the lead times through the operation.

1.38   There are three distinct steps in preparing an MRP schedule.

- The first step is 'exploding' the bill of materials. As we have seen, this lists how many we need of each item forming part of the finished product.
- The next step is 'netting', in which any stock on hand is subtracted from the gross requirement determined through explosion, giving the quantity of each item needed to manufacture the required finished products.
- The final step is 'offsetting'. This determines when manufacturing should start so that the finished items are available when required. To do so a 'lead time' has to be assumed for the operation. This is the anticipated time for manufacturing.

1.39   Here is an example of how the MRP process works. We assume that the gross requirement (GR) for Product X in Week 4 is 270 units. The required safety stock (SS) for this item is 30 units. The stock currently on hand (OH) is 40 units. There are currently no orders due (OD) from suppliers.

1.40   The net requirement in Week 4 can be calculated as follows.

NR = GR – OH – OD + SS
NR = 270 – 40 – 0 + 30 = 260 units

1.41   We therefore need to place an order for 260 units with the appropriate supplier. When we place the order depends on the supplier's lead time. If we assume that this is one week, the order will need to be placed in Week 3 so that the net requirement becomes available when it is needed, in Week 4.

Benefits of MRP systems

1.42   The production of the MPS and the running of the MRP program lead to a detailed and timetabled approach to planning orders and production. The system is based on customer demand and software is increasingly capable of responding to changes in demand by producing revised schedules. The emphasis on end customers is in line with modern management thinking, which stresses that customer needs should shape action throughout the organisation.

1.43   MRP systems emphasise the importance of precise and accurate ordering and production policies, which if successfully followed will lead to reduced inventory levels. By focusing management attention on production schedules well in advance, MRP systems can give an early warning of potential problems in production or hold-ups in the supply chain.

1.44   The MRP system offers the following benefits.

- Provides accurate and timely information to procurement staff
- A scheduling tool in that it tells planners if due dates remain valid
- Anticipates shortages and/or slow moving stock
- Communicates priorities (what is wanted and in what sequence)
- Professional business discipline with the ability to build on and expand

1.45   An MRP system does not suit all organisations. It is a complex system to introduce and administer successfully. Once launched it may be difficult to make changes. While results are good in batch production and some assembly processes, the application elsewhere is less straightforward.

2   Manufacturing resource planning

2.1   The disciplined approach introduced by MRP has been further developed over the years. Manufacturing resources planning (MRPII) builds on key areas of MRP by considering all the resources needed for production, not just materials. For example, it deals with manpower, machinery and money.

2.2   The differences are made clear in their respective names. Materials requirements planning concentrates on securing the right materials to enable the production run to go ahead. Manufacturing resources planning examines the manufacturing resources required for the production to go ahead, eg the labour costs involved, the costs of machinery and proportion of overheads attributable etc. MRPII enables materials and work to be costed accurately.

2.3   MRPII is a method for planning manufacture and assessing the costs involved. It draws on the aggregate plans via the MPS not only to develop the areas covered by an MRP system but also to allow for such areas as personnel deployment, maintenance planning, and financial analysis.

2.4   Building on the discipline required for traditional MRP systems the MRPII model has led some to say that MRPII adds the financial function to MRP.

2.5   Managers can determine the dates when suppliers must be paid by studying MRP timing of purchase orders and their due dates. Accurate costing of manufacturing can be obtained as the system can look at machines and personnel used and analyse the information to provide accurate costings on production runs. The analysis can be further used as a benchmark for future production runs in order to seek operational improvements.

2.6   MRPII is often described as a closed-loop system, in that there is an automatic feedback from the manufacturing function to the MPS, leading to changes in the MPS. This in turn leads to adjustments in manufacturing plans, thus closing the information loop as illustrated in Figure 8.3.

Figure 8.3 *A closed-loop MRPII system*

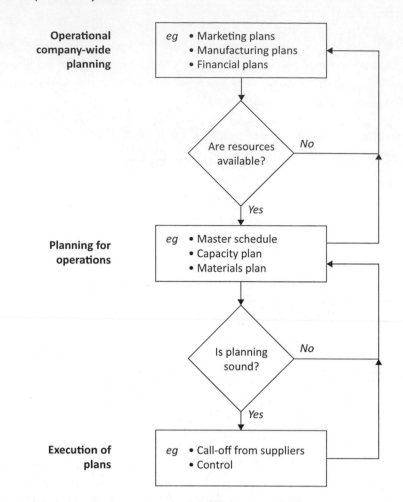

2.7 Closing the loop involves comparing production plans against the availability of resources. MRP makes the assumption that resources required are available. Closed loop MRPII checks whether the required resources are available. If this is not the case then the MPS is modified.

2.8 Oliver Wright has classified MRP/MRPII implementation and effectiveness under four headings. Starting with Class D status they have the ability to graduate to Class A status: Table 8.1.

Table 8.1 *Implementation and effectiveness of MRP/MRPII*

CLASS	CHARACTERISTICS
D	MRP working in data-processing department only Poor inventory records Master schedule mismanaged Reliance on shortage lists for progressing
C	Used for inventory ordering, not scheduling Scheduling by shortage lists Overloaded master schedule
B	System includes capacity planning, shop floor control Used to plan production, not to manage the business Help still required from shortage lists Inventory higher than necessary
A	Uses closed-loop MRP Integrated capacity planning, shop floor control and vendor scheduling Used to plan sales, engineering and procurement No shortage lists to override schedules

2.9 MRP and MRPII systems have proven themselves particularly in batch manufacture. Although they require ongoing investment in people and system development the rewards in increased professionalism as the system integrates into the organisation can be impressive.

2.10 Manufacturing on a larger scale brings a new range of issues that goes beyond the design of MRP and MRPII systems. Just in time (JIT) systems can utilise MRP and MRPII, but MRP shows to best advantage in batch production systems where the need is to schedule production around customer demand and supplier lead times.

3 Enterprise resource planning

Defining ERP

3.1 Enterprise resource planning (ERP) is the practice of consolidating an enterprise's planning, manufacturing, logistics, supply chain, sales and marketing efforts into one management system.

3.2 To integrate systems across an organisation is a tall order. Each department has its own system designed to meet its particular needs (known as 'legacy' systems). ERP combines them together to form a single, integrated software program that operates off a single database enabling the sharing of information and enhanced communication.

3.3 ERP systems are increasingly being used, at this stage primarily by multinational organisations, to integrate all aspects of the business into one unified database that interfaces across the entire organisation.

3.4 ERP helps the communication between all aspects of a business including human resources, financial accounting, manufacturing, supply chain management, logistics and sales.

3.5 ERP systems are a development of the MRP approach that enables an examination of the consequences that changes will bring. The same principle forms the basis of ERP systems but on a far wider scale.

3.6 ERP (despite the name) is not a planning system but is more about resources and enterprise. It can have a defined purpose (particularly with supply chain management and financial accounting where resources can be more finely monitored and discrepancies become more apparent), but its main purpose is about gaining competitive advantage for the enterprise as a whole.

The origins of ERP

3.7 ERP has its origins in MRP, which has been common in business practice from the 1970s onwards. The driver from MRP to ERP has been the application of information technology which served to make MRP an essential manufacturing business tool, in turn leading to the development of MRPII in the 1980s.

3.8 During this period computer power was developing rapidly. MRPII built on MRP by allowing forward modelling. In other words, 'what if?' scenarios could be developed, allowing for better planning and better responses if unplanned situations occurred.

3.9 A foundation stone of ERP systems was the theory of relational data management as originally designed by Edgar F Codd in 1969. This led to the development, in 1970, of the concept of a relational database at an IBM advanced research lab. According to relational database theories data is held in tables which are linked to each other through the use of key fields unique to each table, and used to identify each record in that table.

3.10 An example of this is a customer number that uniquely identifies that customer in every transaction. Using the customer number in a sales order, credit note, or other transaction eliminates the need to copy all of a customer's information (such as name, address, post code) to every transaction. This significantly reduces the amount of data stored in a database. As a result, this data structure has facilitated very fast and powerful reporting capabilities allowing companies to quickly and easily analyse historical data.

3.11   Relational databases were a huge advance in the field of data management and were a significant improvement over previous data storage techniques.

3.12   This concept unfolded from order inventory management of materials to plant and personnel planning and distribution planning, which in turn became MRPII. This incorporated financial accounting and human resource management functions, distribution management functions and management accounting functions and came to globally cover all areas of enterprise and eventually came to be called ERP.

The structure of a common ERP system

3.13   The essence of ERP is the fundamental approach which takes a wider, holistic view of the organisation. Traditional application systems treat each transaction separately. They are built around the strong boundaries of specific functions that a specific application is meant to cater for.

3.14   ERP, however, considers all transactions to be the part of the interlinked processes that make up the total business and financial impact. Almost all the typical application systems are nothing but the data manipulation tools. They store data, process them, and present them in the appropriate form whenever requested by the user. In this process, the only problem is that there is no link between the application systems being used by different departments.

3.15   An ERP system does the same thing, but the transactions are not confined within any departmental or functional boundaries. These are rather integrated for the speedy and accurate results required by multiple users, for multiple purposes, for multiple sites, and at multiple times.

3.16   An ERP solution is designed so that it exhibits the following features.

- **Flexible.** An ERP system should be flexible to respond to the changing needs of an enterprise.
- **Modular.** The ERP system has to have modular application architecture. This means that various functionalities are logically clubbed into different business processes and structured into a module which can be interfaced or detached whenever required without affecting the other modules. It should support multiple hardware platforms for companies running a heterogeneous collection of systems. It must support some third party add-ons also.
- **Comprehensive.** It should be able to support a variety of organisational functions and must be suitable for a wide range of business organisations.
- **Beyond the company.** It should not be confined to the organisational boundaries; rather, it should support online connectivity to the other business entities within the overall organisation. This feature is referred to as **web-enabled ERP.**

3.17   ERP architecture must be designed using advanced information technologies and environments. Thus, ERP is typically implemented through a client-server environment. This technology divides the applications fundamentally into two or more components, called server and clients. The client portion uses the functions of the server. Servers are centralised while clients tend to be spread out in multiple locations.

Implementing ERP

3.18   When implementing ERP, an organisation must go through a careful period of strategic planning that will involve a strong and ongoing commitment from senior management. Implementation will take from three months to two years and will prove a costly operation. Existing systems (legacy systems) must be integrated into the new software, and packages and features required from the new system will require development.

3.19   ERP systems provide a generic business model for an organisation to follow. This may cause problems, as most businesses will not fit neatly into this model. It may prove necessary to reconfigure or re-engineer aspects of the business. Software can be customised to meet requirements but at a price.

3.20   Many companies have successfully integrated ERP software systems. Others have not been as successful. Hershey Foods issued two profit warnings in the run-up to Christmas 2004 as huge distribution problems followed a flawed implementation. In November 1999, domestic appliance manufacturer Whirlpool also blamed shipping delays on ERP implementation problems.

3.21   Clearly the strategic considerations and possible implementation pitfalls of ERP systems require detailed thought. Here are some relevant considerations.

- Who are our stakeholders?
- Which processes are most important now and why?
- Does the system meet our needs or go beyond them?
- Do we integrate over stages and if we do what sequence should we use?
- Who will be responsible for change management?
- Who will be our change champions?
- What is our business culture and what are its strengths?
- How can we maximise those strengths?
- What are our weak areas and how will we address issues caused by them?
- What will be the toughest changes and how will we address them?

Web integrated and supply chain integrated ERP systems

3.22   The problem of integrating ERP applications is as old as ERP itself. Not long after ERP originated in the early 1990s companies struggled to improve the level of integration between their ERP packages and other applications such as legacy systems and e-commerce sites.

3.23   To deal with the problem, developers have several options for integrating legacy systems, e-commerce, customer relationship management, and other applications with ERP suites. Each integration approach, naturally, comes with its own challenges, and each has limitations.

3.24   Developers can use off-the-shelf data-sharing products such as middleware, EAI tools (enterprise application integration) and ERP connectors. Alternatively, they might opt to develop their own home developed connector components or use the application programming interfaces (APIs) shipped with the ERP systems themselves. But, as you might expect, each method is not suitable for all integration projects.

3.25   Having said that we have entered a new phase in ERP development as many of the integration problems are increasingly resolved. In the era of closer, collaborative relationships, web integrated and supply chain integrated ERP systems are becoming an effective and practical tool for business.

3.26   Web integrated and supply chain integrated ERP systems have also paved the way for what has become known as **collaborative commerce**. This refers to online business-to-business interaction between two or more parties, focused on the exchange of knowledge and the mutual interconnection of business processes in order to optimise value creation. It enables online collaboration and interactions among the employees, business partners, and customers of diverse firms belonging to a trading community or industry segment

3.27   Collaborative commerce enables retailers, suppliers, and distributors to share information with one another in a standard business language, benefiting all members of the supply chain. This initiative includes the processes, technologies, and supporting standards that allow continuous and automated communication of electronic information between trading partners.

Chapter summary

- An item is subject to dependent demand if its demand depends on the demand for a larger product of which it forms part.
- Independent demand items are goods that are required for an operation in quantities independent of those used in the production process. There are very few independent demands in supply chains.
- The MRP program works by 'exploding' the BOM by reference to the production schedule
- MRP systems emphasise the importance of precise and accurate ordering and production policies, which if successfully followed will lead to reduced inventory levels.
- Manufacturing resources planning (MRPII) builds on key areas of MRP by considering all the resources needed for production, not just materials.
- MRPII is often described as a closed-loop system, in that there is an automatic feedback from the manufacturing function to the MPS, leading to changes in the MPS.
- Enterprise resource planning (ERP) is the practice of consolidating an enterprise's planning, manufacturing, logistics, supply chain, sales and marketing efforts into one management system.

Self-test questions

Numbers in brackets refer to the paragraphs above where your answers can be checked.

1   What is the distinction between dependent and independent demand? (1.3, 1.4)

2   An MRP system is a system for controlling stocks of independent demand items. True or false? (1.11)

3   How does the MRP program act on the MPS? (1.17)

4   List benefits of an MRP system. (1.44)

5   Distinguish between MRP and MRPII. (2.2)

6   Sketch a closed-loop MRPII system. (Figure 8.3)

7   Define ERP. (3.1)

8   List key features of an effective ERP system. (3.16)

CHAPTER 9

Improving Performance

Assessment criteria and indicative content

4.1 Analyse the main tools for improving performance in operations management

- The use of performance measurement in operations management
- Setting performance targets
- Benchmarking in improving operations management
- Building continuous improvement
- The use of business process re-engineering

Section headings

1 Performance measurement
2 Benchmarking
3 Continuous improvement
4 Business process re-engineering

1 Performance measurement

1.1 Measuring the performance of an operation is a fundamental part of business management. By putting effective performance measures in place an organisation can quantifiably assess how well they are doing overall or in specific areas. The application of performance measures can identify if and where improvements are necessary, if specific goals are being met and if customers are being satisfied.

1.2 Performance measures quantitatively demonstrate something about an organisation's products, services and the processes that produce them. Performance measurement can be defined as the process of quantifying the efficiency and effectiveness of an action.

1.3 To accurately assess how well a business or operation is performing, quantifiable measures must be developed. Those measures should clearly identify the aspects of processes that need improvement and those that are working well. Performance measures also assist in the evaluation of organisational and operational productivity over a period of time.

1.4 The significance of performance measurement is that it allows operations managers to compare performance with the stated requirements. Established performance objectives quantify to operations managers what is expected of them in order to meet customer expectations.

1.5 Each of the performance objectives (quality, speed, dependability, flexibility and cost) can be measured. These performance objectives can be broken down further. For example, in relation to quality we can look at the number of defects per I,000 items produced, the level of customer complaints, the amount of scrap etc. The role for operations managers is to identify those broad performance objectives which are important and then use specific performance measures or key performance indicators (KPIs) as targets to measure results against.

1.6 The five performance objectives are made up of many smaller measures which will vary in importance from company to company and from time to time. Slack *et al* give typical partial measures of performance: see Table 9.1.

Table 9.1 *Performance objectives and measures*

PERFORMANCE OBJECTIVE	SOME TYPICAL MEASURES
Quality	Number of defects per unit Level of customer complaints Scrap level Warranty claims Mean time between failures Customer satisfaction score
Speed	Customer query time Order lead time Frequency of delivery Actual versus theoretical throughput time Cycle time
Dependability	Percentage of orders delivered late Average lateness of order Proportion of products in stock Mean deviation from promised arrival Schedule adherence
Flexibility	Time needed to develop new products or services Range of products and services Machine changeover time Average batch size Time to increase activity rate Average capacity and maximum capacity Time to change schedules
Cost	Minimum delivery time and average delivery time Variance against budget Utilisation of resources Labour productivity Added value Efficiency Cost per operation hour

1.7 As the table demonstrates, the five performance objectives can be broken down into many smaller parts. Equally you can argue that each performance objective is a combination of a number of composite elements that together form the overall performance measure. The skill for operations is in deciding the right combination of performance measures that together achieve the performance objective in a manner that provides meaningful results for the organisation.

1.8 Performance measurement cannot be carried out in isolation. It is only relevant within a reference framework against which the efficiency and effectiveness of an action can be judged. Choosing the right performance measures is clearly an important consideration. A wide range of factors outside of operations come into consideration – such as the organisational strategy, competitors' actions, technological advances – which all impact on the measures appropriate to operations.

1.9 Performance measurement is not carried out against a static background. Customers' needs, wants and expectations are constantly changing. It is no good to have the quickest delivery from order time (speed) if the customers want a range of finishes (flexibility).

The balanced scorecard approach

1.10 The balanced scorecard model was developed in 1990 by *Kaplan and Norton*. They argued that financial objectives and measures are insufficient to control organisations effectively. Organisations need other parameters and perspectives, in order to avoid the problem of 'short-termism', which arises when managers are judged by criteria which do not measure the long-term, complex effects of their decisions.

1.11 *Karlof & Lovingsson* suggest that: 'Few can withstand the simple and obvious logic underlying balanced scorecard: namely, that there are factors other than the financial which are important to control and follow up and that it can be a good idea to establish which factors these in fact are.'

1.12 Kaplan and Norton proposed four key perspectives for a balanced scorecard (sometimes called a balanced business scorecard or BBS).

- Financial – how do we create value for our shareholders?
- Customers – what do they value?
- Internal business processes – what is our internal CSF process? (CSF = critical success factors)
- Innovation and organisational learning – what new products and services do our customers need?

1.13 Other management thinkers have proposed different categories, around the same basic themes: internal perspectives (processes, efficiency, employees and co-workers, innovation and learning, organisation, products, environment and quality); external perspectives (customers, stakeholders, business environment, suppliers, community); and profit or performance perspectives (finance, economy, owners or shareholders, profit). The scorecard has been designed to balance decision-making by focusing on the interrelationship between the differing competitive pressures facing the organisation and stimulating continuous improvement.

1.14 The 'balance' of the balanced scorecard is thus between: financial and non-financial performance measures; short-term and long-term perspectives; and internal and external focus.

1.15 Working with a balanced scorecard requires describing, for each 'perspective' selected:

- The organisation's long-term goals
- The success factors established to achieve those goals
- The key activities which must be carried out to achieve those success factors
- The key performance indicators which can be used to monitor progress

1.16 According to Kaplan and Norton's model, managers' performance should be evaluated on a range of financial and non-financial key performance indicators (KPIs): Figure 9.1.

Figure 9.1 *The balanced scorecard*

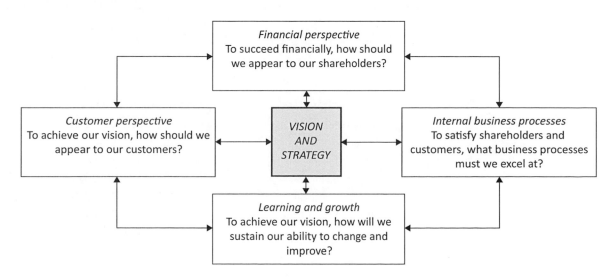

Setting performance targets

1.17   Measuring performance does not, in itself, indicate what should be done. Taking quality as an example: is a 94% satisfaction rate good or bad? At first sight it may look good but how is it being judged? What rate are other firms in the same business areas achieving, how does the satisfaction rate look when we compare it to previous years' figures, how does it compare to the target figure? Performance depends on what you are comparing against.

1.18   There are a number of approaches that can be used when setting targets.

- Historically-based targets – we compare current measures with those that we achieved in the past
- Strategic targets – we set targets to reflect how the operation is doing against stated strategic aims and objectives
- Externally performance-based targets – we set targets to match or exceed the performance level achieved by a competitor, external operations or recognised performance standards within the industry (refer to benchmarking later in this chapter).
- Absolute performance targets based on the theoretical upper level of performance

1.19   The results obtained from performance measurement must be considered and, if necessary, refined over time in order to get meaningful results.

Performance judgement

1.20   Performance measurement has an impact on the environment in which it operates. Starting to measure, deciding what to measure, how to measure and what the targets will be, are all acts that influence individuals and groups within the organisation. Once measurement has started, the performance review will have consequences, as will the actions agreed upon as a result of that review. Performance measurement becomes an integral part of the management planning and control system of the organisation or operation being measured.

1.21   By setting performance targets we move from performance measurement to performance judgement. For that reason it is crucial that the comparators are accurate and that they are meaningful to the particular organisation. Judgement will be made using the hard data from performance measurement but will also consider soft data: the internal and external factors and considerations that influence the business. Hard figures are effective as comparators but judgements have to be made about their meaning and how best to interpret the results.

1.22   Performance management needs to ensure co-ordination and coherence between all levels of performance measurement in order that overall the organisation is better equipped to meet its strategic objectives.

2   Benchmarking

What is benchmarking?

2.1   Benchmarking is a business discipline that has been utilised over many years. It has gained widening appeal as technology has enabled comparable measures to be used, contrasted and evaluated within tight time-frames and with greater accuracy.

2.2   A dictionary definition demonstrates the basic concept of benchmarking: *'A standard point of reference against which things can be assessed.'* This suggests using an acceptable reference point to assess against. In storage and distribution this reference point could be deliveries on time, warehouse space allocated or order fill, as examples.

2.3 A further definition serves to demonstrate that benchmarking can have a significant role in improving supply chain and logistics performance by identifying and learning from best practice in other organisations: *'The continuous process of measuring products, services, and practices, against the toughest competitors or those companies recognised as industry leaders.'* (Rank Xerox)

2.4 Other definitions of benchmarking illustrate the importance of benchmarking in a competitive world.

- 'The process of identifying, understanding and adapting practices from anywhere in the world to help your organisation improve its performance.'
- 'Knowing the standards expected by your customers of yourself and competitors, and (a) measuring yourself against those standards on a regular basis and (b) setting management systems in place to improve against those benchmarks.'

2.5 Benchmarking is about comparing your organisation with others to identify areas for improvement and putting in place systems and procedures to ensure effective delivery.

A historical perspective

2.6 During the 1980s Rank Xerox found that its dominant position in the photocopier market was increasingly under threat from Japanese companies. Rank Xerox responded by developing and using benchmarking to identify areas of weakness and opportunities for improvement.

2.7 Rank Xerox developed a five-phase approach to benchmarking that suited its needs: Table 9.2.

Table 9.2 *Rank Xerox's five phases of benchmarking*

Planning	Identify benchmark outputs Identify best competitor Determine data collection method
Analysis	Determine current competitive gap Project future performance levels
Integration	Establish functional goals Develop functional action plans
Action	Implement specific actions Monitor results and report progress Recalibrate benchmarks
Maturity	Leadership position obtained Processes fully integrated in our practices

2.8 Rank Xerox developed benchmarking by incorporating it into a total quality strategy ('Leadership Through Strategy') that converted benchmarking into a process of continuous improvement. This represented a long-term commitment to benchmarking supported at strategic level.

2.9 Many organisations will not become as committed to benchmarking as Rank Xerox and may use it at a tactical level without the perceived need to integrate benchmarking fully into the organisation. However individual organisations use benchmarking it represents a powerful tool for continuous improvement and performance breakthroughs.

Interfirm comparison

2.10 'Benchmarking' as an improvement tool started in the UK in the 1960s as 'interfirm comparison'. Burman Associates for some years ran interfirm comparisons for several company groupings to compare various aspects of their respective distribution efficiencies. The many ratios compared showed each firm where attention was needed in its distribution structure and management. As this centered around one business area, comparison of like with like could be immediately relevant.

2.11 Benchmarking is not necessarily a comparison between enterprises operating in the same business area but whatever benchmarking data and information is used it needs to be applicable to the benchmarking exercise being undertaken. Benchmarking can be most useful if it can be arranged between non-competitors, that is, enterprises that address different markets from their fellow benchmarking companies. This, of course, heightens the problem of comparing like with like. Delivering milk, for instance, is not the same as delivering personal computers.

How to benchmark a function or process

2.12 Three types of benchmarking can be distinguished: internal benchmarking, competitive benchmarking and functional benchmarking.

2.13 *Internal benchmarking* means identifying best practice within a single organisation and sharing it. This type of benchmarking exercise will involve a structured approach using cross-functional and/or cross-site teams and developing measurement criteria of similar functions within an organisation such as warehousing or distribution with the aim of ensuring that the best practice within the company can be shared and realistic targets set to bring other internal areas in line with identified best practice.

2.14 *Competitive benchmarking* means comparing an organisation's performance with that of a similar competitor. Reliability and the direct comparability of data can often be a problem. Many organisations will keep data and information in house for competitive reasons; others make data and information readily available. Specialist organisations collect and collate data for comparison purposes or can carry out tailored research in specific business areas.

2.15 *Functional* (or *generic*) *benchmarking* compares specific industry functions such as storage and distribution. This area is possibly more advanced in using and applying benchmarking data than many others. Third-party logistic and delivery companies often benchmark their processes against others in their class as a means of ensuring continuous improvement and gaining a competitive edge that can be demonstrated to clients. Within this and other business areas are a number of 'clubs' where exchange of data and information is managed on a mutually reciprocal basis.

Benchmarking in practice

2.16 Benchmarking is as its most effective when looking at processes such as deliveries, downtime, idle time, and so on. The process triangle has been developed as a tool to help managers differentiate the type and importance of the various processes that may impact on customer service. The process triangle examines the three different bases for process requirement, and then uses these to highlight development areas.

- *Basic processes:* looks at processes such as receiving, administration and effective storage that underpin the service delivery.
- *Benchmark processes:* examines those processes that are important in delivering the required level of customer service and in consequence must be of a high standard.
- *Competitive processes:* examines those areas that may serve to give a competitive advantage and help differentiate the organisation against its competitive market.

2.17 An assessment of these interlinked areas will evidence gaps where improvements can be made to efficiency, processes and customer service. Benchmarks that might be applicable to customer service could include:

- Correct and on-time delivery
- Speed of response
- Correct invoicing

2.18 Martin Christopher proposed that when undertaking a benchmarking exercise organisations should start by asking themselves three basic questions.

- How relevant are our standards?
- How do we justify the way we do things?
- How competitive are we?

2.19   We need to consider a range of factors: see Table 9.3.

Table 9.3 *Preparing to benchmark*

Be well organised – prepare thoroughly.
Determine what the customers really want.
Undergo an appropriate self-analysis.
Set and understand priorities. It is impossible to measure every dimension of the operation. Aim for 'best in class'.
Identify companies for comparison. Aim for an organisation comparable in scale and aim for an organisation that is a recognised leader in the particular area you are looking to benchmark against.
Realistically assess the competition.
Identify best practice.
Understand the aims and objectives of the exercise.
Learn from related and other business sectors.
Introduce relevant best practice.
Provide a means to continuous improvement.
Select the appropriate measures.
Select benchmarking partners.
Structured approach determines information needs, where it can be found, deciding how to gather the information, collecting, collating and analysing the information.
Identify the resources and processes that will influence the outcome.
Establish benchmarking teams.
Enable cross-functional working.
Highlight process areas that you feel require priority.
Provide research feedback in a useful format.
Adapt to the results of the benchmarking exercise. Put in place new or modified processes, set targets, plan and implement change.
Measure the results. Measurement for its own sake achieves nothing. The outcome should be continuous improvement.

2.20   To quote Martin Christopher: 'By undertaking a benchmarking exercise the company is embarking on a journey that will fundamentally change the way it sees itself. Such companies can never stand still. For them the phrase 'continuous improvement' is not just a cliché, but a way of life'. Benchmarking can lead to the elimination of a practice or process or the redesign of the entire supply chain. Once benchmarking has been implemented and has proven itself successful it will become an integral part of the organisation's operating process.

Ethics of benchmarking

2.21   Modern benchmarking has its main roots in Japan and measures an organisation's operations, products and services against those of its competitors in a ruthless fashion. It serves as a means by which targets, priorities and operations that will lead to competitive advantage can be established.

2.22   According to John S Oakland in *Total Quality Management* the concept of benchmarking is based on the ancient Japanese quotation: "If you know your enemy and know yourself, you need not fear the result of a hundred battles". (Sun Tzu, *The Art of War, 500BC*). In Japanese the word *dantotsu* (or benchmarking) means striving for the best of the best.

2.23   Some business sectors such as warehousing and distribution readily release information enabling organisations to benchmark against each other. Most do not. Information is gained through benchmarking clubs or via specialist agencies who examine financial information, press reports and releases, annual accounts and other relevant sources and interpret that information in such a way as to provide their clients with comparable benchmarking information.

Benefits of benchmarking

2.24   Benchmarking brings a range of benefits and, if developed as an integrated process, becomes a tool for continuous improvement. Benefits quoted by the Public Sector Benchmarking Service include the following.

- Learning from others who have enjoyed success and greater confidence in developing and delivering new approaches
- Greater involvement and motivation of staff engaged in benchmarking and change programmes
- Heightened awareness about performance levels
- Increased willingness to share solutions to common problems
- Wider understanding of the strategic implications
- Increased collaboration and enhanced working relationships

2.25   Benchmarking aids an organisation in its understanding of competitors and the methods by which they operate. They bring successful ideas from proven practice that can be adapted or built upon. With benchmarking more options become available as different approaches are introduced and these can help lead to superior performance over time.

2.26   Benchmarking is a pro-active approach that establishes credible goals and objectives enabling a considered understanding of real problems and issues supported by proven business responses.

Limitations of benchmarking

2.27   Benchmarking is complex and time-consuming to instigate properly. To succeed requires a high level of consistent commitment over the long term. Clear systems and procedures need to be put in place and followed.

2.28   Toyota freely give benchmarking information to their competitors each year. This enables their competitors to bring their systems up to the standard of Toyota. Toyota are then forced to improve over the following year. By the time their competitors catch up they are a year ahead. Benchmarking is copying and adapting what other organisations have successfully achieved. Its limitation is that it can stifle creativity and original thought. You follow – you don't lead.

3   Continuous improvement

3.1   Continuous improvement is a quality philosophy in modern business. For the operations manager, no matter how effective and efficient the processes, they are still capable of improvement. Continuous improvement has its roots in the work of Deming and Juran in Japan after the Second World War (as we will discuss further later in the text). However the approach to continue to make improvements, in a structured and measurable way, has become embedded in business today.

3.2   The term relates to a number of incremental steps that occur over time to improve a process. The philosophy is about the ongoing nature of the improvement rather than about speed or consistency of any gains. Continuous improvement is also known by the Japanese term *kaizen*.

3.3   Continuous improvement is a type of change that is focused on increasing the effectiveness and/ or efficiency of an organisation to fulfil its policy and objectives. It is not limited to quality initiatives. Improvement in business strategy, business results, customers, employees and supplier relationships can be subject to continuous improvement.

3.4 Continuous improvement is fundamental to operations irrespective of whether it is in the manufacturing or service sector. Improvements can reduce costs, improve quality, and motivate managers and employees as well as providing a better product or service to customers.

3.5 It is possible to identify ten steps in the process of continuous improvement.

- Determine current performance
- Establish a need to improve
- Obtain commitment and define the improvement objective
- Organise the diagnostic resources
- Carry out research and analysis to discover the cause of current performance
- Define and test solutions that will accomplish the improvement objective
- Produce improvement plans which specify how and by whom the changes will be implemented
- Identify and overcome any resistance to the change
- Implement the change
- Put in place controls to hold new levels of performance and begin all over

3.6 Improvement is not about using a set of tools and techniques. Improvement is not going through the motions of organising improvement teams and training people. Improvement is a result, so it can only be claimed after there has been a beneficial change in an organisation's performance.

3.7 The focus and role of operations has changed over recent years. Not too long ago the business emphasis was placed on planning and control, with operations managers concerning themselves with day-to-day, week-to-week activities. Activities such as design, including process design, layout and quality were controlled by specialists who worked with operations management.

3.8 The advance of technology and the development of a more integrated approach to business have combined to enhance the role of operations to a more inclusive role where operations managers now have a wider remit.

Improvement cycles

3.9 W Edwards Deming introduced what has become known as the **Deming cycle** – Plan-Do-Check-Act (PDCA) – to Japanese manufacturing following the Second World War. The improvement cycle demonstrates a never ending cycle of questioning and re-questioning of operations and processes with the objectives of improving on previous performance.

3.10 This improvement cycle commences with **planning** an operation or examining the current method or identified problem area. **Doing** is the implementation stage, carrying out the operation. **Checking** is the collection, analysing and evaluation of data in order to see whether the anticipated results or improvement gains have been made. The final stage is **acting** on the results, incorporating them into new processes if the plan has been successful or, if the production run or trial run has not been successful, developing a new plan before commencing the cycle again.

3.11 A development on the Deming cycle is the DMAIC cycle (Define – Measure – Analyse – Improve – Control). This begins by **defining** the issues or problems in order both to understand what needs to be done and to define the exact requirements of the intended process improvement. Following definition is the **measurement** stage which involves validating the issue or problem to ensure it is actually a problem worth solving. Once the measurements of the process or operation have been taken, they can be analysed.

3.12   The **analysis** stage enables operations to look at the root cause of the problem and possibly develop hypotheses as to how to **improve** the issue or problem. In this respect it can be seen that the DMAIC cycle is more exploratory and experimental than the PDCA Cycle.

3.13   Following analysis and development of a workable solution the improved process needs to be implemented, monitored and **controlled** to ensure the expected level of gain is as anticipated. Following the outcomes the cycle commences again. The DMAIC cycle is in common use in the Six Sigma approach to quality management which will be discussed further in a later chapter.

3.14   Every system, process or project should have provision for an improvement cycle. Therefore when an objective has been achieved, work should commence on identifying better ways of doing it. There is no improvement without measurement. An organisation must establish current performance before embarking on any improvement. If it does not, it will have no baseline from which to determine whether its efforts have yielded any improvement.

4   Business process re-engineering

Definition of business process re-engineering (BPR)

4.1   BPR is another stage in the evolution of quality thinking. It is not totally new: often it involves taking a new look at a number of established ideas and concepts such as JIT, work study, agile manufacturing and supply chain management.

4.2   BPR has been defined by Michael Hammer and James Champy.

'The fundamental rethinking and radical redesign of business processes to achieve dramatic improvements in critical, contemporary measures of performance such as cost, service and speed.'

4.3   Hammer and Champy put forward views on the radical redesign of an organisation's processes. Rather than considering the organisation in its traditional functional divisions (procurement, production, marketing etc) we should look at complete processes from materials acquisition through production through to distribution and on to the customer. The organisation should be engineered as a series of processes, each of which may cross functional boundaries.

4.4   Hammer and Champy argued that it is more efficient to put forward a team who have responsibility for all the tasks in the process. Later, they extended this idea to include suppliers, distributors and business partners.

4.5   BPR contrasts with the gradual improvements over time of total quality management and puts forward a more radical, innovative approach. BPR is applied to selected initiatives that are designed to achieve radically redesigned and improved work processes within a given time frame.

4.6   The quality tools and methods already discussed remain relevant in this changing setting. The emphasis shifts from one of management control to one of empowerment, commitment and trust.

4.7   Hammer and Champy propound IT as the principal enabler of 'radical change'. The business power of IT can be harnessed in other ways than as an extension of existing business organisations. IT should be used as an automating or mechanising force fundamentally reshaping the way business is perceived.

4.8   They argue that the current rules of work design are based on assumptions regarding technology, people and organisational goals that are no longer valid. They put forward the following 'principles of re-engineering'.

- Organise around outcomes, not tasks. This gives one person the role to perform all the steps in a process. This in turn provides job enlargement and increased job satisfaction.
- Have those who use the output of the processes perform the processes. An example might be employees buying their own equipment (within guidelines) without going through the procurement department.
- Integrate information processing work into the real work that produces the information. Those who collect information should have responsibility for progressing it (eg statistical information through to final report or invoice through to payment).
- Treat geographically dispersed resources on a centralised basis. Refer back to ERP systems. Technology is increasingly making this approach workable.
- Link parallel activities instead of integrating their results. The use of cross-functional teams, simultaneous engineering and early supplier involvement are examples of integrating activities.
- Place the decision point where the work is performed and build control into the process. Educate the workforce and allow IT supported decision making to the more empowered workers.
- Gather information once and at the source. Avoid the mistakes of inaccuracy of data capture from the outset.

4.9 BPR is essentially to do with fundamental change. One aspect is that of the 'clean slate' – do away with what existed before and start again. Walter compared this to running an old car. You can work on it to keep it going. The BPR approach is to get a new car.

4.10 Michael Hammer has said 'Don't automate, obliterate!' However, the clean slate approach is rarely found in practice. A more practical approach is to adopt clean slate thinking at the commencement of a new product or service.

4.11 The view given by Hammer and Champy is that re-engineering is driven by open markets and competition. The protectionism that existed in the past no longer applies today and organisations find themselves in a highly competitive and demanding global economy.

4.12 Management has been based on fragmentation and specialisation with repetitive jobs within a business structure based around departments, functions and strategic business units. Hammer and Champy put forward the view that in the future there will be fewer layers of management but more highly skilled workers who will be involved in more complex tasks.

Implementing BPR

4.13 Davenport and Short give a five-stage approach to the implementation of BPR.

- *Develop the business vision and process objectives.* BPR is driven by a vision that states specific objectives such as cost reduction, time reduction, quality improvement etc.
- *Identify the processes to be redesigned.* Two approaches seem to have developed: the high impact approach and the exhaustive approach. High impact means that focus is placed on those processes identified as the most important or those that conflict with the business vision. The exhaustive approach attempts to identify all processes and then set priorities for redesign.
- *Understand and measure the existing processes.* These will provide a measure against which to gauge improvements and help avoid the mistakes of the past.
- *Identify the contribution of IT.* An awareness of IT and its present and evolving capabilities can and should influence process design.
- *Design and build a prototype of the new process.* The actual design is evolving but the focus will usually be on quick delivery of results and customer involvement and satisfaction.

4.14 BPR must have top-level management support to succeed. It is a radical approach and one that causes concern at all levels of the organisation. Change management, in the accepted sense of identifying leaders or champions, keeping stakeholders informed and phasing change, may not always be fully appropriate with BPR.

4.15   Owing to the radical nature of BPR, if resistance is encountered the champion must be prepared to enforce change, even to the point of ruthlessness.

4.16   Clearly after change has been achieved the role of people is paramount. They are expected to be better and able to handle more complex tasks. This will not be achieved without focused and appropriate ongoing training.

Reasons for BPR failure

4.17   BPR has gained a poor reputation over the years. One of the main drivers, particularly in the early years (1990 on), was a focus on cost reduction. This tarnished BPR with a link to high levels of job reductions that it has yet to recover from.

4.18   This reputation was further hurt as many BPR initiatives were poorly run or poorly understood using inappropriate methodology or approaches.

4.19   Failure rates for BPR projects are put as high as 70 per cent. The reasons are understandable: poor top management understanding and support, unrealistic expectations and resistance to change. Bashein outlines the positive preconditions for success, and some of the reasons for failure: Table 9.4.

Table 9.4 *BPR: preconditions for success and reasons for failure*

PRECONDITIONS FOR SUCCESS OF BPR	REASONS FOR FAILURE OF BPR
Senior management support	The wrong sponsor
Realistic expectations	Cost-cutting focus
Empowered and collaborative workers	Narrow, technical focus
Strategic context of growth and expansion	Unsound financial condition of the organisation
Shared vision	Too many projects underway
Sound management practices	Fear and lack of optimism
Appropriate people participating full-time	
Sufficient budget	

The benefits of BPR

4.20   Rohm, in his review of BPR at the Principal Financial Group Inc, gives an example of the impact of BPR on its field support transaction (called 'licensing and contracting'). The impact on processes was significant.

'Under the old system, this was a 16-step process requiring input from nine people stationed in different areas and on different floors of the home office. The new structure enabled this process to be cut to six steps, requiring the work of only three people.'

4.21   As a result, customers were provided with a single contact person who could execute and manage the whole process.

4.22   Rohm has subsequently summarised the benefits of BPR.

- *Revolutionary thinking* – organisations need to abandon conventional thinking and make a paradigm shift to the new way of thinking.
- *Breakthrough improvement* – BPR helps organisations take a more radical approach to quality, seeking big gains rather than on a more continuous basis.
- *Organisational structure* – a genuine focus on identifying customer needs with a structure built to do just that.

- *Corporate culture* – reducing management while at the same time genuinely empowering workers.
- *Job redesign* – more rewarding and satisfying jobs where workers are involved in the entire process.

4.23 BPR has been largely concentrated in the US to date. However, the thinking and the commercial reality of doing business in today's commercial environment combine to develop new ways of looking and doing things. We have seen established production methods evolving, we have seen the service sector becoming more dominant but still without an established modern management approach. Operations management continues to be at the heart of these changes.

9

> ## Chapter summary
>
> - Performance measurement is an essential part of performance improvement. Increasingly, organisations attempt to measure performance across a number of dimensions, perhaps using a balanced scorecard approach.
> - Benchmarking is widely used as a technique for performance improvement. The idea is to measure current performance against a 'best in class' standard so as to identify where improvements can be made.
> - Continuous improvement is an incremental approach. It may be pursued systematically by means of the Deming PDCA cycle.
> - By contrast, business process re-engineering aims at radical, transformational change. The aim is to structure a business around its core processes, which will often stretch across functional boundaries.

Self-test questions

Numbers in brackets refer to the paragraphs above where your answers can be checked.

1   Give some typical performance objectives and list typical measures that can be applied to each. (Table 9.1)

2   What are the four perspectives in Kaplan and Norton's balanced scorecard? (1.12)

3   List possible approaches that can be taken in setting performance targets. (1.18)

4   Define benchmarking. (2.2–2.4)

5   Distinguish between internal, competitive and functional benchmarking. (2.13–2.15)

6   List benefits of benchmarking. (2.24)

7   List ten steps in systematic process of continuous improvement. (3.5)

8   Explain the steps in the PDCA cycle. (3.10)

9   List five stages in an approach to implementing BPR. (4.13)

10   List benefits of BPR. (4.22)

CHAPTER 10

Failure Prevention and Recovery

Assessment criteria and indicative content

4.2 Explain the main techniques in failure prevention and recovery that can be applied in operations management

- Measuring failure and the impact of failure
- Mechanisms to detect failure
- Failure mode and effect analysis
- Improving process reliability
- Maintenance and approaches to maintenance
- Failure distributions
- Business continuity

Section headings

1. Detecting and preventing failure
2. Improving process reliability
3. Asset maintenance and replacement
4. Business continuity

1 Detecting and preventing failure

The definition and causes of failure

1.1 Quality is inherent in any product or service. It is, however, subject to change with the age or acceptability of the offering. The acceptability of a product will depend on its ability to perform satisfactorily over a period of time. The reliability of a product is its ability to meet customer requirements over time.

1.2 Reliability ranks alongside quality in importance to customers. It forms the basis of many procurement decisions where comparisons are being made. There is clearly a close inter-relationship between quality and reliability as one of the goals of quality production will be to produce a reliable product. However, every product will eventually fail.

Preventing failure through design controls

1.3 Reliability is an important aspect of the acceptability of a product. There is a need to plan and design reliability into products and services. Earlier in the text we examined the design and development phase of product design. Proven methods of this type enable products to be designed to meet customer needs not only in marketing terms but also in terms of quality and reliability.

1.4 When a product, system, component or service no longer performs its required function, it is said to have failed.

1.5 This definition assumes that the required function is being attained exactly. A car could be described as working or broken down, or something in between (eg the clock is not working or performance has deteriorated over time). Failure can be built in (eg a car headlight may be designed to last three years where the car may have an anticipated life of ten years). The engineering and costs involved in producing a headlight may be excessive, technologically too difficult or perceived as being an acceptable failure by users.

1.6   To understand failure it is useful to consider the various types and causes of failure.

- **Total failure**: is the complete lack of ability of the product or service to perform or fulfil its function
- **Partial failure**: where the item does not work as expected but has not completely failed
- **Gradual failure**: which takes place progressively over time. Gradual failure can often be anticipated or built in.
- **Sudden failure**: occurs unpredictably and is not easily planned for.

1.7   Failure may be built-in following an acceptable working life, or it may be caused by misuse or by a weakness in design. Misuse is frequently caused by the stresses caused outside the anticipated design and use. Weakness can frequently be traced back to the design or production stage where the ramifications of use have not been fully evaluated.

1.8   Where failure is 'built-in' this is normally evaluated following extensive testing. An example would be a car seat that is subject to one million machine 'visits' to see how it will wear in everyday use. The failure rate of products is higher at the introduction or 'infant' stage, usually consistent during the normal or adult period, and high again during the 'ageing' period.

Mechanisms to detect failure

1.9   Identification of failures provides a chance to examine the root causes and put in fixes to avoid recurrence.

1.10   At its most straightforward 'failure' is when something does not work as it should do. In operations management the term failure will denote a more dramatic event such as something ceasing to do what it should do. For example, a piece of material fails, or a process fails. Yet there is clearly a spectrum of failure which goes from minor failures (which may occur quite frequently) to very serious and/or catastrophic failure (which hopefully do not occur very often). Relatively minor 'failures' are usually dealt with under the general heading of 'quality management'.

1.11   Operations managers will go to considerable lengths to prevent failures occurring. The paradox is that if they were completely successful they would deprive themselves of opportunities to learn how their systems react when pushed to the extreme. Operations managers will never succeed in preventing failure totally. Things will always go wrong, so in that sense operations managers will always have the opportunity to learn. Their responsibility is, of course, to prevent failures resulting in serious damage, but also to make sure that a failure never occurs without suitable lessons being learnt and applied in order to improve the operation.

1.12   It is of increasing importance in operations to try to detect potential failures before they occur. This will involve visualising all possible reasons why an operation might fail and what would be done should this occur. Operations managers are simulating what might happen to the system should a failure event occur.

1.13   Simulation, particularly computer simulation, may involve working through a sequence of events which may happen and trying to understand the consequence of such events. It is simulation in the sense that it has not occurred in reality as yet. This idea is particularly important since the advent of internet-based technologies. Although companies spend much time and money trying to protect their systems from interference or attack, their defences have to keep ahead of any potential hackers' knowledge. Speculating on what hackers might do and simulating the consequences is a starting point for developing their defences.

1.14   Advances in technology have led to new approaches to business. E-business in particular has grown rapidly due to accessibility by the internet. ERP systems are growing in linkages and information sharing with other companies. Security is a major issue to both companies and consumers.

1.15   If failure does occur then the operation has to cope with it in some way The failure recovery has two objectives.

- To put right whatever has gone wrong. This may involve compensating the customer who is subject to a service failure in such a way that he or she will not actively discourage other people from using the service. Interestingly complaints are often viewed as an opportunity to learn from customers and get their opinions.
- To deal with the longer-term issues of the failure which may include limiting the effects of the failure and learning from it so as to prevent it happening again. This involves making sure that processes are in place to detect failure, providing an appropriate diagnostic process to understand exactly what has happened, and being able to respond quickly to put the failure right.

Failure mode and effects analysis

1.16   Failure mode and effects analysis (FMEA) is a technique for determining the different ways (modes) in which a product can fail, and assessing the seriousness of the effects in each case. By using appropriate numerical parameters, the different modes can be ranked in order of how critical they are. (The term FMECA, or failure mode, effects and criticality analysis, is sometimes used.) Attention can then be concentrated on the most critical areas.

1.17   The most appropriate time for applying FMEA is at the design stage. However, examples of its use at other stages of the product life cycle are not uncommon. To provide the basic data, inputs are required from a variety of different departments: marketing, customer service, design and engineering, procurement, operations and others. In light of their experience in buying in parts and components from suppliers, procurement staff have an important role to play in identifying parts that have given rise to problems in the past.

1.18   To conduct the analysis, the following steps are required.

- Identify the components forming part of the product.
- For each component, list the different ways in which failure may occur and the causes of each.
- For each failure mode identified, list the effects on the overall product.
- Assess the probability (**P**) of each failure on a scale of 1 (not very probable) to 10 (extremely probable).
- Assess the seriousness (**S**) of each failure mode by considering its effects, again, on a scale of 1 (not very serious) to 10 (extremely serious).
- Assess the difficulty (**D**) of detecting the failure before the customer uses the product, on a scale of 1 (easy to detect) to 10 (very difficult to detect).
- Calculate the criticality index (**C**) for each failure mode by use of the formula: $C = P \times S \times D$

1.19   A low figure for C indicates that the failure mode is less important, ie it may have a low probability of occurrence, or a low seriousness level, or may be of such a nature that discovery is likely before the customer uses the product, or all three of these. If C has a high value it would indicate that urgent attention is required.

1.20   Finally, the means of correcting the problem should be indicated in each case.

1.21   By this stage, the required actions should be reasonably clear. Where the means of correction are simple and inexpensive they should normally be adopted in all cases. On the other hand, if correction is complex and costly management must carefully consider the criticality of that particular failure mode before determining what to do.

Failure distributions

1.22   A failure distribution is an attempt to describe mathematically the length of life of a material, a structure, or a device. The modes of possible failure for the item in question will affect the analytic form of the failure distribution.

1.23   The importance of this lies in failure prevention. If the distribution pattern for a particular failure suggests that it will usually occur at approximately a particular time, then prevention measures taken just before that time will pay large dividends. Whereas if the pattern for another type of failure is more random, then such a plan will not be feasible.

1.24   Materials and structures can fail in several ways, with two or more types of failure sometimes occurring at once. Examples of the different types of failure are: static failure when fracture occurs during a single load application; instability of a structure; chemical corrosion; fatigue due to cyclic loading; and the sticking of mechanical assemblies. Electronic devices may fail when certain critical parameters drift out of tolerance bounds with changes in time, temperature, humidity, and altitude. Early failures can result from improper design, improper manufacture, and improper use.

1.25   The failure rate is the frequency with which an operation system or component fails. The failure rate of a system usually depends on time, with the rate varying over the lifecycle of the system. For example, a new car is likely to experience more failures in Year 5 than in Year 1. The failure rate is calculated as the number of failures over a period of time. It can be measured either as a percentage of the total number of products tested or as the number of failures over time.

1.26   In practice, the **mean time between failures** (MTBF) is often reported instead of the failure rate. This can prove valid and useful if the failure rate may be assumed to be constant. For example, new cars may experience initial problems that will be rectified (the infant-mortality stage); following rectification the normal-life stage where failures are less and more random will occur; as time progresses components become worn-out (the wear-out stage) and more failures will occur. The **bath-tub curve** illustrates this process: see Figure 10.1.

Figure 10.1 *The bath-tub curve*

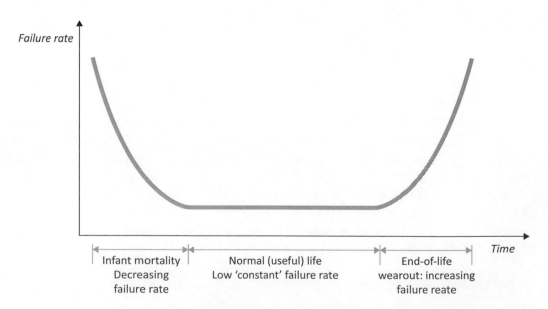

1.27   The MTBF is an important system parameter in systems where the failure rate needs to be managed, in particular safety systems. The MTBF appears frequently in engineering design requirements and governs the frequency of required system maintenance and inspections.

2   Improving process reliability

Measuring reliability

2.1   Reliability is a measure of the ability to perform as expected over time. Suppose an interdependent system has three components each with their own reliability ($R_1 = 0.96$, $R_2 = 0.90$, $R_3 = 0.94$). The reliability of the system (RS) is calculated as follows:

RS = $0.96 \times 0.90 \times 0.94 = 0.812$

2.2   The reliability of the entire system is 0.812 although the reliability of the specific components are individually higher. The greater the number of components in this example, the more interdependent the system and the lower reliability will be. The Japanese approach which revolutionised the car and motorcycle industries in the 1980s onward placed considerable emphasis on component reliability by putting in place rigorous quality processes. With over 400 components in a modern car you can visualise the issues in making cars to the level of reliability that is found today.

Building redundancy into a process

2.3   Once failure and the causes of failure have been understood by operations managers there is a clear responsibility to try and prevent failures from occurring. We will look at three areas to prevent failure: building redundancy into a process; fail-safeing some of the activities of the process; design for reliability.

2.4   Redundancy means having back-up systems or components should failure occur. This approach can prove expensive but when compared to the cost of a breakdown or lost production is generally regarded as cost effective. Regular pre-planned maintenance can prolong the life of an asset, but failure can often be anticipated with components. A stock-holding of those with a high statistical failure rate may be a worthwhile investment.

2.5   By building redundancy into a process the risk of failure can be reduced. The reliability of a component together with its support component reduces, although it does not eliminate, the risk of total failure.

Fail-safeing (poka-yoke)

2.6   The concept of fail-safeing is based on the idea that human mistakes are to some degree inevitable. The key consideration is how to prevent these errors becoming defects. Poka-yoke systems are simple fail-safe devices and methods initially designed to reduce human failures on production lines. One illustration of the simplicity of Japanese manufacturing lines was the use of hand signals to indicate errors or issues. This simplicity of approach is evident in fail-safeing.

2.7   The goal of mistake-proofing or poka-yoke is to eliminate mistakes. In order to eliminate mistakes, we need to modify processes so that it is impossible to make them in the first place. With mistake-proofing solutions, many repetitive tasks that depend upon the memory of the worker are built into the process itself. Mistake-proofing frees the time and minds of the workforce to pursue more creative and value-adding activities.

2.8   Poka-yoke is implemented by using simple objects such as fixtures, jigs, warning devices, and the like to prevent people from making mistakes. These objects, known as poka-yoke devices, are usually designed to stop the machine and alert the operator if something is about to go wrong. In addition to these types of devices, concepts such as colour coding, texturing, and visual indicators are also used.

2.9   Poka-yoke concepts are not only used in manufacturing and assembly processes; they are also used in the product design process, designing parts that cannot physically be assembled incorrectly. Connection points are often colour coded to prevent wiring or piping errors. Colour coding is also used to allow the quick identification of the correct materials.

2.10   Slack *et al* give a number of examples from manufacturing.

- Limit switches on machines which allow the machine to operate only if the part is positioned correctly
- Gauges placed on the machine through which a part has to pass to be loaded-on or taken-off a machine
- Light beams that activate an alarm if positioned incorrectly

2.11   Here are some examples from service contexts.

- Colour-coding cash register keys
- The McDonald's French-fry scoop which picks up the right quantity in the right orientation to go in the pack
- Trays with indentations for food ensuring all items are present

Design for reliability

2.12   Design for reliability (DFR) is a concept that has begun to receive a great deal of attention in recent years. The use of analysis techniques is increasingly important although analysis itself is not enough to achieve reliable products. There are a variety of activities involved in an effective reliability program and in arriving at reliable products. In achieving an organisation's reliability goals there is a requirement for proper planning, sufficient organisational resource allocation and the integration into development projects.

2.13   Design for reliability, however, is more specific than these general ideas. It is actually a process that describes the entire set of tools that support product and process design (typically from early in the concept stage all the way through to product obsolescence) to ensure that customer expectations for reliability are fully met throughout the life of the product with low overall lifecycle costs. DFR is a systematic, streamlined, concurrent engineering program in which reliability engineering is an integral part of the total development cycle.

2.14   DFR relies on a wide array of reliability engineering tools along with a proper understanding of when and how to use these tools throughout the design cycle. This process encompasses a variety of tools and practices and describes the overall order of deployment that an organisation needs to follow in order to design reliability into its products.

2.15   Understanding when and where to use the reliability engineering tools available will help to achieve the reliability goals of an organisation. This approach is becoming more important with the increasing complexity of systems as well as the complexity of the methods available for determining their reliability. System interactions, interfaces, complex usage and stress profiles need to be addressed and accounted for.

2.16   With such increasing complexity in all aspects of product development, it becomes a necessity to have a well defined process for incorporating reliability activities into the design cycle. Without such a process, trying to implement all of the different reliability activities involved in product development can become a difficult situation, where different reliability tools are deployed too late, randomly, or not at all, resulting in the waste of time and resources.

The distinction between reliability and quality

2.17   Traditional quality control assures that the product will work after assembly and as designed; whereas reliability provides the probability that an item will perform its intended function for a designated period of time without failure under specified conditions. In other words, reliability looks at *how long* the product will work as designed, which is a very different objective than that of traditional quality control. Therefore, different tools and models apply to reliability that do not necessarily apply to quality and *vice versa*.

3 Asset maintenance and replacement

The objectives of maintenance

3.1 The purpose of maintenance is to optimise the performance of equipment by attempting to prevent breakdowns or failures. An understanding of the nature and purpose of maintenance regimes and schedules enables the operations manager to view production schedules with greater confidence as the incidence of delays or breakdowns in production will be reduced.

3.2 There is a close correlation between maintenance and quality as only those machines that operate within anticipated parameters will be able to deliver the required quality of product. Without effective maintenance there will clearly be concerns relating to product quality.

3.3 Muhlemann, Oakland and Lockyer cite the following objectives of maintenance.

- To enable product or service quality and customer satisfaction to be achieved through correctly adjusted, serviced and operated equipment
- To maximise the useful life of the equipment
- To keep the equipment safe and prevent the development of safety hazards
- To minimise the total production or operating costs directly attributable to equipment service and repair
- To minimise the frequency and severity of interruptions to operating processes
- To maximise production capacity from the given equipment resources

3.4 In the operations environment the objectives of maintenance must be balanced against the objectives of production. This is explained below.

Differences between preventive and repair maintenance

3.5 There are two approaches to repairs and maintenance: repair maintenance and preventive maintenance.

3.6 **Repair (or breakdown) maintenance** is involved with failures and related problems as they occur. This is reactive in nature. The operations manager must have in place details with regard to guarantees, warranties or specialists to call on.

3.7 Unscheduled maintenance of this type can be highly disruptive to any production process and consideration should be given to the appropriate level of after-sales support in this area at the time of unit purchase. The availability of spares, response times and costs should all be fully evaluated prior to purchase.

3.8 **Preventive maintenance** requires a proactive approach and is concerned with the reduction of failure by the implementation of a rigorous preventive regime.

3.9 Preventive maintenance is defined as 'a system of daily maintenance, periodic inspection, and preventive repairs designed to reduce the probability of machine breakdown'.

Preventive maintenance

3.10 When maintenance is delayed, one risks premature equipment failure, product damage and production delays.

3.11 The primary reason for preventive maintenance is to reduce unexpected downtime and repair costs caused by machine breakdown. Preventive maintenance is largely precautionary and will be undertaken according to a predetermined and regular schedule.

10

3.12   A regular schedule should be established for items that have manufacturers' maintenance guidelines, predictable reliability or known breakdown characteristics. Preventive maintenance will also be undertaken where there is evidence of a reduction in manufacturing capability of a unit.

3.13   Preventive maintenance plays an important role in operations management with benefits ranging from cost reductions and decreased downtime to safety and improved performance. It involves routine machine inspection, servicing, cleaning, and keeping accurate maintenance records.

3.14   Preventive maintenance will normally be undertaken when the operating facility is idle. This allows for work to be planned with the minimum amount of disruption to production schedules. This may not always be possible and, apart from any unscheduled maintenance requirements, it is inevitable that some maintenance will be required during production hours.

3.15   The total cost curve demonstrates that increased effort in preventive maintenance should reduce the cost of repair.

Figure 10.2 *Cost effects of preventive maintenance*

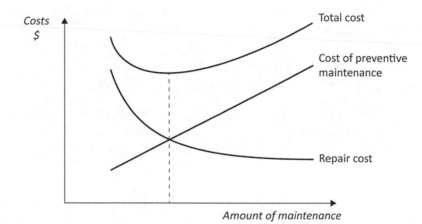

3.16   The more frequently preventive maintenance is carried out then the less need there should be for repair or breakdown maintenance. With no preventive maintenance the cost of repair would be substantial. However, often a balance must be struck between the operating needs of the production system and the scheduled maintenance requirement. The short-term production requirement may win over the longer-term objectives of preventive maintenance.

Maintenance decisions

3.17   To establish a maintenance policy for an operation we consider three linked aspects.

•   Which machines, items or facilities, etc, are to be maintained?
•   What is the appropriate maintenance in each case?
•   How will the maintenance work be organised?

3.18   There is often an interdependence between machines of similar capacities. These are often operated together in a production run. If one is undergoing preventive maintenance it will often make sense to carry out maintenance on the other at the same time.

3.19   The development of a maintenance policy that meets the needs of the organisation (eg both operations staff and maintenance staff) is difficult. Clearly there are conflicting needs and these must be addressed by a mutual understanding of each other's aims and objectives.

3.20   Preventive maintenance policy should consider the alternative approaches that can be used and decide on the appropriate mix of approaches. The options available are as follows.

- **Work-based**: where maintenance is carried out after a set number of operating hours or usage. Usage can be gauged by counting (eg after 10,000 miles, 5,000 units or 50,000 copies).
- **Time-based**: where maintenance is based on time intervals irrespective of usage. This system is easy to schedule and monitor but often neglects the problems that may become apparent if high usage in an area is not recognised.
- **Opportunity-based**: where maintenance takes place outside work hours (evenings and holidays) or when machine breakdowns provide downtime on other machines that can then be used for maintenance.
- **Condition-based**: often relies on planned, visual or measured inspection in order to ascertain the need for maintenance (eg when brakes wear down to a 1mm minimum). Many manufacturers will use a tougher material that causes audible noise when the minimum recommended level is reached to alert operatives that replacement is due. Or they may include electrical systems (as in cars) that indicate when maintenance should be carried out.

3.21 Maintenance, which involves inspection, servicing, preventive maintenance and repair maintenance, can be carried out at various levels of operation. In certain cases the operators who use the machine can carry out routine maintenance tasks as part of their role. The organisation can supplement this with their own team of maintenance engineers, and/or external maintenance personnel can be brought in either on contract or as provided by machine manufacturers under a guarantee, warranty or after-sales arrangement.

3.22 Total productive maintenance (TPM) is a development from total quality management thinking and is designed to encourage the unit operative and those linked with the production process to take 'ownership' of their role. The key features are as follows.

- To optimise the use and effectiveness of equipment and eliminate unplanned failures
- To involve the operator in maintenance activities where appropriate in order to develop a sense of ownership, involvement and responsibility
- To encourage employees to be involved in continuous improvements in machinery and equipment operation

3.23 The replacement of worn, defective or damaged parts is an integral part of preventive maintenance. When the cost of repair is becoming substantial a new approach may need to be taken. A common method is to set a repair limit and if the estimated cost of repair exceeds this limit then the machine is due for replacement.

Asset replacement

3.24 The costs involved in operating machinery and equipment will normally increase with the age or high usage of the piece. These costs (eg the cost of maintenance necessary to keep the piece operational and the obsolescence of the equipment particularly in the light of technological advances) will together eventually present an economically viable case for replacement.

3.25 Asset replacement is dependent on a number of factors. One of these factors is the repair limit but other considerations are dependent on the nature and value of the item to be replaced. This can include replacement cost and whole life costing, cashflow implications, downtime costs, obsolescence, and projected long-term production requirements. These factors are discussed in turn below.

3.26 **Replacement cost and whole life costing**. Asset replacement will be considered before it is immediately necessary. If a high-value unit is being replaced a case must be put forward by the operations team and discussed with other business functions (most notably finance and procurement). Finance will need to evaluate the implications of future purchase and consider options such as hire or leasing. Procurement are the specialists in supply and increasingly have a wider remit. They will evaluate the purchase over the whole life of the unit. This includes such areas as running costs, power usage, emissions and recycling and/

10

or disposal costs, which are very much a feature of the modern view of procurement when buying capital equipment.

3.27 **Cashflow implications**. Organisations should have a structured replacement plan with anticipated replacement dates and cost estimates in order that funds will be available when required. The role of finance will involve a full appraisal of alternatives to purchase (such as leasing and hiring) and they will need a fully justified case for the purchase of a major unit. Procurement will negotiate with an aim of spreading the payment period over time. This is often linked to scheduled payments related to hours used, output or reliability.

3.28 **Downtime costs**. These can be minimised by careful planning that allows for linked machines to be maintained in the same time interval. Maintenance outside normal work hours is often the preferred option as it causes minimum disruption to the production process.

3.29 **Obsolescence**. This is an increasing concern to modern business, owing largely to the rapid advances in technology that are taking place. Particularly with computer-based equipment, consideration should be given to the ease and effectiveness of upgrades during the product's life. The impact of fast-moving technology can be seen in the way that many organisations handle their office PC requirement: by outsourcing supply, maintenance and upgrades to a specialist or by leasing equipment where upgrades are an essential part of the renewal arrangements. Similar decisions will be relevant to the operations manager.

3.30 **Projected long-term production requirements**. As discussed earlier in the text, the purchase of high-value items, in particular, should be viewed and costed over the long term. Consideration should be given to strategic aims and objectives to justify the purchase decision. Other aspects such as compatibility, future product plans, and possible requirements for increased output will all be areas for discussion and evaluation.

3.31 Advances in technology have enabled the development of systems that reduce the overall cost of maintenance while improving production performance. The impact of technology can be compared to that found in modern cars (warning lights indicate problems, interval times are flagged-up, temperature sensors indicate status, vibration sensors indicate a machine operating outside acceptable parameters, etc).

3.32 Computers can analyse the feedback from units to give an early warning of possible maintenance requirements. **Predictive maintenance** can work alongside preventive maintenance as an additional way of ensuring maintenance objectives are met.

3.33 The role of modern maintenance is broadening in scope and sophistication. Failure of any one part can cause major problems in manufacturing and the maintenance role is crucial in ensuring that failures of this type are minimised and that machines continue to work accurately within the parameters laid down for the operation.

4 Business continuity

4.1 Business continuity is a management process that provides a framework to ensure the resilience of a business to any eventuality, to help ensure continuity of service to key customers and to protect brand and reputation. It provides a basis for planning to ensure long-term survivability following a disruptive event.

4.2 Business continuity management (BCM) is a generic management framework that is valid across the public, private and voluntary sectors. It is about maintaining the essential business deliverables of an organisation during a disruption and forms part of the organisation's wider resilience policy.

4.3   Figure 10.3 is an article by Wanja Eric Naef that appeared in *Infocon* magazine (October 2003 issue).

Figure 10.3 *Business continuity planning – a safety net for businesses*

The events of 11 September 2001 were a drastic reminder to all companies that business contingency planning (BCP) should not be disregarded. According to the *Information Security News* magazine (2000), an effective BCP and disaster recovery plan can reduce losses by 90% in the event of an incident. According to another study 81% of CEOs indicated their company plans would not be able to cope with a catastrophic event like the 9/11 attacks.

There are numerous examples of companies suffering because of poor business contingency planning. In the 1993 World Trade Center bombing, 150 companies went out of business (out of 350 affected) – scarcely an encouraging statistic. But an incident does not need to be a dramatic terrorist attack to have a massive impact on an organisation. For instance, in the case of fires, 44% of businesses fail to reopen and 33% of those that do fail to survive beyond three years. The examples could be continued endlessly. The bottom line is that businesses need to have plans in place to cope with incidents (whether they be major terrorist attacks or a minor hardware problem) and thereby avoid major business interruptions.

4.4   Business continuity is not to be confused with either contingency planning or disaster recovery. A contingency plan is a fallback position should anything go wrong, enabling the business to recover over time. Contingency planning is often about 'unlikely' events. This differs from business continuity in that the aim of BCP is to minimise the risk of business failure by enabling the business to continue without interruption following a 'disaster'.

4.5   It is also not be confused with disaster recovery which concentrates on the restoration of facilities after a major incident (eg loss of IT systems, recovery after a fire or flood etc). In general disaster recovery plans are written on the basis of recovery after an event. BCM examines the entire business.

4.6   BCP involves the processes and procedures for the development, testing and maintenance of a plan (or a series of plans) that will enable an organisation to continue operating during and after a disaster. Plans are typically designed to cope with incidents affecting all the organisation's business-critical processes and activities, from failure of a single server, or server room, all the way through to complete loss of a major facility. BCP is a response to an enterprise level risk assessment.

4.7   Disaster recovery planning (DRP) usually takes place within the BCP framework. Disaster recovery plans are usually relatively technical and will focus on the recovery of specific operations, functions, sites, services or applications. A single BCP might contain or refer to a number of DRPs.

The BCM process

4.8   Before even starting to create a BCP it is important to get the full support of the management and governance of the organisation. Without this it will be very difficult to push BCP plans through the entire company. Directors should be involved in the strategic design of the BCP as this will help to create a realistic plan that will be focused on the business interests of the company.

4.9   A BCP team should then be formed. The team will be responsible for designing the BCP and for initiating the BCM process. The team will serve as a central focus point during the entire process. It is also important to set a timescale for the BCP delivery and to create a budget for the process.

4.10   The BCP team must identify threats and conduct a risk assessment, which will help to design the areas on which the plan should focus; it is impossible to avoid or mitigate all risk. The team will have to prioritise depending on likelihood of the risk and business impact. It is very important to analyse all risks and threats: technical, economic, internal, external, human or natural.

4.11   Once the risk assessment has been done the risk must be managed. Preventive, detective and reactive means must be put in place in order to protect the company. For example, it might be possible to migrate risks by using insurance, contracting out some services, implementing safeguards and controls and so on. Risks with high potential impact, but low probability, and which cannot be mitigated, are prime candidates for BCP.

Failure recovery

4.12   Business continuity planning presents operations managers with the need to consider how to respond when failures occur. 'Normal' failures are well-considered with well tried and tested plans, as we have discussed, in place. In the event of a situation where business contingency planning is involved operations managers must ensure there is a sound failure recovery plan in place.

4.13   In a BCP situation operations would be expected to have contributed throughout the forming of the plan, discussing different scenarios and how they could affect the operations role. Situations would be considered and solutions developed for inclusion in the BCP.

4.14   Operations also face failure recovery situations when something unexpected happens to or within a process or project (eg goods due being delayed due to strike action, machinery breakdown, etc). Operations managers would consider various scenarios in advance and would have put in place actions that will be taken to resolve the situation.

4.15   Recovery procedures will also affect how the organisation and the operation is viewed by customers. Customers' perceptions can be improved by the way an organisation responds to failure. Most customers will understand the problem if explained correctly. If the recovery response is robust and effective a negative could be turned into a positive in the way customers view the company.

Chapter summary

- Reliability is highly valued by customers, which makes it vital for organisations to minimise instances of product failure. Quantitative approaches to this include FMEA and use of probability distributions.
- Improving process reliability can be attempted using such methods as building in redundancy, fail-safeing (poka-yoke), and 'design for reliability'.
- Both repair maintenance and preventive maintenance will be necessary to ensure continuing use of organisational assets. The costs involved typically rise as assets become older, so it is important to have a systematic approach to asset replacement.
- Business continuity is a management process to ensure the resilience of the organisation in the event of major disruption to operations.

 ## Self-test questions

Numbers in brackets refer to the paragraphs above where your answers can be checked.

1   List different types of product failure. (1.6)

2   Explain the steps in FMEA. (1.18)

3   Why are operations managers interested in failure distributions? (1.23)

4   Give some examples of fail-safeing. (2.10, 2.11)

5   Distinguish between reliability and quality. (2.17)

6   What are the objectives of asset maintenance? (3.3)

7   Describe four different approaches to the planning of preventive maintenance. (3.20)

8   List factors involved in the asset replacement decision. (3.25–3.33)

9   Distinguish between business continuity and disaster recovery. (4.5)

CHAPTER 11

Total Quality Management

Assessment criteria and indicative content

4.3 Evaluate the role of total quality management in operations management

- Approaches to total quality management
- The differences between total quality and quality assurance
- The work of pioneers of total quality management (such as Deming, Juran)

Section headings

1 Definitions and dimensions of quality
2 Approaches to TQM
3 Pioneers of TQM
4 The benefits and criticisms of TQM

1 Definitions and dimensions of quality

Defining quality

1.1 In recent years the issue of product and service quality has assumed overwhelming importance in the search for competitive advantage. Partly this is a natural development as Western economies have become wealthier, and consumers more discriminating and demanding. Partly it is a reaction to trends in Japanese manufacturing that have caused European and American organisations to look afresh at their principles and practices particularly in regard to quality issues.

1.2 Initial definitions of quality focused on product quality. Generic definitions such as 'fitness for use', 'fitness for purpose' and 'meeting specification' have their roots in the early stages of the quality movement. The movement to total quality management brought together the 'quality triangle' advocated by Juran in a definition by Armand Feigenbaum that extended quality definitions to include customers: 'an effective system for integrating the quality development, quality maintenance and quality improvement efforts of the various groups in an organisation so as to enable production and service at the most economical levels which allow for full customer satisfaction'.

1.3 There remains a debate on what exactly constitutes quality, and this is reflected in the variety of definitions that can be found in the literature. Most definitions with wide acceptance emphasise the central position of the customer. That of IBM is cited by Arjan J van Weele: 'Quality is the degree in which customer requirements are met. We speak of a quality product or quality service when supplier and customer agree on requirements and those requirements are met'.

1.4 These requirements relate not only to technical specifications of a product, but to the whole range of benefits that the customer is purchasing. For example, they might include ease of use, after-sales service, short delivery lead-time and so on. Supplying products and services that meet the definition of quality is a task that calls for a wide-ranging management effort.

Dimensions of quality

1.5   David Garvin lists eight main dimensions for quality. (Later in this chapter we look at the Servqual approach, which identifies five such dimensions in a service context.)

- **Performance**: the operating characteristics of the product or the delivery of the service.
- **Features**: aspects such as customer care policy, availability of spare parts and credit facilities. Features assist the marketing effort in differentiating one product from another.
- **Reliability**: the ability of a product or service to perform with consistency and certainty over a period of time.
- **Durability**: the length of time a product will last without deterioration under stated conditions of use.
- **Conformance**: the degree to which agreed standards are met
- **Serviceability**: the time between service periods and the ease and availability of service support.
- **Aesthetics**: how the overall product is perceived by the customer in regard to its design, shape, texture, taste etc.
- **Perceived quality**: the subjective view a customer develops from the influence of advertising, brand image and price etc, that indicates the level of quality the customer anticipates.

1.6   Quality means different things in different operations. A motor manufacturer is looking for parts and components that meet the specification, an assembly operation that is automated to reduce human error in order to produce a product that is reliable and meets customer needs and wants. A contrasting view would come from a hospital: patients require the correct treatment within an acceptable time-frame (which could be quite varied), patients want to be kept informed, the staff to be knowledgeable and the hospital to be clean.

1.7   Garvin considered the various definitions of quality and the different approaches to it and categorised the various perspectives into his 'five approaches' to quality.

- **The transcendent approach**: this view equates quality with excellence.
- **The user-based approach**: concerns the making of a product that is fit for purpose and use (Juran). Quality is designed to meet the needs of the customer. This does not necessarily mean to excel: it means to produce a product or service that meets customers' needs. The two are not the same.
- **The product-based approach**: the product-based perspective sees quality as precise and measurable. For example, the product will travel 12,000 miles between oil changes or will download data three times faster. The assessment of quality is based on measurable factors.
- **The manufacturing-based approach**: quality is the manufacture of a product that precisely meets specifications. The product is free of errors as a result. It is a product that will do the job.
- **The value-based approach**: develops the manufacturing perspective further by incorporating both cost and price. This involves a trade-off in the customers' mind of what represents value. As an example I could fly direct from London to Orlando with British Airways, or get the flight cheaper with Delta via Atlanta, but with a six-hour transfer delay.

Customers' expectations

1.8   Customers' views and expectations will all be shaped by a variety of factors such as product knowledge, personal history, lifestyle, etc. Customers may perceive quality in different ways.

1.9   Quality must be understood from the customer's perspective. The customer's view of quality is what they expect the quality to be. The expectations are based on a range of factors that have been communicated to them. If we fail to meet those expectations we are either putting our message across wrongly or are failing operationally to match customer expectations.

1.10   As an example, call centres are one of the most rapidly growing industries in the world today as many service providers are seeking to lower the cost of providing services and increasing the time period during which customer access is available.

1.11   Call centre operators are often required to answer a great number of calls and they are sometimes judged on how quickly they deal with the call, regardless of the quality of the call (eg satisfaction of the customer).

1.12   The performance statistics relating to this become an efficiency measure rather than an effectiveness measure. In a service industry the 'product' is often the employee's service. The rapid growth of call centres emphasises the importance for service delivery in this context. It is important to attain the correct balance between efficiency and effectiveness.

The Servqual approach

1.13   Quality and customer service have been identified as critical strategic issues in today's business environment. The Servqual approach to the measurement of service quality was first introduced by Parasuraman *et al* (1995).

'The approach starts from the assumption that the level of service experienced by customers is critically determined by the gap between their expectations of the service and their perceptions of what they actually receive from the service provider.'

1.14   The Servqual model puts forward five **dimensions** on which customers evaluate service.

- **Tangibles**: the appearance of the physical facilities and materials related to the service. There is little tangible about a call centre with the exception of voice contact.
- **Reliability**: the ability to perform the service accurately and dependably. A consideration is the number of operators to receive calls and the need to address operational issues such as scheduling operators to be available at peak times.
- **Responsiveness**: the willingness to help customers and provide a good level of service. Clearly this is compromised by an emphasis on the number of calls answered rather than other performance measures such as problems resolved or customer satisfaction.
- **Assurance**: confidence in the competence of the operation, its systems, security and credibility. This is not easy to develop, particularly at first call.
- **Empathy**: approachability and individual attention to customers. This can be achieved by a knowledgeable operator who is aware of the surrounding issues.

1.15   The Servqual method can serve as an operations management tool in a wide range of operations. To operations managers in the service sector it is useful to have a widely accepted tool to help analyse their operation. If your role is primarily service based consider applying the five points of the model to your organisation and see what the results tell you.

1.16   The purpose of understanding perceived quality is that it can be used to diagnose quality problems. Slack *et al* identify four distinct areas that could explain a perceived quality gap between customers' perceptions and expectations.

- **The gap between the customer's specification and the operation's specification**: the customer's perception of quality could be poor as the operation's specification is lower than he expects or requires.
- **The gap between concept and specification**: the perceived quality could be poor as the product or service was not conceived and developed with adequate consideration being given to customer expectations.
- **The gap between quality specification and actual quality**: perceived quality may evidence a mismatch between the actual product or service quality and its internal specification (eg the product may suggest to the customer a higher level of after-sales support than is actually available).
- **The gap between actual quality and communicated image**: there may be a mismatch between what is actually delivered and what the customer expects, particularly following positive advertising and promotion.

11

1.17   The key consideration with quality gaps is to understand why they exist. Once this has been established, action can be taken to reduce or eliminate the gap areas.

1.18   More recent definitions of quality reflect this more rounded approach and consider both the production and customer service aspects but also look to place quality in a modern business context. Philip Crosby stated that 'quality is free'. His meaning is that if effective quality systems are in place then production will continually improve and customer service will meet or exceed expectation leading to repeat business and a philosophy that will continue to drive the business forward. The idea of 'zero defects' puts forward a quality objective for companies to aspire to.

2   Approaches to TQM

The TQM philosophy

2.1   For an organisation to be effective each part of it must integrate and work together. With the modern views of supply chain management and closer supplier relationships this role of integration and working effectively together will often extend outside an operation and cascade through the supply chain. Total quality management (TQM) is conventionally a commitment to quality adopted by an organisation but with the increasing drive toward supply chain management the TQM philosophy is one that impacts along the supply chain as suppliers strive to meet customer needs in relation to quality.

2.2   TQM is an extension of quality thinking. Quality has long been achieved by inspection of products to check that they meet the required specifications. As we have discussed earlier in the text there is an increasing emphasis placed on building quality in to new products, processes or services from the beginning. The customer is at the heart of this thinking. Terms such as 'satisfying customer needs' or 'delighting the customer' are not only marketing terms – they are the drivers for delivering quality.

2.3   Recognising customers and discovering their needs is a crucial aspect of quality thinking. Designing processes that lead to the cost-effective meeting of those needs underpins the quality process. Management have a responsibility for setting the guiding philosophy and supporting it over the long term, providing motivation through leadership and equipping people to achieve quality. TQM is as much a philosophy as a set of techniques; it requires everyone in the organisation to view everything in terms of meeting customer needs.

2.4   Customers are becoming increasingly intolerant of poor goods and services and the delivery of a quality product and/or service gives organisations a competitive edge over the opposition. TQM is a philosophy that must be introduced, integrated, supported and continually improved. Those in the organisation, and those supporting the organisation, need to see the tangible and intangible benefits that a TQM approach can bring and need to see this continuing over time and leading to noticeable quality improvements. TQM thrives on its own success.

2.5   John S Oakland in *Total Quality Management* puts forward a ten point plan for senior management to adopt when implementing a TQM approach.

- The organisation needs long-term commitment to constant improvement with constancy of purpose fully supported by senior management.
- Adopt the philosophy of zero errors/defects to change the culture to right first time.
- Train people to understand the customer-supplier relationships.
- Do not buy products and services on price alone – look at the total cost.
- Recognise that improvement in the systems must be managed.
- Adopt modern methods of supervision and training – eliminate fear.
- Eliminate barriers between departments by managing the process – improve communications and teamwork.

- Eliminate: arbitrary goals without methods; all standards based on numbers; barriers to pride of workmanship; fiction – get to the facts by using the appropriate tools.
- Constantly educate and retrain – develop the 'experts' in the business.
- Develop a systematic approach to manage the implementation of TQM. It requires a carefully planned and fully integrated strategy.

2.6 TQM requires a 'core' of management: appropriate systems, tools for analysis and corrections, and teamworking. These underpin the 'softer' aspects that involve the organisational culture, communication and commitment.

2.7 Business culture has put quality at the heart of competitiveness over recent years and new ways of thinking and considering quality issues have been developed.

- Quality control has developed a more refined and systematic approach, particularly with the increasing impact of information technology across all operations, and this has led to recognisable gains and improvements for many organisations.
- Quality assurance has widened the concept and responsibility for quality management by introducing a formalised approach that extends beyond production and encompasses the service element of organisational operations.

2.8 TQM has been developed as a way of management that seeks to improve the effectiveness, flexibility, reputation and competitiveness of a business overall. TQM can be defined as 'a continuous improvement in quality, efficiency and effectiveness' and has the following features.

- It aims towards an environment of zero defects at a minimum cost.
- It involves measuring and examining all costs that are quality related.
- It requires awareness by all personnel of the quality requirements involved in supplying the customer with products that meet the agreed specification.
- It is a philosophy that involves all parts of the organisation and everyone working in it.
- It aims at the elimination of waste, where waste is defined as anything other than the minimum essential amount of equipment, materials, space and workers' time.
- It must embrace all aspects of operations from pre-production to post-production.
- It involves an emphasis on supply chain thinking (working with suppliers to improve quality along the supply chain).
- It works toward a continuous process of improvement.

2.9 TQM will seek changes in methods and processes that will help in achieving these objectives and lead to measurable quality improvement.

2.10 TQM comprises three major components.

- A documented and auditable quality management system such as ISO 9000 and derivatives
- The application of relevant online and offline controls
- The development of cross-functional teams

The three components are complementary and support each other. They share the same requirement – a commitment to quality.

2.11 TQM is designed to include everyone in the organisation. It is designed with the 'internal customer' very much as a focus. The concept of 'total quality' is just that. No one, no part of the organisation, is excluded. All have a role to play in attaining total quality.

2.12 TQM develops this concept by stressing the role of 'micro-operations'. To use procurement as an example: internal customers could be marketing, operations, quality control or warehousing; external customers would be suppliers, logistics operators and supplier reference agencies etc. The procurement department has a role to manage all these relationships by defining as clearly as possible their customers' requirement and how they are going to meet it.

11

Quality circles

2.13   An important element of TQM is that every one in the organisation should be involved and that anyone with an idea should be heard. One approach is to form groups of managers and employees into 'quality circles'. These groups (normally consisting of around 10 people) meet on a regular basis to discuss quality issues and put forward ideas. The mix and nature of the team will vary, depending on individual circumstances.

2.14   Based on the Japanese model the quality circle approach has met with mixed success in Europe and the United States, perhaps because many organisations continue to operate them beyond their useful life. Quality circles must be flexible in membership and skills in order to meet changing situations.

2.15   Other approaches that are adopted include quality councils, quality improvement teams and corrective action teams. The approach will depend on the organisation and its needs.

ISO 9000

2.16   ISO 9000 was launched in 1987 and comprises a group of quality management standards laid down by the International Organisation for Standardisation (ISO). Although not an essential within the philosophy of TQM the integration of ISO 9000 standards provides a quality assurance structure that ensures good practice is applied and is seen to be applied.

2.17   The ISO 9000 standards are built around business processes, with an emphasis on improvement and on meeting the needs of customers.

2.18   The ISO 9000 model contains eight quality management principles, on which to base an efficient, effective and adaptable quality management system. The principles reflect best practice and are designed so as to enable continuous improvement in the business.

- **Customer focus**. Customer needs and expectations must be determined and converted into product and/or service requirements.
- **Leadership**. Good leaders establish a direction and a unity of purpose for an organisation. They formulate an acceptable and appropriate quality policy and ensure that measurable objectives are set for the organisation.
- **Involvement of people**. The role of people in the organisation and their full involvement in the quality ethos enables their abilities to be used for the organisation's benefit while also enhancing their own personal role. Management must act as the enablers of this process.
- **Process approach**. A desired result is achieved more efficiently when related resources and activities are managed as a process. In consequence a quality management system must have, at its core, a process approach, with each process transforming one or more inputs to create an output of value to the customer.
- **Systems approach to management**. Identifying, understanding and managing a system of inter-related processes for a given objective contributes to both the efficiency and the effectiveness of the organisation. These processes must be fully appreciated and understood in order that the most efficient use is made of them.
- **Continuous improvement**. This is a permanent and ongoing objective. Customer satisfaction is a moving target and the quality management system must take this into account. Monitoring of customer feedback and proactive research supported by the measuring and monitoring of performance delivery must be an integral part of the system.
- **Factual approach to decision-making**. Effective decision-making is based on the logical, intuitive analysis of data and information. This requires that a system is in place that provides current and relevant information to managers to assist in the decision-making process.

- **Mutually beneficial supplier relationships**. These types of relationships between an organisation and its suppliers (commonly known as 'win-win' relationships) enhance the ability of both organisations to create value. Each organisation is just one of the links in a much larger supply chain. In order to serve the long-term needs of the community and the organisation itself, mutually beneficial relationships must exist at all points in the supply chain.

2.19 The most recent family of ISO standards for quality management systems comprises:

- **ISO 9000: 2000**: Quality management systems – fundamentals and vocabulary.
- **ISO 9001: 2000**: Quality management systems requirements. This specifies the key requirements of an efficient, effective and adaptable quality management system.
- **ISO 9004: 2000**: Provides guidelines and focuses on performance improvement.

2.20 The ISO 9000 and ISO 9004 standards are designed to be used together but can be operated separately if required. The year 2000 standards are intended to be generic and adaptable to all kinds of organisations including those that are primarily service based.

2.21 The ISO 9001: 2000 standard specifies the requirements for a quality management system that can be used by organisations for internal application, contractual purposes, or certification. The standard identifies quality management systems as comprising four processes: management responsibility, resource management, product realisation and measurement, analysis and improvement.

2.22 The majority of organisations who adopt the ISO 9000/9001 route will have their systems approved by an independent certification body to reinforce in-house disciplines and to demonstrate compliance to customers and purchasers. A number of other potentially relevant standards (such as ISO 10012 measurement systems and ISO 10014 managing the economics of quality) are also in place.

The differences between total quality and quality assurance

2.23 In earlier decades, an organisation would tackle quality entirely in-house. Goods received from suppliers would be inspected and faulty items rejected. Similarly, goods emerging from the buying organisation's own production processes would be inspected as they emerged from the production line. This is the idea of **quality control**.

2.24 More recently, there was a shift from quality control to **quality assurance**. In relation to external suppliers, this meant that the buyer would work hard to identify suppliers who could provide goods and services 'right first time'. By identifying suitable suppliers, and monitoring their performance clearly, the buyer could greatly reduce the need for rejection and rework of faulty inputs.

2.25 More recently still, buyers have recognised that quality is best achieved by starting right at the beginning. Rather than checking for quality once items have been produced, the aim is to design quality into products. And rather than restricting this process to the in-house operations, buyers have sought to extend it along the supply chain. Buyers work with suppliers, who in turn work with their suppliers, the objective at all stages being to design quality into the components that will ultimately form part of finished products in the hands of consumers. (We adopt a manufacturing perspective in this discussion, but these ideas are now well developed in the services sector as well.)

2.26 These developments are the key difference between the modern approach to TQM and the earlier approaches of quality control and quality assurance.

11

3   Pioneers of TQM

The development of TQM

3.1   The philosophy of TQM has evolved over the years both through practical experience and through the researches of certain influential authorities on the subject (who are often referred to as the 'quality gurus'). We look in turn at three of these 'gurus'.

W Edwards Deming

3.2   Deming was a statistician who worked with Walter Shewhart at Bell Laboratories in the 1920s. Shewhart pioneered the statistical measurement of product deviation from an accepted norm – the process that Deming developed further to become statistical process control. After a period of considerable success in the US Census Office, Deming was sent to Japan as one of the consultants that supported the Marshall Plan following the Second World War.

3.3   Deming's initial message was about the need to measure product deviations and to continually reduce them. This message, now known as the 'Deming Cycle' (Plan-Do-Check-Act), forms the basis for **kaizen** or **continuous improvement**. His message was well received in Japan where a thorough and meticulous approach to manufacture has long been appreciated.

3.4   Deming placed considerable importance on the role of management, both at the individual and at the company level, believing managers to be responsible for 94 per cent of quality problems. His view was that inappropriate systems, processes and procedures were the root cause of many quality concerns and that workers could do little to influence these issues unless they were empowered to do so.

3.5   In his 1986 book *Out of Crisis* he published his 14 points for management (although these had been published in Japan much earlier).

- Create constancy of purpose towards improvement of product and service.
- Adopt the new philosophy for the new economic age. We can no longer live with commonly accepted levels of delay, mistakes and defective workmanship.
- Cease dependence on mass inspection. Instead, require statistical evidence that quality is built in.
- End the practice of awarding the business on price; instead minimise total cost and move to single suppliers for items.
- Improve constantly and forever the system of production and service to improve quality and increase productivity.
- Institute modern methods of training on the job.
- Institute modern methods of supervision of production workers. The responsibility of foremen must be changed from numbers to quality.
- Drive out fear, so that everyone may work effectively for the company.
- Break down barriers between departments.
- Eliminate numerical goals, posters and slogans for the workforce asking for new levels of productivity without providing methods.
- Eliminate work standards that prescribe numerical quotas.
- Remove barriers that stand between the hourly worker and their right to pride of workmanship.
- Institute a vigorous programme of education and retraining
- Create a structure in top management that will push towards the transformation.

Philip Crosby

3.6 Philip Crosby is one of the most highly regarded of the modern quality gurus. His two leading publications *Quality is Free* (1979) and *Quality Without Tears* (1984) help to expound his philosophy. In these books he defines quality as 'conformance to requirements' and develops (some already existing) themes such as 'quality is free', 'zero defects' and 'do it right first time'.

3.7 In these publications Crosby laid down his original four absolutes for quality.

- Quality is conformance to requirements.
- The system of quality is prevention.
- The performance standard is zero defects.
- The measurement of quality is the price of non-conformance.

3.8 Crosby also published a 14-step plan to quality improvement.

- Management must commit to a formalised quality policy.
- Form a management level quality improvement team with responsibility for quality issues.
- Determine where current and potential quality issues are.
- Evaluate the cost of quality and explain its effectiveness as a management tool to measure waste.
- Raise quality awareness and involvement amongst all employees.
- Take corrective actions, using formal systems to expose the root causes.
- Establish a zero defects committee and programme.
- Train all employees in quality improvement.
- Hold a zero defects day.
- Encourage groups and individuals to set improvement goals and targets.
- Encourage employee communication.
- Give formal recognition to those involved.
- Establish quality councils for information dissemination and sharing.
- Do it all over again – the quality process never ends.

3.9 Quality management is not easy to achieve. Crosby offers his **quality management maturity grid**, a five-stage progression in awareness and application of quality and quality thinking in an organisation.

- **Stage 1: Uncertainty**. 'We don't know why we have problems with quality.'
- **Stage 2: Awakening**. 'Is it absolutely necessary to always have problems with quality?'
- **Stage 3: Enlightenment**. 'Through management commitment and quality improvement we are identifying and resolving our problems.'
- **Stage 4: Wisdom**. 'Defect prevention is a routine part of our operation.'
- **Stage 5: Certainty**. 'We know why we do not have problems with quality'.

Dr Joseph M Juran

3.10 Juran, a former co-worker at Bell Systems, followed Deming to Japan and developed the **quality trilogy** (quality planning, quality improvement and quality control), the implementation of which requires management actions and processes to be planned, measured, managed and continuously improved.

3.11 Juran's approach is more formal than Deming's, with a greater emphasis on a structural approach within the organisation. Juran defined quality as 'fitness for use' in which he categorised quality under four headings with three subheadings for each.

- **Quality of design**: market research, product concept, design specifications.
- **Quality of conformance**: use and application of technology, human resources, management.
- **Quality of availability**: distribution (perhaps more correctly logistics with the modern understanding), reliability and maintainability.
- **Field service**: promptness, competence and integrity.

3.12   In 1951 he published the highly influential *Quality Control Handbook* which encouraged top management involvement, introduced the Pareto principle into quality, defined quality as 'fitness for use' and propounded a project-by-project approach to quality improvement.

3.13   His later **quality planning map** provides a stage process for understanding quality.

- Identify the customers both internal and external.
- Determine the needs of these customers.
- Translate those needs into our language.
- Develop a product designed to meet those needs.
- Optimise the product features so as to meet both our needs and our customers' needs.
- Develop a process that is able to produce the product.
- Optimise the product.
- Prove that the process is effective under operating conditions.
- Transfer the process to operations.

4   The benefits and criticisms of TQM

4.1   The evolution of the quality movement has led to dramatic changes in product and service delivery. The increased emphasis on meeting customer needs is a business essential in a competitive world. Quality, often viewed as a tool that would help organisations gain competitive advantage, is now a 'given' in many industries. Those who do not offer quality products or services are increasingly at risk.

4.2   The phrase 'quality is free' (Philip Crosby) demonstrates the main benefit gains of a TQM approach. Quality is gained over time. The Deming Cycle underpins many of the quality processes. The PDCA cycle ensures continuous improvement. It ensures that processes and procedures are scrutinised with the objective of improvement (better manufacturing techniques, tighter tolerances, improved customer communications, reduced waste etc), and when integrated into an organisation's culture the philosophy brings intangible benefits to staff and stakeholders.

TQM implementation

4.3   Implementation of TQM can be seen as time-consuming, bureaucratic, formalistic, rigid, impersonal and the property of one group within the organisation. The implementation of TQM requires good management practice particularly in regard to change management and communications in order to introduce and then embed TQM within the organisation.

4.4   There are two main approaches to TQM implementation. The 'blitz' approach introduces TQM very rapidly with mass education and communication programs. This can lead to problems in not knowing what to do next (or even first!) and can prove highly disruptive to existing business. The second approach is more measured and gradual, requiring a commitment to change to be identified, supported and communicated at a strategic level and integrated into strategic and business plans.

4.5   Criticism of TQM differs over time. Initially the introductory phase may be poorly communicated or managed, perhaps seen as another 'management fad' rather than a long-term commitment. During the implementation phase the TQM process may be seen as under the ownership of a particular group rather than the whole organisation and when implemented it may be seen as inflexible and too bureaucratic.

4.6   The challenge for management is to understand TQM and how the implications of fundamental change will impact on the organisation.

4.7   TQM offers a comprehensive approach to improving competitiveness, effectiveness and planning throughout the organisation but requires long-term commitment and organisational policies to succeed.

TQM starts at the top where a serious long-term commitment to quality should be demonstrated. Chief Executives must accept responsibility for commitment to a quality policy that encompasses organising for quality, understanding customer needs, appreciating the abilities of the organisation, developing suppliers, education and training and ongoing review of manufacturing and management systems.

4.8 TQM takes time to implement and embed successfully. The introduction of this new approach will change the culture of an organisation. The culture of an organisation is formed by the traditions, beliefs, behaviours, norms, values, rules and approach. The introduction of a TQM philosophy is concerned with allowing and encouraging individuals to take 'ownership' of their role and responsibilities and having the means to communicate their respective issues in a way that leads to 'micro-improvements' and in turn to overall improvement.

4.9 Individuals require to understand the TQM process, its purpose, the reasoning behind it and why it is important for the organisation. A key word in successful implementation is 'empowerment'. The empowerment of individuals lies in their ability to put forward ideas, discuss issues and influence changes in their area or over the organisation as a whole.

4.10 Building a quality culture is of crucial importance and, if achieved successfully, is a major intangible benefit that can serve to drive an organisation forward. Management commitment and cohesion are created as processes develop.

- Employees are more involved in managing.
- Managers are obligated to recognise the operational difficulties that employees work under.
- TQM demonstrates management commitment to quality by deed rather than words.

4.11 TQM is difficult and time-consuming to implement. It requires long-term cohesive commitment from senior management that must be successfully cascaded throughout the organisation. Quality thinking must be embedded in the organisation. Manufacturing gains are measurable and a clear benefit. Cultural change is less measurable but can be of equal or greater benefit.

11

Chapter summary

- Quality is the degree in which customer requirements are met. Customers may perceive quality in different ways.
- Total quality management aims for a continuous improvement in quality, efficiency and effectiveness and will develop methods and processes that help to achieve these objectives. It is based on the idea that everyone has a responsibility for quality.
- TQM has evolved from a long process of analysis, involving the work of numerous 'quality gurus' such as Deming, Crosby and Juran.
- TQM is increasingly seen as a vital discipline. However, it is time consuming and difficult to implement.

Self-test questions

Numbers in brackets refer to the paragraphs above where your answers can be checked.

1   Define quality. (1.2, 1.3)

2   What are David Garvin's eight main dimensions for quality? (1.5)

3   What is the name of the management tool developed by Parasuraman *et al*, which looks at the 'gap' between customer expectations and what is delivered? (1.14)

4   List the ten points (John S Oakland) for senior management to adopt when implementing TQM. (2.5)

5   What are the eight quality management principles in ISO 9000? (2.18)

6   Distinguish between quality control and quality assurance. (2.23, 2.24)

7   List as many as you can of Deming's 14 points for management. (3.5)

8   What are the five stages in Crosby's quality management maturity grid? (3.9)

9   What criticisms have been made of TQM implementation? (4.5)

CHAPTER 12

Techniques for Quality Improvement

Assessment criteria and indicative content

4.4 Analyse the main techniques for quality improvement that can be applied in operations management

- Diagnosing quality problems
- The use of statistical process control
- Variation in process quality
- The Taguchi loss function
- Poka-yoke
- The six sigma approach to quality management

Section headings

1 Diagnosing quality problems
2 Statistical process control
3 Tools for quality improvement

1 Diagnosing quality problems

Online and offline controls over quality

1.1 Quality is a philosophy that organisations embrace as part of their work culture. Quality assurance puts in place systems and procedures that ensure that quality standards will be met. Quality controls are the operational activities that are used to meet quality requirements.

1.2 In a quality control and improvement process the measurement or examination of data will form the basis for decisions and actions. The control of quality is achieved by some form of inspection or by the application of processes that lead toward reducing the need for inspection.

1.3 Quality control techniques can be divided into two main types.

- **Online controls**: these are controls of quality when the product is in the supply chain or on the production line. Examples include inspection and statistical process control (SPC).
- **Offline controls**: these are designed to prevent failure from occurring by intervening early in the design process. Examples include Taguchi methodology and failure mode and effects analysis (FMEA).

Online controls: the reactive approach

1.4 Inspection forms an integral part of most quality control systems (with the possible exception of just in time production systems). Inspection is usually based on the statistical process of **sampling**: a smaller number is considered as representative of a higher number. For example, from 1,000 items delivered 50 selected at random will be inspected. These 50 will be assumed to be representative of the whole.

1.5   This is not only a process that has proven statistical rigour (if carried out correctly) but clearly reduces inspection costs and speeds up the inspection process.

1.6   Inspection can be categorised under four headings.

- **Receiving inspection**: where materials, parts or components from suppliers are inspected for conformance to agreed specifications. This should be part of a formal process where records are kept.
- **Classification inspection**: the inspection of materials, parts or components into separate categories according to specifications. This allows for the inspection to be more tailored and specialised.
- **Control inspection**: the inspection of work in progress in order to correct variations from those expected (statistical process control).
- **Audit inspection**: the audit of procedures and processes such as ISO 9000.

2   Statistical process control

2.1   Statistical process control (SPC) is one of the most influential quality processes developed, in that its use and application aided Japan to become a major trading nation. Developed primarily by W Edwards Deming it involves the measurement of a production run, comparison against expectations, an investigation into why variations have occurred and a gradual reduction of variations. In essence, every time you do a production run, measure it and do it better next time (continuous improvement).

2.2   SPC is a technique for identifying the possibility of quality defects at an early stage of production. It is designed:

- to impose **control**
- over **processes**
- using **statistical methods**.

2.3   Complete uniformity is not to be expected in the output from any manufacturing process. (That is what is meant by the syllabus reference to **variation in process quality**.) Even in the most accurate and highly automated process for producing, say, steel rods it would be possible, given sufficiently accurate measuring instruments, to detect differences between one rod and the next. If the process is working well these random differences will usually cause no concern: it would take very accurate measurements to detect them, and they are probably well within the allowed tolerances.

2.4   The situation is different if the process is out of control. Perhaps the cutting tools have become blunt, or the machine has gone out of adjustment. In this case the variances from specification are potentially very serious, and (even worse) unpredictable. It is this kind of fault that SPC can detect to enable remedial action to be taken. By testing samples of output again and again throughout the production run, an operator skilled in the use of SPC can detect when the pattern of variances indicates a fault in the process.

2.5   The principles are relatively simple. Quality assurance and/or maintenance specialists determine that the process is working the way it should be. The operator begins production and takes samples of output for inspection at short time intervals. The measurements are recorded and, by using statistical analysis, it is established what average measurement is expected for all units of output. A determination of the expected range of measurement is provided. If the measurements taken from samples cluster around this predetermined measurement or average within expected parameters then the process is in control. If the results are outside the expected parameters then they are not.

2.6   This is the strength of the SPC concept, because at this stage the operator can halt production to seek and rectify the fault. Few defective units will have been produced. Once the fault is remedied, production begins again.

2.7   Fortunately the operator does not need to be an expert in statistics in order to perform these tasks. For the most part SPC relies on computer-based systems applying control charts. The control limits are determined after the operator's first few samples. These are taken just after the quality assurance team have ensured that the process is in control, so they provide reliable benchmarks for what should be expected throughout the production run. Control charts vary, but typically the operator will be concerned with two measurements.

- The average diameter, weight, length etc, of each sample
- The range of variation in each sample (the idea being that a narrow range of variation should be expected, while a wide variation around the average is a bad sign)

2.8   The average measurement of units in a sample is often denoted by the symbol $\overline{X}$, while the range of measurements within a sample is denoted by R. As the operator measures the units in a sample and calculates their average value ($\overline{X}$), the result should fall within defined limits, the upper and lower control limits, around the expected value. Similarly, the value computed for R should not exceed the expected value by more than a certain amount, marked by an upper control limit.

2.9   All of this is illustrated in Figure 12.1.

Figure 12.1 *SPC charts*

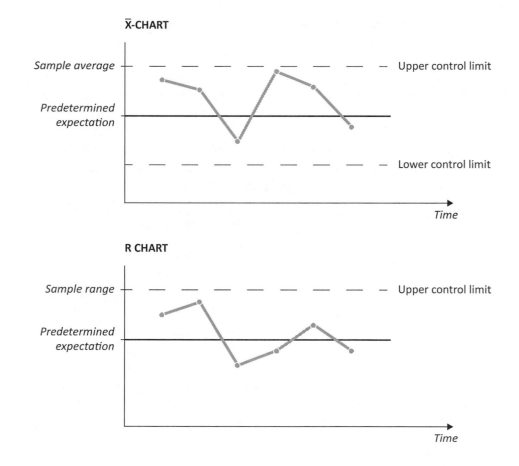

2.10   SPC is a mathematical technique that is applicable under defined conditions. It works best in situations where the production task is continuous and repetitive. It is a technique for ensuring that the production process remains in control (operating within its normal level of precision). The refinement that Japanese manufacturers added to the process was to work to tighter and tighter tolerances, over time. This led to a gradual and sustainable improvement in product consistency.

12

Offline control: the proactive approach

2.11   Offline (off the production line) approaches are based on ensuring that quality considerations are considered from the concept stage through to delivery of the final product. They involve planning, teamwork and measurement. The most influential of the offline processes (but by no means all) are: Taguchi methodology, quality function deployment (QFD) and failure mode and effects analysis (FMEA). Of these, the latter two have been discussed in earlier chapters; Taguchi methodology is discussed below.

3   Tools for quality improvement

The Taguchi Loss Function

3.1   The Taguchi Loss Function Model (Figure 12.2) was introduced by Dr. Genichi Taguchi. It is used to approximate the financial loss for any particular deviation in a product using the best specification target and for the amount of variation in any process. The Taguchi loss function is a way to show how each non-perfect part produced results in a loss for the company. Deming states that it shows:

'a minimal loss at the nominal value, and an ever-increasing loss with departure either way from the nominal value.'

3.2   Taguchi suggests that every process has a target value and that as the product moves away from target value, there is a loss incurred by society. This loss may involve delay, waste, scrap, or rework.

3.3   The parabolic curve describes the cost to society as the product moves away from the target value (centre point between the lower specification limit and upper specification limit). A technical definition of the curve is given by William Duncan (in *Total Quality: Key Terms and Concepts*):

A parabolic representation that estimates the quality loss, expressed monetarily, that results when quality characteristics deviate from the target values. The cost of this deviation increases quadratically as the characteristic moves farther from the target value.

Interpreting the chart

3.4   This standard representation of the loss function demonstrates a few of the key attributes of loss. For example, the target value and the bottom of the parabolic function intersect, implying that as parts are produced at the nominal value, little or no loss occurs. Also, the curve flattens as it approaches and departs from the target value. This shows that as products approach the nominal value, the loss incurred is less than when it departs from the target. Any departure from the nominal value results in a loss.

3.5   Loss can be measured per part. Measuring loss encourages a focus on achieving less variation. As we understand how even a little variation from the nominal results in a loss, the tendency would be to try and keep product and process as close to the nominal value as possible. This is what is so beneficial about the Taguchi loss. It always keeps our focus on the need to continually improve.

3.6   The Taguchi Loss Function Model argues that there is an increasing loss *(both for producers and for society at large)*, which is a function of the deviation or variability from the best or perhaps target value of a parameter. The greater the deviation from target, the greater is the loss. The notion that loss is dependent on variation is very well established in some design theories, and at a technique level is associated with the cost related to dependability.

Figure 12.2 *The Taguchi loss function*

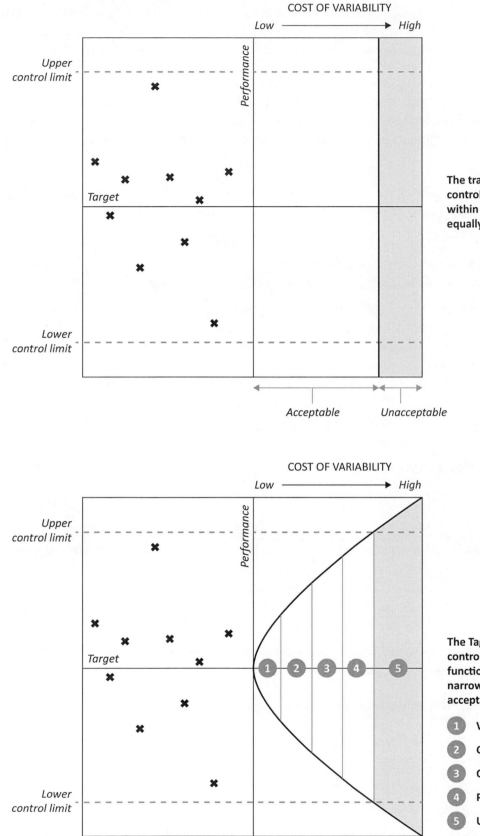

The traditional view of process control regards all performance within control limits as being equally acceptable

The Taguchi view of process control uses a quality loss function which targets a narrower band of acceptance variability:

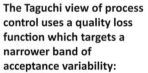

1 Very good

2 Good

3 OK

4 Poor

5 Unacceptable

Poka-yoke

3.7 Poka-yoke (poh-kah yoh-keh) was coined in Japan during the 1960s by Shigeo Shingo who was one of the industrial engineers at Toyota. We have already met this concept in Chapter 10. Here we return to it to provide more detail about how poka-yoke can be implemented as part of a quality management process.

3.8 Poka-yoke helps people and processes work right the first time. The term refers to techniques that make it impossible to make mistakes. These techniques can drive defects out of products and processes and substantially improve quality and reliability. It can be thought of as an extension of FMEA. It can also be used to fine tune improvements and process designs from six-sigma Define–Measure–Analyse–Improve–Control (DMAIC) projects.

3.9 The use of simple poka-yoke ideas and methods in product and process design can eliminate both human and mechanical errors. Poka-yoke is not necessarily an expensive approach.

3.10 Poka-yoke can be used in any number of situations where something can go wrong or an error can be made. It is a technique and a tool that can be applied to any type of process in both manufacturing and service sectors. Errors can occur in a number of situations.

- Processing error: process operation missed or not performed as per the standard operating procedure
- Setup: where the wrong tooling is used or machines are set up incorrectly
- Missing: not all parts included in the assembly or manufacture process
- Improper: wrong parts used in the process
- Operation error: carrying out an operation incorrectly (eg using an incorrect version of the specification)
- Measurement error: errors in machine adjustment, test measurement or dimensions of a part coming from a supplier

3.11 There is a step-by-step process for applying poka-yoke.

- Based on Pareto analysis identify the operation or process to be analysed
- Analyse the 'five whys' (ie consider five reasons why failure may occur) to understand how a process might fail
- Decide on the right poka-yoke approach: such as shut out type (preventing an error being made); attention type (highlighting or the bringing to attention of an error made); take an approach beyond poka-yoke such as limit switches or automatic shutoffs
- Trial the method to see if it works
- Train the operator, review performance and measure success.

3.12 A poka-yoke can be electrical, mechanical, procedural, visual, human or any other device that prevents incorrect execution of a process step

The six sigma approach to quality improvement

3.13 Six sigma is a new form of quality program with its origins in Motorola (1980s). It is a quality management tool that targets three main areas: improving customer satisfaction, reducing cycle time and reducing defects.

3.14 Six sigma has a focus that differentiates it from other quality programs.

- The needs of the customer are the priority. The focus is on the customer's critical-to-quality needs (CTQs).
- It maximises the cross-functional approach that many organisations are taking towards business.
- It concentrates on measuring product quality and improving related processes.

3.15   It has a strategic aspect in that top management commitment is required and implementation introduces new tools, methods and approaches, at all levels, in order to achieve results.

How it works

3.16   The purpose of six sigma is to reduce process variation in order that nearly all the products and services provided by an organisation meet or exceed customer expectations. The name derives from the use in statistics of the Greek character sigma (σ) as a measure of 'standard deviation'.

3.17   An organisation reaching the six sigma stage has its processes in such tight control that only a tiny minority of defects will emerge from its business processes (approximately two defects per billion transactions). At the one sigma stage a high level of defects can be expected. By the time the organisation has improved its processes to the four sigma level only tiny error levels are experienced, but an organisation fully committed to quality will still wish to improve to the five sigma or six sigma level.

3.18   There are three key elements to six sigma: process improvement, process design (or redesign), process management.

3.19   With regard to process improvement, a five-stage approach known as DMAIC is applied.

- **Define**: a serious problem is identified and a project team is formed and given the responsibility and resources to attain the defined project goals.
- **Measure**: the process to determine the existing level of performance. The data gathered is analysed in order to produce initial ideas about what might be causing the problem.
- **Analyse**: based on preliminary ideas, theories are generated and investigated to determine the root cause(s) of the defects.
- **Improve**: the identified root causes are removed by designing and implementing changes to the process.
- **Control**: new controls are designed and implemented to control future process performance and sustain the gains made.

3.20   Each of these stages has a variable number of substages, known as tollgates. These are identified steps that the project team must complete as they progress through each stage.

3.21   With regard to **process design** (or **redesign**) there is again a five-stage model (DMADV) used to achieve design for six sigma (DfSS).

- **Define**: identify and set the goals for the new process taking into account internal and external requirements.
- **Match/measure**: determine customer needs. Benchmark where appropriate and develop performance measures that meet these goals.
- **Analyse**: undertake an analysis of these performance measurements and develop an outline design for the new process that will meet customer needs.
- **Design (and implement)**: detail the process to meet the performance and customer criteria and implement.
- **Verify**: the design performance by introducing controls to ensure the stated goals are being met.

3.22   With regard to **process management**, six sigma fundamentally changes an organisation in the way it is structured and managed. Process management involves the following steps.

- Understanding and defining processes, understanding customer requirements and identifying the process owners, both internal and external.
- Ongoing measurement of performance against customer requirements and key performance indicators.
- Analysing data to monitor and refine measures.

12

- Controlling process performance by monitoring inputs, transformation and outputs and responding to variations outside those anticipated.

Selecting a team

3.23   Having identified a project to be carried out a 'problem statement' is prepared describing specific detail on the problem area. Expressed in measurable terms, the statement forms the basis for the size of the task and the resources and manpower needed. Will it be one project or involve a number of smaller, cross-functional teams reporting back to a central leader?

3.24   Six sigma uses a core of experts who provide the base for the organisational infrastructure to support the program. A typical six sigma team will consist of the following personnel.

- **Champions**: executives who understand six sigma and serve as mentors to black belts and interface with senior management.
- **Mentors** who drive the project forward and give support and direction.
- **Master black belts** are experienced, full-time leaders with a developed knowledge of six sigma. They provide advice, feedback, coaching, project planning advice and training where appropriate.
- **Black belts** who will lead quality projects, usually on a full-time basis until they are complete. It is envisaged that most six sigma projects will be between three and six months in duration.
- **Green belts** who work on projects on a part-time basis but will often lead teams in their own area or function.

3.25   There are six widely accepted themes of six sigma.

- A genuine focus on the customer with improvements measured in terms of customer satisfaction and value.
- It is based on data and fact so that problems can be effectively defined, analysed and resolved.
- Process improvement or design is at the heart of six sigma. Analysing and remedying the process itself leads to measurable improvements in quality.
- Six sigma demands proactive management. Instead of reacting to situations management focus on defining ambitious goals and setting clear priorities, questioning why things are done as they are.
- Boundaryless collaboration: six sigma involves both internal and external providers and contributors to the six sigma program.
- Strive for perfection, tolerate failure. New ideas come with risk. Learn from mistakes but encourage original thinking.

3.26   Quality is important as it demonstrates how risk management can come become embedded within organisations. Many of the themes of quality and quality management are reflected in the risk management approach (eg the need for systems, cross-functional teamwork, support from the top of the organisation and a customer focused approach).

Product liability and consumer confidence

3.27   Apart from aiming to satisfy their customers, manufacturers have strong legal reasons for trying to ensure product quality. In the UK, for example, the Consumer Protection Act 1987 imposed **strict liability** on manufacturers whose defective products cause damage. Strict liability means that the law is not concerned with whether or not the manufacturer was negligent; if his products were defective, he is liable even if he was not negligent.

3.28   This of course makes things very difficult for manufacturers, but the need for **consumer confidence** is paramount. With a régime of strict product liability consumers can be confident that their claims in respect of defective products will be upheld. Without it, consumers would have to prove what a manufacturer did or did not do during the manufacturing process, and for most ordinary citizens that is not a realistic possibility.

3.29   Manufacturers must naturally consider the possibility of product liability claims and will have to cover this cost, along with all others, in the pricing of their products. In effect, an amount will be included in the selling price as a kind of insurance premium. We come back to the question of quality-related costs: it is preferable to ensure quality first time round than to bear the costs of product failure, which could include product liability claims.

3.30   From the buyer's perspective, this applies not just within the boundaries of his own firm. Product defects in a bought-in component can lead to defects in the buyer's own products. For this reason, it is vital to ensure quality right along the supply chain.

Chapter summary

- Online controls occur when the product is in the supply chain or on the production line. Offline controls occur early in the design process.
- Statistical process control, as the name suggest, is designed to impose control over processes using statistical methods. The main idea is to identify very early on when a process is out of control, and then immediately halt it for rectification.
- Tools for quality improvement include the Taguchi loss function, poka-yoke, and six sigma.

Self-test questions

Numbers in brackets refer to the paragraphs above where your answers can be checked.

1   Distinguish between online and offline quality controls. (1.3)

2   Give four different types of inspection. (1.6)

3   Explain the main principles of SPC. (2.5)

4   What two measurements will an operator be concerned with in implementing SPC? (2.7)

5   Explain how a Taguchi chart should be interpreted. (3.4–3.6)

6   What are the five stages in DMAIC? (3.19)

Subject Index